VOICES OF
Resistance

VOICES OF
Resistance

((((((((((((/((((/((((((((

TESTIMONIES OF CUBAN AND CHILEAN WOMEN

EDITED AND TRANSLATED BY
Judy Maloof

THE UNIVERSITY PRESS OF KENTUCKY

Publication of this volume was made possible in part
by a grant from the National Endowment for the Humanities.

Editorial and Sales Offices: The University Press of Kentucky
663 South Limestone Street, Lexington, Kentucky 40508-4008

03 02 01 00 99 5 4 3 2 1

Library of Congress Cataloging-in-Publication Data

Maloof, Judy, 1957-
    Voices of resistance : testimonies of Cuban and
Chilean women / Judy Maloof.
        p.   cm.
    Includes bibliographical references and index.
    ISBN 0-8131-2079-9 (alk. paper)
        1. Cuba—Politics and government—1933-1959.
2. Cuba—Politics and government—1959-   3. Chile—
Politics and government—1973-1988.   4. Government,
Resistance to—Cuba—History—20th century.
5. Government, Resistance to—Chile—History—20th
century.   6. Political persecution—Cuba—
History—20th century.   7. Political persecution—
Chile—History—20th century.   8. Women political
activitists—Cuba—History—20th century.   9. Women
political activists—Chile—History—20th century.
I. Title.
F1787.5.M34   1999
972.9106'3—dc21   98-21801

Manufactured in the United States of America

This book is dedicated to the mothers and families of tens of thousands of disappeared in Latin America whose only crime was to dream of and fight for a more just and equitable world.

Contents

Acknowledgments

First and foremost, I want to express my sincere gratitude to the women in Cuba and Chile who graciously granted me interviews, especially those whose voices are the heart of this book. I appreciate their willingness to share their life stories and their trust in me to translate and edit their oral histories. I interviewed dozens of other women whose stories could not appear in this volume for practical reasons, such as space and the need to provide a sampling of women from a range of diverse backgrounds and experiences. Nevertheless, I was informed, touched, and enriched by these conversations; in particular, I thank Vivian Acosta, Irma Armas Fonseca, Mercedes Blanco Mesa, Maruja Iglesias, Marta Rojas, Mirta Rodríguez Calderón, and Reina María Rodríguez for taking time out of their busy schedules to talk with me. I am further indebted to Miguel Barnet, director of the Union of Cuban Writers and Artists, for his initial interest in my project and the valuable contacts that he provided. I also thank Chiloé Sasso's family for their generous hospitality and friendship and the wonderful conversations I had with Chiloé's mother and her sister, Angela.

The Ohio State University provided institutional support through a Small Research Grant from the College of Humanities. In addition, the Department of Spanish and Portuguese hired several graduate research assistants to help with this project. The bulk of the transcription of the tape-recorded interviews was done by Janet Luttetke. Derek Petrey and Allison Moser helped with technical computer assistance as well as useful editorial comments.

Other readers of parts or all of the manuscript whose suggestions for revision I appreciated include Maureen Ahern, Migue Galam, Donna Long, and the two anonymous readers for the University Press of Kentucky. I am also grateful to Amy Kaminsky, María Inés Lagos, Luis Rodríguez, and Tey Diana Rebolledo for reading my manuscript and believing in the value of my contribution to Latin American testimonial narrative. Also, Patricia Sterling did an excellent job of improving the narrative flow of my manuscript.

Finally, I thank my loving family and terrific friends for always being there when I need them to laugh, to share, and to care. *Gracias* from the depths of my soul to my mother, grandmother, and sisters, and to my close friends Hilda Chacón, Helena Kaufman, Sandra Luz Pedregal, Melinda Robinson, Cecilia Ruiz, Antonio Scuderi, and Margie Shehee.

Acronyms

CEM	Centro de Estudios de la Mujer (Center for Women's Studies)
CEMAS	Centros de las Madres (Mothers' Centers)
CDR	Comité en Defensa de la Revolución (Committee in Defense of the Revolution)
CNI	Centro Nacional de Información (National Center of Information)
CODEM	Comité en Defensa de los Derechos de la Mujer (Committee in Defense of Women's Rights)
CODEP	Comité en Defensa de los Derechos del Pueblo (Committee in Defense of the People's Rights)
COPACHI	Comité de Cooperación para la Paz en Chile (Committee of Cooperation for Peace in Chile)
CTC	Comité de Trabajadores Cubanos (Organization of Cuban Trade Unions)
DINA	Dirección Nacional de Inteligencia (Directorate of National Intelligence)
FAR	Fuerzas Armadas Revolucionarias (Revolutionary Armed Forces)
FCMM	Frente Cívico de Mujeres Martianas (Martí Women's Civic Front)
FLN	Frente de Liberación Nacional (National Liberation Front)
FMC	Federación de Mujeres Cubanas (Federation of Cuban Women)
FPMR	Frente Patriótico Manuel Roderíguez (Manuel Rodriguez Patriotic Front)
FRAP	Frente de Acción Popular (Popular Action Front)

JAP	Juntas de Abastecimiento y Precios (Organizations of Provisions and Prices)
JCC	Juventudes Comunistas de Chile (Chilean Young Communists League, also referred to as La Jota)
MAPU	Movimiento de Acción Popular Unificada (Movement of Unified Popular Action)
MDP	Movimiento Democrático Popular (Democratic Popular Movement)
MEMCH	Movimiento pro Emancipación de la Mujer Chilena (Movement for the Emancipation of Chilean Women)
MIR	Movimiento de la Izquierda Revolucionario (Movement of the Revolutionary Left)
MOMUPO	Movimiento de Mujeras Pobladoras (Movement of Shantytown Women)
MUDECHI	Mujeres de Chile (Women of Chile)
OEP	Organizacion Económica Popular (Popular Economic Organization)
SNM	Secretaría Nacional de la Mujer (National Secretariat of Women)
UNEAC	Unión Nacional de Escritores y Artistas Cubanos (National Union of Cuban Writers and Artists)
UNED	Unión Nacional de Estudiantes Democráticos (National Union of Democratic Students)
UP	Unidad Popular (Popular Unity)

Introduction

WOMEN'S TESTIMONIES OF REVOLUTION AND REPRESSION

Let's all brandish our heart
never fearing that it will burst
for a heart the size of ours
resists the cruelest tortures
and nothing can placate its devastating love
which grows
beat by beat
stronger,
stronger,
stronger.

—Gioconda Belli, "Until We're Free"

This book contains testimonies of Cuban and Chilean women who come from different walks of life: revolutionaries, human rights organizers, homemakers, workers, and intellectuals. Included here are the personal narratives of a poet, a tobacco worker, a maid, a social worker, a university professor, a journalist, a political prisoner, a secretary, an artist, and a documentary filmmaker, among others. The women are of diverse races—black, white, and mestizo. A Chilean woman proudly asserts that she is of Mapuche (indigenous) descent and attributes her strong fighting nature to that heritage.[1] Some of the women are from large cities, others from small towns or rural areas. Some are married; others are single, divorced, or widowed. They range in age from about thirty to over eighty. Most are Catholic, but several are Protestant, atheist, or agnostic, and one practices Santería (an Afro-Cuban religion similar to the voodoo of the West Indies and southern United States). They have a wide range of socioeconomic and educational backgrounds, strong political beliefs, and a variety of party affiliations—though several refuse to join any political party because of what they consider to be deeply embedded sexism in the androcentric

Latin American political parties of the traditional left as well as of the right and center. Despite that patriarchal tradition, however, it is important to note that there is a history of the participation of a small minority of mostly (but not exclusively) upper-class and professional women in politics. Indeed, Latin American women were among those who led suffrage movements during the nineteenth century, and there are examples of feminists in early twentieth-century Latin America.[2]

The common thread among the women I interviewed in Cuba in 1992 and in Chile in 1993 is their involvement in a cause larger in scope than their own or their families' private lives. This book documents the ways in which each one constructs herself via language as a politically aware, gendered social subject and as an agent of social transformation. Each narrator tells an intimate, personal story about her evolving social and political consciousness. Many of their stories are heart-wrenching and tragic; all are impressive examples of heroism and courage. The oral histories of these Chilean and Cuban revolutionary women shed light on the intersection between private and public realms in the configuration of feminine subjectivity.

In collecting these testimonies I was always conscious of the process of self-creation that occurs through the act of narrating one's life story. Each narrator selects, orders, and interprets what she recalls as significant events and meaningful moments from her past. Each storyteller connects crucial, defining incidents and memories from her childhood with her present, concrete reality and projects her dreams and aspirations (for herself, her family and her loved ones, her community and homeland) onto the screen of an uncertain future in order to construct a unified identity from the fragments of her life. Her words illustrate how each woman structures a coherent self, in and through language, from the myriad of subjective and objective experiences that make up her life. Many of these stories help make up an unofficial record of torture, imprisonment, censorship, forced exile, and mass graves, refracting the history of Batista's or Pinochet's military repression against her community from the particular vantage point of a feminine speaking subject.

I began this project during the summer of 1992 under the supervision and guidance of the Cuban writer Miguel Barnet, an authority on Latin American testimonies and director of the National Union of Cuban Writers and Artists (UNEAC). He provided valuable contacts with women who had played an important role in the Cuban Revolution as members of a women's organization called Frente Cívico de Mujeres Martianas (FCMM), the Martí Women's Civic Front; now in their late seventies and early eighties, they had participated directly in the opposition to the dictatorship of Fulgencio Batista (1952-58). I also interviewed women who were active combatants in the Cuban Revolution, and others who evinced varying degrees of support for, or discontent with, the present regime. In December 1993 I interviewed Chilean women who had been involved in the struggle against human rights abuses during the dictatorship of Augusto Pinochet (1973-90) and who recounted their experiences of painful contact with the repression in Chile under his military rule.

These Chilean and Cuban women used the interviews as an opportunity to reinvent themselves through the act of narration. When I met them, they were already engaged in this process of self-invention. They had picked up the shattered pieces of their lives and fought back by speaking out and by organizing against the abuses and repression they and their families had endured. For many, speaking out was not only an act of personal liberation (a means of expressing grief and rage) but also a *collective* act of solidarity, a *political* act of protest against an unjust authoritarian regime.

Why did I choose to combine testimonies from Cuba and Chile, given the radically different geo-political economies of these two nations? Generally speaking, Cuba is an underdeveloped Communist country, suffering today from its worst economic crisis since Fidel Castro's 1959 Revolution. This present period in Cuban history is referred to by the Cubans as the "Special Period in times of peace," brought about by the collapse of the Soviet Union in 1989.[3] By contrast, Chile's export economy is rapidly expanding with the transnationalization and privatization that began during the authoritarian rule of the 1970s and 1980s and continue today as part of the so-called transition to democracy. It is in fact regarded by conservative U.S. economists as a model for the rest of Latin America.[4] The two countries thus represent the economic extremes in Latin America.

In deciding which countries to study, and then which of more than forty interviews to include, I wanted first of all to demonstrate the continuity of women's political activism in Latin America from the early 1950s through the 1990s, to show why I consider the women activists of the 1950s to be the precursors of the tens of thousands of Latin American women of the 1970s and 1980s who participated in the New Left and other human rights and women's organizations and who courageously fought against dictatorial regimes and in national liberation wars in Central and South America.

Second, I chose Cuba and Chile because both countries at different times implemented socialist political economies. Allende's Popular Unity

(UP) government survived only three years before it fell on September 11, 1973, to the bloodiest CIA-sponsored military coup d'état in Latin American history. In contrast, the Castro regime is still hanging on after thirty-eight years. The Cuban revolutionary government easily and quickly defeated the counterrevolutionary invaders at the Bay of Pigs in 1961, and Castro himself has survived more than twenty (CIA-orchestrated) assassination attempts.[5]

Despite so much clamor in the post–Cold War Western industrialized nations about "the end of history" and "the death of socialism," many of the Cuban and Chilean women I interviewed have remained committed to the ideals of socialism; they still consider some form of socialism to be a more just and equitable political and economic system than unbridled, free-market capitalism with its inherent structural inequalities between the small minority of owners of capital and the "masses" of laborers. These women maintain that everyone has a right to education, health care, employment, adequate food, and decent shelter—humanitarian and economic rights supposedly guaranteed to all people living in socialist countries. Nevertheless, most of the women I talked with were also critical of the flaws and imperfections of the former and present "socialist" governments throughout the developed and developing world.

Generally speaking, vestiges of patriarchy are still present in Latin America today. According to the epistemology of the modern Latin American nation-state, formulated after the wars for emancipation during the first two decades of the nineteenth century (with the exception of Cuba and Puerto Rico, whose wars for independence were fought much later), the notion of "citizen" implied a landed, upper-class white or mestizo male. Women and the large indigenous populations were ignored and excluded from the symbolic configurations of the nation except as icons of subalternity and otherness or as symbols of liberty, justice, or motherhood. Women were sometimes depicted as the "mothers of the nation" or as the feminine embodiment of the nation itself. On their place in masculinist conceptualizations of nation, Mary Louise Pratt has written:

> The nation by definition situates or "produces" women in permanent instability with respect to the imagined community. . . . Women inhabitants of nations were neither imagined as nor invited to imagine themselves as part of the horizontal brotherhood. . . . So it is that women inhabitants of modern nations were not imagined as intrinsically possessing the rights of citizens; rather, their value was specifically attached to (and implicitly conditional on) their reproductive

capacity. As mothers of the nation, they are precariously other to the nation. They are imagined as dependent rather than sovereign. [1990, 51]

Pratt's notion of women as "other" in an unstable relation with the imagined community explains why women in Latin American societies have been historically relegated to the private domain of home and family and excluded from the male core of real political and economic power. This general exclusion from the public sphere is not, however, total and absolute; in wars for independence, revolutions, and guerrilla wars many Latin American women have taken part in armed struggle, participated in street demonstrations and organized strikes, and played significant roles in clandestine political movements. Vilma Espín, the head of the Federation of Cuban Women (FMC) and member of the Central Committee of the Cuban Communist Party, recalls the tradition of Latin American women fighting in the wars for emancipation from the yoke of Spanish colonialism:

> In the battles for our first independence, together with the popular and internationalist armies of San Martín and Bolívar, women were present. Outstanding fighters such as Colonel Juana Azurduy de Padilla who fought in the area then called Upper Peru; Manuela Saenz, the companion of Bolívar; Remedios Escalada de San Martín; and our own Ana Betancourt who in 1869 demanded that women's rights be included in the new constitution; Mariana Grajales, the mother of the Maceo brothers, the heroes of our independence; Captains of the Liberating Army, Adela Azcuy and Rosa Castellanos, the Bayamesa, and many others . . . not only helped the combatants but were also combatants themselves. [1976, 170-71]

And more recently, especially as a consequence of the growing women's movement in Latin America since the mid-1970s, the participation of women in politics—especially in grassroots and human rights organizations—has increased substantially.

Jane Jaquette suggests that the rise of the women's movement in Latin America needs to be understood as a new political force with the potential to reshape the political future of Latin America. From a position of marginality, the women's movement, in its many different forms, has had a significant impact on the male centers of political power. Among the most obvious examples are such women as the mothers of the disappeared who organized the Madres de la Plaza de Mayo in Argentina.

Women led the human rights struggle in many nations, including Argentina, Brazil, Uruguay, and Chile. In the late 1970s women's groups in Latin America organized around various issues; as Jaquette states: "Women's human rights groups were organized by women who were mothers or grandmothers of the disappeared; feminist groups formed to combine consciousness-raising with political and social action; and neighborhood-based organizations of poor women banded together to ensure the survival of their families under increasingly harsh economic circumstances." (1989, 186-187). Although these different strands of the movement involved women with different goals, styles, and political agendas, they worked together to play a decisive role in the process of transition from authoritarian rule to "democracy."

Since women's resistance to military dictatorships significantly galvanized and shaped feminist movements in Latin America, the juxtaposition of Cuban and Chilean stories of women at the juncture of private and public crises offers an original contribution to the field of Latin American women's history and testimonial literature. Of course, the transformation of orality into textuality, the conversion from human voice to written page, is always problematic. Much of the "humanity" and uniqueness of the narrator is lost in the process of transcribing a tape-recorded conversation: the facial gestures, body language, and expressiveness (or its lack) in the eyes; the tone of voice, the particular accent, the pattern of intonation, the rhythm of speech, the pauses and silences; the laughter and tears and, most of all, the intimacy of the telling and listening situation.[6]

Even more has been lost as a result of the translation of these testimonies from Cuban and Chilean Spanish—both rich in regional variations, brimming with colorful expressions and popular sayings that are not easily translated—into standard English.[7] All the women in this book are therefore "translated women," to use the phrase coined by anthropologist Ruth Behar. In the introduction to her book *Translated Woman: Crossing the Border with Esperanza's Story* Behar eloquently explains that as she reshaped into a book the life story of a Mexican street vendor of indigenous descent, she somehow "cut out Esperanza's tongue": "As the one who is no longer just expanding her capacities to listen, but sitting here snipping and snipping at the historias Esperanza told me, only to sew them back into this book as a life history, I fear I am somehow cutting out Esperanza's tongue. Yet when I'm done cutting out her tongue, I will patch together a new tongue for her, an odd tongue that is neither English nor Spanish, but the language of the translated woman." (1993, 19).[8]

Likewise, through the process of recording, transcribing, translating, and editing these personal narratives, I too have in a sense cut out the tongues of the Cuban and Chilean women whose oral histories form the heart of this book. Still, it would be a fallacy to presume that I am the only mediating agent. Historical events have translated these women's lives beyond my investigative intervention, and in effect the women themselves are translating the stories of their lives into objectified speech acts.

Whatever the consequences of my editorial "translation," I want to stress that my main objective is to allow these voices to speak for themselves to a wide English-speaking audience. I have avoided including my questions and interruptions in order to make these testimonies more readable. I have tried to preserve their orality, only eliminating some of the repetitious phrases and stock expressions of everyday conversation ("you know," "as I was saying," and the like). I have taken the liberty of selecting those parts of each interview that are relevant to my overall project and have therefore excluded some anecdotes and digressions. I have sometimes reordered the chronology of the telling so as to frame the fragments into a more coherent narrative.

The length of my tape-recorded interviews varied from about one hour on a single day to four or five hours over several consecutive meetings. My goal was to conduct loosely structured, *informant-centered* interviews, allowing each narrator to tell her story as she herself wished to tell it. It is interesting to note, however, that the level of discourse often shifted to a more formal and less colloquial use of language when the tape recorder was turned on. Several women organized their thoughts as though they were giving a public speech, whereas they had been relaxed and "natural" in our prior informal discussions. Their reluctance to speak freely and spontaneously was not merely the consequence of gender-based censorship; men also feel an uneasiness in becoming recordings, transcripts, multilingual artifacts. There are several complex movements here involving politics, discourse, identity, and personal will. It is important for the reader to keep in mind the special nature of texts that are shaped by their concrete origin as a series of taped interviews.

The particular role of women in the Cuban Revolution and in human rights organizations has been studied elsewhere; however, the special ways in which major historical events make their impact on everyday life is the focus of my work—and of recent research by feminist scholars in the areas of oral history and ethnography. The life history is a distinctive type of personal document that differs from the autobiography, diary, letter, or personal memoir. The following distinction is useful for my purposes: "As we see it, the 'life history' is any retrospective account by the individual of his life in whole or part, in written or oral form, *that has been elicited or prompted by another person*. We use the term 'autobiography,' by contrast, to refer to a person's *self-initiated* retrospective account of his life, which is usually but not always in written form" (Watson and Watson-Franke, 1985, 2).

Life history research is a growing area of interdisciplinary, feminist scholarship. A volume edited by the Personal Narratives Group at the University of Minnesota, *Interpreting Women's Lives: Feminist Theory and Personal Narratives* (1989), offers rich insights into the ways that women's voices and life stories can inform scholarly research. This diverse group of women comprises North American feminist anthropologists, historians, literary scholars, and social scientists—all engaged in research dealing with women's oral history. Their introduction points out that whereas "traditionally, knowledge, truth, and reality have been constructed as if men's experiences were normative, as if being a human being meant being male," recent movements for social change throughout the world have challenged this white, patriarchal construction, recognizing that "what had been presented as an objective view of the world was selectively the dominant white, male view" and that what had been "accepted as normative was . . . the limited and limiting perspective of a particular gender, class, and race" (1989, 3). Therefore, women's oral history research that incorporates many classes and ethnic groups validates women's experiences and records a feminine perspective of both everyday social reality and significant historical events.

In the same vein, Susan Geiger regards women's life histories as "primary sources for the content of women's lives, and life history research as a feminist method for the broader and deeper understanding of women's consciousness, historically and in the present" (1986, 335). This feminist perspective and methodology, emphasizing the category of gender, were largely ignored by official historians, anthropologists, and social scientists until the rise of the women's movement forced them to reexamine critically and self-consciously the sexism and ethnocentrism embedded in their professions.

Too often, however, North American and European feminists have sought to celebrate commonalities among women rather than acknowledging their significant *differences*. Some Third World feminists and American women of color make the strong point that sisterhood is not necessarily global and that class, ethnic, and cultural differences among women need to be taken into serious consideration. It is necessary to "see the individual variety in women's lives, to embrace that, to learn from it before we try to generalize—since generalizations can so easily become the imposition of self and erasure of other" (Geiger 1986, 334). I consciously foreground my own subject position so as not to erase the cultural and class differences between me and my interviewees.

When Domitila Barrios de Chungara—whose oral history is recorded in *Let Me Speak! Testimony of Domitila, A Woman of the Bolivian Mines*—addressed the United Nations–sponsored International Women's Year conference in Mexico City in 1975, her remarks to the chair of the Mexican delegation emphasized the class differences that separate women:

> Madam, I met you a week ago. Each morning you arrive with a different outfit; and nevertheless I do not. Each day you arrive made up and with your hair styled like someone who has time to go to a very expensive beauty salon and can afford to spend good money there; and nevertheless I do not. I see that you have a car with a driver waiting for you every afternoon to take you home; and nevertheless I do not. And in order to look the way you look, I am sure you live in a very elegant home in an area that is also elegant, right? And, nevertheless, we miners' wives have only a small, borrowed place to live in, and when our husband dies, or when he is ill or retired from the company, we have ninety days to leave our home and we are in the street.
>
> Now, tell me, Madam, do you have anything similar to my situation? Do I have anything similar to you? Then what "equality" are we going to talk about between us? If we are not at all similar, if you and I are so different? Right now you and I cannot be equals, not even as women. (1978, 225)

Essays in the anthology *Women's Words* (Berger Gluck and Patai 1991) address the unique interplay of voices between interviewers from hegemonic cultures and subjects from subaltern cultures in contemporary feminist oral history research; their authors agree about the importance examining the distribution of power and knowledge between the ethnographer and the informant.[9]

Some feminist anthropologists have argued in favor of the politically committed "advocacy oral history" that Sherna Berger Gluck, who coordinates the oral history program at California State at Long Beach, practices in her research on women's liberation in occupied Palestine. She maintains that although oral histories can be used as instruments and agents of social change, those of us who collect them must be sensitive to the ways in which our political beliefs affect our scholarship and aware of its potential misuses and abuses: in the hands of the wrong people, the research we generate may be used to harm the community or the individuals we think we are serving. But advocacy oral history, Berger Gluck asserts, which attempts to combine the roles of scholar and advocate, can keep us "rooted in the social movement from which we sprang. . . . Advocacy scholarship retains the potential for informing the movement and for activating the academy" (1991, 218).

Because many previous U.S. studies of Cubans have had propagandistic ends, seeking to pervert testimonies into justification for anti-Castro politics, many of the Cuban women I spoke with were hesitant to believe that I was willing or able to offer a sympathetic ear and a space where their words might be taken at face value. But my goal is to let these voices speak for themselves and thus offer the English-speaking public an alternative point of view to that represented in the mainstream North American media. My own position, one of solidarity with the perspectives expressed by most of my informants, classifies my project as an example of the "advocacy scholarship" proposed by Berger Gluck, based on an intersubjective model of ethnographic practice.

Clifford Geertz, James Clifford, George Marcus, Paul Rabinow, and others have posited an intersubjective model of interpretive anthropology, arguing that any anthropologist's claim of "objectivity" (intended to give the discipline a "scientific" veneer) is false and often serves to obscure and conceal the operations of bias, interests, and motives in a study.[10] As ethnographer Roger Lancaster succinctly asserts in his defense of anthropology as an intersubjective practice, "I would not claim an 'absence of subjectivity' here, any more than I would claim to a lack of personality, or to be cut adrift from my own experiences or social relations" (1988, 4). This model stresses the notion that the ethnographer is a subjective observer who studies the subjectivity of her informants.[11]

My project builds upon and has been shaped by existing scholarship in feminist ethnography, cultural anthropology, cultural studies, and Latin American testimonial discourse by women.[12] Contemporary critics of Latin American cultural studies provide several definitions of the *testimonio* and have begun to theorize about this emerging and growing corpus of non-canonical texts. With some minor disagreements, most of these scholars would accept John Beverley's definition: "The general form of the testimonio is a novel or novella-length narrative, told in the first-person by a narrator who is also the actual protagonist or witness of the events she or he recounts. The unit of the narration is usually a life or a significant life episode (e.g., the experience of being a prisoner)" (Beverley and Zimmerman 1990, 173). Beverley goes on to say that in many cases the narrator is someone who is either functionally illiterate or, if literate, not a professional writer, so that "the production of a testimonio often involves the tape recording and then the transcription and editing of an oral account by an interlocutor who is an intellectual, journalist, or writer. . . . The nature of the intervention of this editorial function is one of the more hotly debated theoretical points in the discussion of the genre" (1993, 70-71)—as is the intervention of the interviewer. It is important to note, however, that my informants are *not* illiterate, and many of them are not subaltern subjects; therefore, the oral narratives in this book do not entirely fit Beverley's definition of testimony.

Other definitions by Latin American scholars and critics are more relevant to my research. For example, building on the studies of Barnet (1969, 1981), Vidal and Jara (1986), Beverley (1990, 1993), Kaminsky (1993), and others, George Yúdice emphasizes the notions of urgency, social agency, and the denunciation of oppression in the testimony: "It is an authentic narrative, told by a witness who is moved to narrate by the urgency of a situation (e.g., war, oppression, revolution, etc.). Emphasizing popular, oral discourse, the witness portrays his or her own experience as an agent (rather than a representative) of a collective memory and identity. Truth is summoned in the cause of denouncing a present situation of exploitation and oppression or in exorcising and setting aright official history" (1991, 17).

This is an adequate working definition for many of the Chilean testimonies here, which denounce a situation of oppression and express a sense of urgency to to tell the world about the repression suffered under Pinochet. Likewise, most of the Cuban women articulated a sense of urgency to put an end to the U.S. embargo, which is strangling the Cuban economy and inflicting hardship on Cuban civilians. I agree with Yúdice that the notions of urgency and social agency distinguish testimonial discourse from other oral histories. Within the context of Latin American literary and cultural studies, oral narratives denouncing oppression—many produced in a social context of concrete resistance—are studied under the rubric of testimonies; in ethnography and women's studies the terms oral history and life history are usually used to denote any oral accounts that have been recorded, transcribed, and edited by a professional researcher.

It is important to note that the testimonial form of non-fictional discursive practice is not new in Latin America. One of the first eyewitness accounts of the genocide of indigenous peoples following the Spanish invasion and conquest of the "New World" is Bartolomé de las Casas's *Brevísima relación de la destrucción de las indias* (Short account of the destruction of the Indies), first published in 1552.[13] Nor is testimonial writing by any means homogeneous. As Beverley rightly observes, "a variety . . . of texts—some of which would be considered literature, some not—can fit under the label of testimonio: for example, oral history, memoir, autobiography, chronicle, confession, life history, *novela-testimonio*, documentary novel, nonfiction novel, or 'literature of fact'" (1993, 71).

Elena Poniatowska's *Hasta no verte, Jesus Mío* (And Here's to You, Jesusa, 1969), about the life of a poor Mexican woman who fought in the Mexican Revolution, and Manlio Argueta's *Un día en la vida* (One day in a life, 1980), about the guerrilla war for national liberation in El Salvador, are just two examples of Latin American novels that have a testimonial structure. They are based on the oral accounts of real human beings, transformed by professional authors into what the Guatemalan writer Mario Roberto Morales has called *testi-novelas*.[14]

Elena Poniatowska allows others to speak for themselves also in *La noche de Tlatelolco* (Massacre in Mexico, 1971), a documentary novel that uses a collage technique in order to include in its graphic account many different voices of those who witnessed the massacre of some three hundred peaceful demonstrators at a rally of 10,000 at Tlatelolco (the Plaza of Three Cultures) in Mexico City. On October 2, 1968, government soldiers and police armed with tanks and machine guns mowed down innocent protesters, mostly young members of the student movement but also workers and housewives who were protesting repressive measures taken by the government against labor activists, teachers, and university students. In another testimonial narrative, *Nada, Nadie: Las voces del temblor* (Nothing, nobody: Voices about the earthquake, 1988), Poniatowska uses the same collage technique to incorporate oral accounts from a broad spectrum of the urban population that mobilized in response to the tragic earthquake in Mexico City in September 1985.

Testimonial literature emerged in Nicaragua and El Salvador during the 1930s and again starting in the 1970s in response to widespread popular insurgency in the region. According to the Nicaraguan critic Ileana Rodríguez, testimonial writing in Central America "reveals the hidden secrets of popular tradition in relation to questions of resistance" and is also an important means of popular-democratic cultural practice (1982, 85-86).

Barbara Harlow (1987) analyzes testimonial discourse as a strategy of cultural and political resistance within Third World liberation movements. She presents a powerful critique of the cultural imperialism of the West, especially regarding the imposition of traditional categories and models of critical practice and theories (structuralism, deconstruction, psychoanalytic theory, postmodernism, and the like) on texts produced by the periphery. According to Harlow, "resistance literature" can be defined as the writings that emerged significantly as part of the organized national liberation struggles and resistance movements in Africa, Latin America, and the Middle East.

Another important contribution of Harlow's work is her analysis of the changing role of Third World women whose lives have been radically altered by political forces, historical circumstances, and economic pressures.[15] Many Latin American women became active combatants in Cuba, Nicaragua, El Salvador, Chile, Guatemala, and elsewhere. Often because their husbands, brothers, or sons had been killed or imprisoned or were otherwise absent, women took on responsibilities in the larger social order that transformed their relationships with their husbands and families. The oral histories I present illustrate the transformation of women's daily lives as a result of their participation in political resistance movements, often subsequent to the death, disappearance, or imprisonment of a husband, son or daughter, brother or sister, friend or lover.

Daphne Patai (1988) uses the oral histories of "ordinary" women from many walks of life in contemporary Brazilian society to explore the relation between gender and power in the transnational context.[16] Margaret Randall, who has gained international recognition as a poet, editor, translator, author, and photographer, is another woman who has shown sustained interest in the participation of women in Latin American revolutionary struggles. She has collected hundreds of interviews with Cuban and Nicaraguan women, whose testimonies have been published in both Spanish and English. The oral histories in Randall's books *Sandino's Daughters: Testimonies of Nicaraguan Women in Struggle* (1981a), *Doris Tijerino: Inside the Nicaraguan Revolution* (1978), *Mujeres en la revolución* (1972), and *Cuban Women Now* (1974) have shed light on the important role of women in both the Nicaraguan and Cuban Revolutions.[17] Shortly after the Sandinistas' victory against the forty-year Somoza dictatorship, Randall interviewed scores of women who had fought in Nicaragua—as field commanders, rank-and-file guerrillas, messengers, intelligence agents—and mothers and daughters engaged in the reconstruction of their country. As she explains in the introduction to *Sandino's Daughters*, the book is about "the women of Nicaragua—the peasant, working–class, professional and bourgeois women who joined with their brothers in the struggle to defeat Somoza. They tell us openly about their lives—in the days of Somoza, during the Revolution, and today as they work to build a free country. They describe the brutality of the old regime and their participation in the movement which finally defeated the tyrant. They speak very personally about their fears and losses, but mostly of their victory as women and as militants" (1981a, v-vi).

One of the most interesting aspects of Randall's presentation of women's testimonies from Nicaragua and Cuba (where she herself lived for many years) is the focus on the interaction of the political and the personal. Randall is interested in the intimate, everyday lives of these revolutionary women as mothers, daughters, and *compañeras* (partners), as well as their public lives as active participants in the efforts to carve out a new space for women in revolutionary societies.

The Chilean journalist Patricia Politzer has published moving testimonial narratives that convey the experience of individual citizens from many different sectors of the population during the Pinochet dictatorship. Her *Miedo en Chile*, translated as *Fear in Chile* (1989), presents fourteen interviews with a range of informants including priests, soldiers, Communist activists, a bank employee, a copper miner, the mother of a *desaparecido* (a "disappeared" prisoner of conscience), and a "Chicago Boy" economist. Politzer observes that their common denominator was the element of fear: "At some point in each conversation, fear surfaced more or less explicitly, with more or less profound roots. For some, it was fear of the army; for others, of unemployment; for still others, of poverty, informers, repression, Communism, Marxists, chaos, violence, or terrorism" (1989, xiv). My interviews with Chilean women likewise reveal the experience of fear as something that they all had in common—along with courage to resist the repression.

More testimonies from women active in the resistance to Pinochet appear in *We, Chile: Personal Testimonies of the Chilean Arpilleristas*, edited by Emma Sepúlveda (1996) and based on taped interviews with eight members of artisan workshops and the Folkloric Troupe of Families of the Detained-Disappeared. Sepúlveda's stated objective is similar to my own: "I recorded their stories so the pain and suffering of so many human beings would not be totally in vain and so that, upon reading their testimonies, we might learn the immeasurable worth of human rights and teach future generations to defend them throughout the world" (1996, 36).

Other examples of Latin American women's testimonial writing about resisting authoritarian regimes are Alicia Partnoy's *The Little School* (1986) and Claribel Alegría's *They Won't Take Me Alive* (Alegría and Flakoll 1987).

Partnoy relates her own experiences and those of her companions who were held in an Argentine concentration camp in 1977, before she was transferred to prison for another two and a half years.[18] Alegría's testimonial book—a composite recounting of the life of Salvadoran Commander Eugenia as told by friends, family, and comrades who knew her before she was killed by the military—is "dedicated to Salvadoran women engaged in political struggle, to Ana Patricia (Eugenia's daughter), to the next generation and a new civilization" (1987, 32).

Three well-known and widely read testimonies of Latin American subaltern women that have been translated into English are Nobel Peace Prize winner (1992) Rigoberta Menchú's *I . . . Rigoberta Menchú: An Indian Woman in Guatemala* (1984), edited and introduced by the Venezuelan anthropologist Elizabeth Burgos-Debray; Domitila Barrios de Chungara's account, with Moema Viezzer, of daily life in the Bolivian mines, *Let Me Speak!* (1978); and Elvia Alvarado's story as told to and edited by Medea Benjamín, *Don't Be Afraid, Gringo: A Honduran Woman Speaks from the Heart* (1987). Each of these employs a rhetorical strategy that constructs not just a personal record but the collective reality of a community's struggle against oppression and exploitation—a major difference between testimony and autobiography. In all three the speaking subject, the "I," is replaced by a collective "we," for each narrator represents herself not as an isolated individual but as a member of her community. For example, Menchú emphasizes that her story is something that she learned neither in a book nor alone: "I'd like to stress that it's not only *my* life, it's also the testimony of my people. My story is the story of all poor Guatemalans. My personal experience is the reality of a whole people" (1984, 1). Similarly speaking for a whole population, Barrios de Chungara begins: "I don't want anyone at any moment to interpret the story I'm about to tell as something that is only personal. Because I think that my life is related to my people. What happened to me could have happened to hundreds of people in my country" (1978, 15). Alvarado too indicates that her story is the story of all the poor *campesinos* (peasants) in her country: "I thought about our struggle, how we suffer hunger, persecution, abuse by the landowners. How we fight with all the bureaucrats at the National Agrarian Institute. How we fight the police, the army, the security forces. . . . I decided I couldn't pass up a chance to tell the world our story" (xiii). In contrast to male-gendered testimonial writing (Che Guevara, Omar Cabezas[19]), which often fails to represent a collective subject, these female-gendered works (Partnoy, Alegría, Menchú, Barrios de Chungara, and Alvarado) highlight the significance of solidarity and of the collective rather than the individual struggle for social justice.[20] This element is evident in many of the women's testimonies in this book as well.

Claudia Salazar argues convincingly that Menchú's testimony "represents the intersection of many and contradictory discourses/voices, including that of the ethnographer."[21] She focuses on the complexities in the production and translation of cultural "otherness" in this text. Rigoberta Menchú's way of introducing herself can be read, asserts Salazar, "as a rhetorical attempt to restructure the relationship between the personal and the political through a subversion of Western individualism." She goes on to explain that Menchú is not simply doing away with the private/public opposition; on the contrary, she is "recoding it in such a way that the private becomes public and vice versa. What is public for Rigoberta Menchú is her private life—thus she tells about *her* story. What is private, on the other hand, are the ways of her community, which she keeps hidden from us" (1991, 97, 94, 96). Salazar is referring to Menchú's "secrets," secrets about a way of life that the Quiché people of highland Guatemala have traditionally refused, as a means of cultural self-preservation, to tell nonindigenous people.[22] As Menchú herself reiterates throughout her testimony, "I'm still keeping my Indian identity a secret. I'm still keeping secret what I think no-one should know. Not even anthropologists or intellectuals, no matter how many books they have, can find out all our secrets" (1984, 247).

The notion of keeping secrets is also relevant to my study. My informants too may have refused to reveal certain information; for various reasons they may have engaged in acts of self-censorship. The process of self-fashioning is very complex; the number of variables is infinite and impossible to comprehend fully. Nonetheless, the parts of their lives that they did share with me are available here. It is interesting to observe the specific ways in which each woman made use of the interview situation to communicate those experiences she considered most important to tell, quite possibly omitting others.

Chapter 1 details the historical, political Cuban context, focusing especially on the role of women in the Revolution; Chapter 2-7 are the testimonies of six Cuban women, each with a brief introduction; Chapter 8 analyzes the construction of the self in the Cuban accounts. Chapter 9 surveys the Chilean historical and political context from the election of Allende through the Pinochet dictatorship, emphasizing the participation of women in the human rights struggle and in the "transition" to democratic rule; in Chapters 10-16 seven Chilean women relate their stories of resistance; Chapter 17 comments on aspects of self-representation revealed in the Chilean testimonies. Finally, the Conclusion explores similarities and differences in the Cuban and the Chilean testimonies, shows how these women's voices complement one another, and also attempts to respond to questions raised in this introduction.

Cuba
SIX VIEWS OF REVOLUTION

Women and the Cuban Revolution

The revolution gave human beings their dignity back; it didn't just give it back to men. Because I don't believe that the words *man* or *men* include women. I don't agree that when one is going to talk about human beings one should say *men*. I don't think men would agree that our saying *women* when what we mean is men and women really includes them.

—Haydée Santamaría

To understand the revolutionary struggle in Cuba and the role of women in Cuban society, one must look first at Cuba's heritage as a colonized country. Unlike the South American nations, which fought and won their wars for independence from Spain early in the nineteenth century (1810-24), the Caribbean islands of Cuba and Puerto Rico remained under Spanish domination until the end of the Spanish-American war in 1898. Cuba's first war for independence—the Ten Years' War of 1868 to 1878—failed; it was not until after José Martí had led the country into its second war for independence (1895-98) that this small island nation achieved its emancipation from Spain.

Martí's writings and his legendary significance as a national hero inspired the leaders of the revolutionary movement of the 1950s; the ideological underpinnings of the Cuban Revolution were not socialist; rather, they were based on Martí's nationalist, democratic, and antiimperialist thought. In the minds and hearts of tens of thousands of Cubans from varying socioeconomic backgrounds, Martí symbolized Cuban freedom and the right to self-determination.[1] He spent the final fifteen years of his life (1881-95) in exile in the United States, where he founded the Cuban Revolutionary Party, organized Cuban tobacco workers living in exile in Tampa and Key West, and prepared for the war that would liberate his country. At the age of forty-two, however, this architect of Cuba's freedom died in Cuba; he was killed on the battlefield in Dos Ríos while leading his country's second war for independence.

Martí was a prolific writer as well as a man of action. As a journalist for Latin American newspapers and the *New York Sun*, he put his pen to use as a weapon in the battle for his nation's freedom. The twenty-eight volumes of his *Obras completas* (Complete works) include speeches, essays, and letters about Latin America and Cuba which reveal his passionate advocacy in the struggle for Cuban independence. He also published essays on life in the United States and on American imperialism, three books of poetry, a play, a novel, and critical essays on art and culture; he even edited a magazine for children.[2]

Martí's famous statement "I have lived inside the monster and I know its entrails" refers to the Cuban leader's growing awareness of the failures of U.S. democracy: the social inequities, racism, and brutal exploitation of workers he witnessed in North America during the late nineteenth century. In a series of articles on the "Haymarket martyrs" he expressed outrage at the condemnation of the Chicago anarchists.[3] This tragic affair marked a turningpoint in Martí's thinking. Although he never embraced socialist ideology, the Cuban leader was thereafter more sympathetic to working-class issues and the proletarian cause. He began to understand more fully the role of the state, especially the courts, in defending the interests of big business over the interests of working-class people; he thus became an inspiration to Fidel Castro, who evoked the figure of José Martí to gather support for the Cuban Revolution.

Martí also warned of the serious threat of U.S. imperialist expansion in Latin America and of U.S. intentions to annex Cuba. As he predicted, following its intervention in the Cuban-Spanish conflict, the United States did seize the island. The infamous Platt Amendment of 1902 converted the new republic into a protectorate. Although this agreement formally granted Cuba a kind of quasi independence, it allowed the United States to retain its naval bases on the island and to intervene to ensure the maintenance of a government that it considered adequate for the protection of private property and individual liberty. Making good use of the Platt Amendment, Washington sent in troops from 1906 to 1909, in 1912, and again from 1917 to 1923 to quell rebellions.[4]

Even more devastating than the political domination of Cuba was the U.S. economic domination. Before 1959 the United States controlled the sugar industry, owned the power and telephone companies, and had invested more in Cuba than in any other Latin American or Caribbean nation. According to Department of Commerce information on investment in Cuba, "When Fidel Castro and his rebel army came to power in January 1959, U.S. firms controlled 40 percent of raw sugar production;

90 percent of telephone, light, and power services; half the public railways; and a quarter of all bank deposits. They also dominated the refining and distribution of petroleum, the exploitation of mineral resources, most of the tourist sector, and a substantial part of the manufacturing" (Barry, Wood, and Preusch 1984, 268).

U.S. hegemony over the Cuban economy can be classified as semi-colonialism; it created the conditions of misery that caused the masses of peasants and workers to take up arms and willingly fight in the Cuban Revolution. Fidel Castro was inspired by the nationalist, antiimperialist writings of José Martí and able to rally support by invoking the national hero's message of freedom and self-determination. Fidel Castro gave a moving five-hour defense speech at his trial after the failed attack on the Moncada Barracks in Santiago de Cuba on July 26, 1953—his first attempt to overthrow the dictatorship of Fulgencio Batista and the event that gave its name to the subsequent July 26 Movement. In this famous "History will absolve me" speech, the twenty-seven-year-old Castro, a lawyer by profession and the son of a wealthy landowner, outlined the aims of the uprising and specified the social conditions requiring radical reform:

> Seven hundred thousand Cubans without work, who desire to earn their daily bread honestly without having to emigrate in search of livelihood.
>
> Five hundred thousand farm laborers inhabiting miserable shacks, who work four months of the year and starve for the rest of the year, sharing their misery with their children, who have not an inch of land to cultivate, and whose existence inspires compassion in any heart not made of stone.
>
> Four hundred thousand industrial laborers and stevedores whose retirement funds have been embezzled, whose benefits are being taken away, whose homes are wretched quarters, whose salaries pass from the hands of the boss to those of the usurer, whose future is a pay reduction and dismissal, whose life is eternal work and whose only rest is in the tomb.
>
> One hundred thousand small farmers who live and die working on land that is not theirs. . . .
>
> In Oriente, the largest province, the lands of the United Fruit Company and West Indian Company join the north coast to the southern one. There are two hundred thousand peasant families who do not have a single acre of land to cultivate to provide food for their starving children. . . .

Ninety percent of rural children are consumed by parasites which filter through their bare feet from the earth. [Qtd. in Keen, 409, 413]

Although by Latin American standards Cuba was an urbanized nation with a large middle class and a high per capita income, prerevolutionary life there was hard. A large sector of the population—men and women alike—suffered hunger and malnutrition, extreme poverty, poor housing, high infant mortality, widespread unemployment and underemployment, illiteracy and disease. Nevertheless, this beautiful island nation had become the tropical playground of foreign tourists, U.S. businessmen and financiers, Mafia bosses, and military personnel stationed at U.S. naval bases. The ceaseless lights of the casinos and nightclubs, the rhythmic sounds of rumba, mambo, and cha-cha-cha, the pristine beaches offering unlimited sand and sun, and the promise of fulfilled sexual fantasies through easy access to voluptuous Cuban prostitutes had lured hordes of North American tourists to the island since the 1920s. The island also served as what Tom Barry has called "a hangout for mobsters like Meyer Lansky, who kept dictator Fulgencio Batista rich while managing their underworld empires unhindered" (Barry, Wood, and Preusch 1984, 268).

The United States was able to maintain tight control over the Cuban economy by propping up several puppet dictatorships to look out for the interests of the United Fruit Company and other U.S. corporations that had come to control 40 percent of the land area of Cuba by 1927. When popular resistance against Gerardo "The Butcher" Machado (1925-33) led to the overthrow of this brutal dictator in 1933, the U.S. government turned to Batista to carry out the dirty work of imprisoning, torturing, and killing members of the growing opposition. Students, workers, and peasants joined the revolutionary movement against this repressive military regime. Finally, on January 1, 1959, the corrupt rule of Batista and United Fruit came tumbling down when Castro and his rebel army from the Sierra Maestra region of eastern Cuba triumphantly marched into Havana and gained control.

Cuban women, both black and white, had participated in the island's struggles since at least as early as the second war of independence. They did not win the rights to divorce, child custody, and administration of their property, however, until 1917. The First National Congress of Women was held in Havana in 1932; as a consequence of the pressures it generated, women finally won the right to vote in 1935 (see Rivero y Méndez 1993, 15).

In prerevolutionary Cuba, however, life for most women remained extremely difficult. For the majority of working-class and poor Cuban women, who made up approximately 17 percent of the work force, there were limited employment opportunities. According to Margaret Randall, "seventy percent of these women worked as domestic servants, with accompanying long hours, oppressive conditions, lack of fringe benefits, and miserable pay" (1981b, 23). The second largest area of employment open to women was prostitution. Young women migrating to the cities from rural areas often found that their options were either working as a maid in the homes of wealthy, bourgeois women or else catering to the sexual whims of U.S. tourists, businessmen, and military personnel in addition to the Cuban male population.

As Alfred Padula and Lois Smith have pointed out, "Prostitution in prerevolutionary Cuba reflected the double standard and patriarchal nature of the old society. At the onset of puberty, boys were taken by their fathers to neighborhood brothels to be initiated into the mysteries of sex." But whereas sexual experience and machismo were encouraged in boys, virginity was a highly valued expectation of any "proper" girl from a "good family" who wished to get married someday and have a family of her own. The centuries-old belief that women were not suited to work outside the home was, generally speaking, unchallenged in Cuba before the revolution. Patriarchal structures remained firmly in place. In many homes, young women were not even permitted to leave the house without a male chaperone. The primary function of women in this society was to reproduce. For most lower-class women, "life was an endless struggle of caring for large broods of children whose fathers were often absent or unemployed" (Padula and Smith 1985, 81).

It was women who suffered most from the effects of underdevelopment: "It was they who did household chores without benefit of electricity and running water. They were the ones with the highest rate of illiteracy. The economic stagnation and low level of industrialization—products of imperialist exploitation—meant that it was almost impossible for a woman without an education or a skill to get a job except as someone else's personal servant" (Stone 1981, 7).

Even Cuban peasant women, in contrast to those in other parts of Latin America, did not participate in direct agricultural labor along with men. As Cuban social scientists Isabel Larguía and John Dumoulin point out, "With rare exceptions, the cutting of sugar cane was exclusively male and seasonal labor. . . . It was unimaginable for women to work in a sugar mill, even as a cleaning woman." Also in contrast to peasant women elsewhere, Cuban women living in the countryside did not make pottery, weave baskets, or produce textiles or leather goods: "The fact that a peasant woman did not produce *visible* commodities with her own hands contributed to her lack of access to commercial activity" (1985, 39). This difference in historical factors aggravated the oppression already imposed upon all women by patriarchal social structures; it also made the task of incorporating Cuban women into the work force after the revolution particularly monumental.

The direct participation of women in the Cuban Revolution was, broadly speaking, limited. In the July 26, 1953, assault on the Moncada Barracks only two women, Haydée Santamaría and Melba Hernández, were present, whereas 165 men took part in this quixotic and disastrous adventure. Likewise, the guerrilla war carried out in the Sierra Maestra was, for the most part, a male enterprise. The small ratio of women to men who participated in direct combat points to the prevailing attitude that women were "too fragile and too soft to kill" and therefore belonged at home and not on the battlefield. This commonly held opinion of both men and women reflects the patriarchal beliefs and attitudes deeply embedded in Cuba's prerevolutionary culture.

This is not to say, however, that women did not play a significant part in this conflict. A small number of women combatants did fight in the hills; some were killed in battle and others, such as Santamaría, Hernández, and Celia Sánchez, "survived to become heroines and to hold high office in the postrevolutionary society" (Padula and Smith 1985, 81).[5] There was also a legendary troop of women guerrilla fighters called the Mariana Grajales Platoon (see Chapter 4). This all-woman unit was named after the mother of the Maceo brothers, who led Cuba's first war of independence; Mariana Grajales, a black woman active in that struggle, came to symbolize Castro's ideal of overcoming both gender and race discrimination. In fact, it was Castro who, when women combatants demanded their right to fight on equal terms with the male guerrillas on the front lines, encouraged the formation of the platoon during the final year of the Revolution. He encountered strong resistance from his male officers, however, who still thought "women would faint at the sight of blood" and "were too soft and delicate" for real combat. In a speech of January 20, 1981, the Cuban leader recalled this opposition among male guerrilla fighters to women's full participation as soldiers, fighting alongside their brothers-in-arms:

> I remember that when I organized the Mariana Grajales Platoon—in fact, I took part in the combat training of those comrades—some of

the rebel fighters were furious, because they didn't like the idea of a platoon made up of women. We had some spare M-1's, and the M-1 was considered a good light weapon and, therefore, we thought it would be the right one for the women. Some of our fighters wanted to know why they had Springfields while the women were going to get M-1's. On more than one occasion I got so annoyed that I would answer, "Because they are better fighters than you are." And the truth is that they showed it. [Qtd. in Stone, 1981, 8][6]

Margaret Randall has written that the Marianas, as they were called, "saw action in some twenty important battles before the enemy capitulated on New Year's Eve, and then they went on to enlarge their ranks and take on peacetime military tasks" (1981b, 23).

Although only a few women were actual combatants in the Revolution, many women organized demonstrations against Batista, distributed leaflets and propaganda, and worked in the clandestine movement, as the following testimonies reveal, they carried messages to political leaders, transported arms under their skirts, participated in action and sabotage units in the cities, and even planted bombs at strategic sites. Some collected supplies for the guerrillas and sold war bonds to raise money for the rebel army; others showed their solidarity by setting up hospitals to care for wounded soldiers, by making uniforms, or by hiding revolutionaries in their houses.[7]

During the summer of 1952, Aída Pelayo (see Chapter 3) and her friends Olga Román and Carmen Castro Porta decided to start an organization made up of women of the so-called Generation of 1930 to oppose the Batista dictatorship.[8] Because the antiimperialist ideas of José Martí formed the group's ideological foundation, and they wished to honor the national hero on the hundredth anniversary of his birth, they originally named their organization El Frente Cívico de Mujeres del Centenario Martiano (the Civic Front of Women on the Martí Centennial). In November 1952 the first assembly of about forty women, mostly students, formally established the Frente Cívico de Mujeres Martianas (the Martí Women's Civic Front), or FCMM. This was a heterogeneous group of women with a range of political ideologies and varying degrees of political experience and militancy; they were from different social sectors (although most were white and middle or upper-middle class). The FCMM grew to include more than one hundred women who coordinated their efforts with the July 26 Movement and other sectors of the revolutionary opposition to Batista. Members joined student protesters in street demonstrations, distributed propaganda, worked as militants in the clandestine movement, helped to organize strikes, cared for wounded soldiers, fought for the rights of political prisoners, and offered support to the families of detainees and revolutionaries killed by the regime.

Following the triumph of the Cuban Revolution in January 1959, the Federation of Cuban Women (FMC) was founded on August 23, 1960. The purpose of this grassroots organization made up of women of diverse backgrounds and ideologies was to incorporate women into the labor force en masse and to integrate them into the revolutionary process. Today, about 80 percent of Cuban women over fourteen years of age are FMC members. Although this organization was successful in channeling women's energies in defense of the Revolution, it did not promote a *feminist* agenda or provide a gender-specific analysis of Cuba's social structure. As Elizabeth Stone explains, its principal activities following the Revolution were to "organize masses of women, house by house, in the cities and the countryside, helping to build the militias and the Committees for the Defense of the Revolution (CDRs), setting up schools for peasant women, and establishing a network of childcare centers" (1981, 9). During 1959 and 1960 the CDRs and a popular militia worked to counteract efforts by the U.S. government and counterrevolutionaries within Cuba to destabilize the Revolution's attempts to carry out radical programs of land reform and the nationalization of large foreign companies.[9]

Although the CDRs, block organizations that reported suspicious activities and guarded important buildings, were necessary during the early years of the Revolution to secure its very survival, they also formed the basis for a sort of "police state." Many Cubans believe that they contributed to a general climate of distrust and lack of openness, pitting neighbor against neighbor. For many years, in which no direct criticism of the Castro regime was tolerated, people feared that any complaints about the government might be considered "counterrevolutionary," reported by the CDRs, or even deemed a legitimate cause for persecution, punishment, imprisonment, or the loss of privileges reserved for the regime's most loyal supporters.[10]

There was, of course, an aggressive counterrevolution—orchestrated and financed by the United States—immediately following the 1959 victory over the Batista dictatorship. There were numerous bombings, sabotaging of factories, the burning of sugarcane fields, and finally the failed military invasion at the Bay of Pigs in April 1961. Fidel Castro (1981) has asserted that a whole arsenal of measures was used against our country. They started with refusing us commercial credits at the beginning of the Revolution, then they stopped their oil deliveries, then they revoked our sugar quota, and finally imposed a harsh and total economic blockade. . . .

Relying for support on the exploiter classes which had been removed from power, and all that gang of politicos allied to imperialism who had plundered our country, they organized hundreds of counterrevolutionary groups—I repeat, hundreds. They were following a methodical plan to eliminate the Revolution's leaders.

The economic blockade has had devastating effects on the Cuban economy. Under U.S. pressure, all Latin American countries except Mexico broke off trade relations with Cuba. The CIA, continuing its covert war against Cuba until the present, embarked on a large-scale campaign of sabotage in order to discredit Cuba as a trade partner and to pressure other countries to cancel their airline and shipping services to the island.[11] The United States has tried to prevent the republic from receiving foreign credit and has financed the broadcast of antirevolutionary and anti-Castro propaganda by Radio Martí, TV Martí, and Radio Free Europe. The CIA even engaged in sinister biological warfare, introducing viral diseases among pigs and poultry.[12] It also planned assassination attempts on Castro's life, including a scheme to poison his cigars. According to the 1975 Senate Select Committee on Intelligence Activities (Church committee), there was "concrete evidence of at least eight conspiracies involving the CIA to assassinate Fidel Castro from 1960 to 1965" (Tarasov and Zubenko 1984, 220). The United States routinely violated Cuba's airspace in its attempt to intimidate and demoralize the Cuban people, trying to instill the fear of another U.S. invasion.[13]

Soon after the Revolution, the Federation of Cuban Women mobilized women to combat counterrevolutionary threats to the new government. A number of women were killed defending against the invasion of the Bay of Pigs. Vilma Espín, president of the FMC, describes the role of women during this conflict: "The Bay of Pigs went down in history as imperialism's first defeat on the continent. We all took up arms against the aggressor. . . . On the front lines, women from the FMC helped bring supplies to the first-aid posts, managed one hundred kitchens and three hospitals—where wounded fighters were taken—and all over the country the federation mobilized to replace militiamen who went into combat. FMC women also participated in the collection of clothing, medicine, and food" (qtd. in Stone 1981, 43).

Perhaps the most important task of the FMC, however, was to raise consciousness about the need to create a new society based on the principle of equality between the sexes. Women were demanding their right to equal education, equal employment opportunities, and the right to full participation in all the activities of the new revolutionary government. In 1961 a major literacy campaign was launched: more than 100,000 young people aged ten to eighteen were sent out into the countryside as literacy *brigadistas* to teach peasants (see Kozol 1978). Even though there was strong resistance by many husbands in rural areas to their wives' attending literacy classes, the campaign not only taught thousands of peasant women how to read and write but also offered them increased self-confidence and a sense of having greater control over their own lives.

Another educational effort designed specifically to address the needs of young women was the foundation of the Ana Betancourt School for Peasant Girls in Havana in 1961. Its purpose was to provide a sixth-grade education, instill "revolutionary" consciousness, and offer vocational training and skills (mainly sewing and dressmaking) to girls from the remote rural areas of Oriente, Las Villas, and Pinar del Río—regions that did not yet have adequate schools. Other schools were dedicated to the education of young women who had formerly worked as domestic servants or as prostitutes, in order to integrate them into the labor force as day-care workers, taxi drivers, secretaries, accountants, translators, bank clerks, and factory workers (see Randall 1981b, 54-59). Many of these women were able to improve their self-esteem and to feel that they had become useful, productive members of a new, more egalitarian social order.

Nicola Murray catalogues the efforts made by the Central Organization of Cuban Trade Unions (CTC) to set up a women's organization in 1969 that would "investigate and initiate new policies to facilitate women's participation in paid labor," including

> *Plan Jaba* [the "shopping-bag scheme"], under which women can leave a shopping list in the morning and pick up the shopping ready-packed in the evening, or else simply jump the queue—thus freeing women from the interminable queuing which causes material shortages in every shop; giving women in paid labor priority for certain material goods; the establishment of holiday camps and weekend play schemes for children; increased provision of laundry facilities and communal eating services; increased manufacture of refrigerators and washing machines, which are distributed through the CTC and for which working women have priority. [1979, 101]

Although the number of child-care centers still doesn't satisfy the demand for enrollment, they have been an important source of support for working parents and also a means of educating future generations. Vilma Espín commented in a 1988 interview that there were "854 childcare centers with a capacity for 109,923 children and some 101,530 working mothers" (qtd. in Shnookal 1991, 13). Strong state support is reflected in the subsidized funding of these centers, making them affordable for most parents by putting fees on a sliding scale according to per capita family income.

Health care became another revolutionary crusade. One result is that the infant mortality rate has declined substantially.[14] Women were admitted into medical school in an effort to increase the proportion of women doctors; by 1993, 65 percent of Cuban general practitioners were women (Modlich 1993, 38). Further, a program of family doctors in neighborhood health clinics and even in the most remote mountainous areas was implemented. In addition to widespread improvements in the general health-care system, huge strides were made in attention to women's specific health needs. For example, contraceptives became readily available at the neighborhood clinics and at local pharmacies throughout the island (Padula and Smith 1985, 83). Prenatal care classes were offered, and more women began to deliver their babies in hospitals.[15] And in 1974, an advanced Maternity Law increased the amount of paid maternity leave provided to women by the 1963 law: Cuban women are now guaranteed six weeks of paid leave before and twelve weeks after childbirth.[16] Cuban women also have full access to legal abortions. (Data on family violence, child abuse, and public violence against women, however, are not readily available, since these problems do not officially exist.)

Although the FMC has been relatively successful in integrating women into the revolutionary process, the vestiges of patriarchal gender relations have not been uprooted. Most Cuban women continue to put in a so-called "double shift." Pastor Vega's 1979 film *Portrait of Teresa* well portrayed the anxiety many Cuban women suffer as they attempt to juggle their multiple responsibilities and roles. Padula and Smith argue that this film, reflecting the state of crisis of the Cuban family, "makes clear that it is in activities outside the home that women's fulfillment is to be found. . . . Teresa, played by Daisy Granados, is the modern *cubana*. Educated and intelligent, Teresa works at a textile plant by day and helps organize a factory musical at night, while struggling to keep her household with three children and oafish husband afloat. She takes tranquilizers. She washes, irons, cooks, and cleans. She dresses and feeds the children. Her husband provides little assistance. He is distressed by Teresa's nighttime activities. They quarrel, he begins an affair. As the film ends it appears Teresa, like so many other *cubanas*, is headed for divorce" (1985, 85).

Just like the protagonist in that film and the women whose testimonies are recorded in this book, many Cuban women struggle to integrate factory or other full-time jobs with voluntary agricultural work on the weekends, participating in the revolutionary activities of political organizations (CDR duty, attending Communist Party meetings or FMC meetings), and perhaps attending night school, as well as taking on the primary responsibility for their children and all the domestic chores. Many women also confront sexist, egocentric partners who maintain a double standard, expecting fidelity from their wives but feeling entitled to have extramarital affairs and use sexual conquest as a means of affirming their masculinity.

In order to combat officially this deeply embedded gender oppression, a milestone measure was taken in 1975. The Family Code gave the force of law to the division of household labor: Article 26 states, "Both partners must care for the family they have created and must cooperate with the other in the education, upbringing, and guidance of the children. They must participate, to the extent of their capacities or possibilities, in the running of the home, and cooperate so it will develop in the best possible way" (qtd. in Stone 1981, 146). Cuba is the only Latin American country that has required, by law, that men and women assume equal responsibility in raising and caring for children as well as in housework, shopping, cooking, and laundry.

Even though this law is on the books, it is far from being implemented in everyday practice. A 1988 survey showed that working men contributed 4.5 hours per week to domestic chores; employed women, 22 hours (Modlich 1993, 38). Most of the Cuban women I talked with told me that the majority of Cuban men still resist the idea of doing housework. Nevertheless, with the severe economic crisis of the "Special Period," more and more men are helping out at home and waiting in long lines to get food and the other basics the family needs for day-to-day survival. Several women explained that their partners had begun to cook and shop out of sheer necessity. Many of the restaurants and dining halls at factories and other workplaces have been shut down because of the fuel shortages and other scarcities. Husbands, wives, and children must often wait for several hours in different lines in order to get whatever fruit, vegetable, or other product may have come to the market on that particular day. Also, electrical blackouts are so common that families are forced to cook their main meal at whatever hour electricity is available in the home. (When I was in Cuba in 1992 the power shortages lasted from twelve to sixteen hours a day, often causing even refrigerated food to spoil).

The economic crisis of the 1990s, the worst in thirty-six years, was brought on by the collapse of the socialist bloc and the disintegration of the Soviet Union; as a direct consequence, Cuba lost its principal trading partners and became increasingly isolated. Given the continued economic blockade and U.S. hostility, many of the Revolution's accomplishments—free education, quality health and dental care, full employment opportunities, the provision of basic shelter (however overcrowded and in urgent need of paint and repair), and a somewhat equitable distribution of food and other basic necessities—were threatened and gradually disappearing as the country began its "transition" from a tightly centralized, state-controlled economy to some form of "mercantile economy" in which the market would play a much greater role. Many Cuban women who had supported the Revolution because of the opportunities it afforded their children began to fear the future and to worry about a rapidly declining standard of living. When Soviet petroleum shipments declined in 1990 and Cuba was forced to purchase oil with dollars, bicycles (imported from China) were substituted for buses, and oxen for tractors. Likewise, with gas and electrical shortages, women could no longer count on the convenience of modern appliances at home. These practical difficulties for everyday survival aroused feelings of discontent among many Cuban women.

The problems are not only economic; the difficulties produced by the "double blockade"[17] have been exacerbated by other disasters. In 1993 a mysterious epidemic spread throughout the island, causing tens of thousands of Cubans to begin to go blind, apparently at least in part because of vitamin B deficiencies. In March 1993 a devastating storm flooded Havana, caused extensive crop damage, and "left some 150,000 people homeless. Official estimates placed the damage at around one billion dollars" (Schultz 1994, 175). Then Hurricane Gordon hit Cuba in November 1994, "leaving more than $123 million of damage in its wake" (Lage-Dávila 1995, 19).[18]

There has been dissatisfaction in political and social matters as well. A charge frequently made against the Cuban leadership, by friends and foes alike, is that of nepotism (several of my respondents complained about it). In the restructuring of the Communist Party in 1965, Castro himself became first secretary of the Cuban Communist Party (PCC) and the top member of the Political Bureau, in addition to being prime minister and commander in chief of the Revolutionary Armed Forces (FAR); thus, he held the top position in the Party, the government, and the military, and his younger brother Raúl ranked second in all three branches. Raúl's wife, Vilma Espín, the most powerful woman in Cuba, has been president of the Federation of Cuban Women since its inception in 1960. She has also served on the Central Committee of the PCC since 1965, the Council of State since 1976, and the Political Bureau since 1980.

The repression of homosexuals in Cuba following the revolution is well documented.[19] Lesbians and gays still live under the shadow of an old law specifying up to twenty years in prison for homosexual behavior in public (Modlich 1993, 38). During the 1960s this law was enforced; since then, however, tolerance in the workplace and the arts has gradually started to prevail. In recent years there have been some successful unofficial efforts to combat homophobia, such as Tomás Gutiérrez Alea and Juan Carlos Tabío's internationally acclaimed 1993 film *Fresa y chocolate* (Strawberry and chocolate). Based on the novella by Senel Paz, it explores the evolving friendship between a gay intellectual, who loves art and literature, and a student—a Party comrade who refuses to spy on his new friend. The film's sensitive handling of homosexuality and homophobia in Cuba during the 1970s suggests a new attitude of openness and the beginning of a greater acceptance of gays.[20]

During my visit to Havana, however, I observed that though the "gay coffee shop" was a meeting place for homosexual men, there were no public spaces where lesbians could openly congregate, and several I spoke with complained that they still felt discriminated against. One young lesbian in her mid-twenties would not allow me to record our interview for fear of reprisals; she had suffered frequent verbal abuse from Cuban men both in the workplace and in the streets. The lack of official support for lesbians in Cuba was illustrated by a leader of the Federation of Cuban Women who acknowledge the presence of lesbians in the FMC but was uncomfortable discussing or promoting the need for lesbian visibility and activism (see Mates 1994).

In its need for hard currency, Cuba has turned to tourism.[21] This reliance has created many social problems and resentments on the island; Castro himself has referred to increased tourism as a *mal necesario*, a "necessary evil," to keep the Cuban economy afloat during the Special Period. With increased tourism, the country has seen a revival of some of the problems previously eradicated by the Revolution, such as a dual market (native and tourist), prostitution, an active black market, and an increase in crime (see Salloum 1996).

Forty years ago, Cuba was a tropical playland, promising "exotic" young women to foreign tourists. Things have, in a certain sense, come full circle now that the Cuban economy is on the brink of ruin (Fusco 1995). Nevertheless, there are aspects of Cuban prostitution today that distinguish it from that of other countries: it is unlike prostitution in most industrialized nations—where the women are marginalized and often turn to prostitution to support a drug habit—or throughout most of Latin America where (as in prerevolutionary Cuba) women resort to "the world's oldest profession" in order to survive conditions of abject poverty. Instead, many young *jineteras* (as prostitutes are now commonly called in Cuba) are teenagers motivated by the possibility of buying new clothes, new shoes, and some cosmetics at the *turi-tiendas* (tourist shops). They are also attracted by the prospect of sexual experience with (and possible marriage to) foreign men and, thereby, access to Cuba's finest restaurants and nightclubs, reserved only for tourists. In the discos of Havana many middle-class, educated *jineteras* sell themselves for money.[22]

For me, a North American tourist, one of the most dreadful aspects of tourism in Cuba is that it has created a kind of "apartheid" in which wealthy and middle-class tourists enjoy fine restaurants, luxurious beach resorts, air-conditioned hotels and taxis, and discotheques featuring live music and entertainment which Cubans are not even allowed to enter, unless accompanied by a foreign tourist. Meanwhile, food has become so scarce that only children under seven years of age are given milk, and each person is limited to only one piece of bread a day. In 1992 there was no beef, pork, or chicken except on the black market (for those who could afford it). Even staple foods such as beans, rice, eggs, coffee, and sugar—rationed by government-controlled stores to assure equitable distribution—were being doled out in smaller and smaller amounts, and many Cubans complained that they were suffering hunger for the first time in their lives.

Because employees of the market-oriented joint venture companies and the tourism sector enjoy advantages and "perks" that other Cuban employees don't have, many relatively skilled workers and even highly educated Cuban professionals, such as doctors and engineers, are leaving other sectors of the economy to work as doormen or waiters; their tips will buy shampoo, soap, deodorant, and cooking oil in the special dollar stores established for Cuban diplomats and foreign tourists. Pedro Monreal, a researcher at the Center for the Study of the Americas and coauthor of *Cuba; La restructuración de la economía: Una propuesta para el debate* (Cuba; Restructuring the economy: Notes for debate), recently commented in an interview with journalist Gail Reed:

I have trouble thinking that a country can function well when highly qualified professionals, technicians or skilled workers, employed in key areas like the sugar industry, have a standard of living and incentives far below people working in tourism; where a hotel waiter earns more in two weeks than a doctor or an engineer in a year. It's an aberration when a chain of special stores sells scarce consumer goods, necessary items, in a currency like the U.S. dollar that hardly anyone earns. The solution begs another discussion about the sole use of the Cuban peso, measures designed to rectify the financial situation in the country, the question of the convertible peso. But that, in turn, requires what I don't think exists yet: an overall plan for a new formulation of the Cuban economy. [Reed 1995, 11]

The economic and social crisis led many Cubans to leave the island on makeshift rafts and inner tubes, hoping to reach the United States. President Bill Clinton's shift in Cuban immigration policy, denying Cuban refugees entry visas to the United States for the first time since the triumph of the Revolution in 1959, has slowed this exodus; nevertheless, many Cubans still dream of emmigrating and settling somewhere outside their country.

Undoubtedly, the Cuban government has made many mistakes regarding its economy; some of the shortages on the island have to do with internal distribution problems. But most of the current economic crisis is the direct result of not having normal economic and diplomatic relations with the United States and of U.S. pressure on other countries not to trade with or invest in the small island nation. The embargo, which includes food and medicine, is causing much suffering in the lives of all Cubans, whose standard of living has dropped significantly.

The U.S. embargo is considered obsolete and outdated in the post–Cold War world by nations such as Canada, Mexico, Argentina, France, and Spain, which want to engage in trade relations with Cuba. These countries resent U.S. policies that blatantly violate international law and interfere with their own rights to trade with whomever they choose. But the right-wing Cuban exile community in Miami—especially the late Jorge Mas Canosa and the Cuban-American National Foundation— wields enormous political clout and influence over both the Democratic and Republican Parties; its lobbyists have been major players in the shaping of U.S. foreign policy, in particular the tightening of the embargo.

In addition, several right-wing Cuban exile groups have committed terrorist acts against Cuba. One of the worst examples occurred on October 6, 1976, when a bomb planted aboard a Cubana Airlines plane exploded after takeoff from Barbados, killing all seventy-three passengers—including Cuba's entire fencing team. Since its founding in 1962 a terrorist organization of Cuban exiles called Comandos L has conducted dozens of raids against targets in Cuba, especially hotels. At a news conference on January 7, 1993, Tony Bryant, a leader of this group, announced more raids and warned tourists to stay off the island. Another anti-Castro, Miami-based group of exiles called Brothers to the Rescue has violated Cuban airspace frequently in recent years. In July 1995 the Brothers flew over Havana and dropped thousands of anti-Castro leaflets encouraging dissidents to rebel against the socialist regime. Since then, their pilots have repeatedly ignored warnings by the Cuban government. Some zealous members of these *all-male* terrorist exile organizations who engage in hit-and-run or sabotage attacks have been caught and imprisoned in Cuba.

This history of exile violence against Cuba was a factor in the February 24, 1996, downing of two small civilian planes piloted by Brothers to the Rescue, following a dispute as to whether the planes were flying in Cuban or international airspace. This tragic event elicited a predictable response from the United States: make the embargo stricter in order to hurt the Cuban economy and punish Fidel Castro. The Helms-Burton Cuban Liberation Bill, enacted in March 1996, was designed to toughen economic sanctions and strongly discourage foreign investment in Cuba.

President Clinton's signing of the legislation evoked outrage particularly in Canada, France, and Mexico—because of their foreign investments and huge trade ties with Cuba. They claim that giving Cuban exiles the right to sue foreign companies that profit from Cuban property confiscated by Castro following the Revolution is a violation of international law and of their sovereignty. Another provision of this controversial bill prohibits executives of foreign countries from entering the United States if they are "trafficking in" expropriated properties abroad. Canada, angered by U.S. attempts to legislate other countries' trade relations with Cuba, is threatening to challenge Helms-Burton in international tribunals. Other critics point out that the United States is punishing the Cuban people, inflicting hunger and economic hardship on a whole nation by denying them food and medicine, and also violating Cuba's right to sovereignty. Critics of U.S. sanctions—the trade embargo, travel restrictions on U.S. citizens wishing to visit the island and on Cubans requesting travel visas to the United States, the expansion of Radio and TV Martí, and the entire anti-Castro propaganda network—say there is no justification for these policies in the post–Cold War era. Nevertheless, the blockade has been tightened, not loosened, since the collapse of the Berlin Wall.

An ever growing number of moderate, younger Cubans, both at home and in exile, are calling for a dialogue, a bridge of open communication, and improved relations between the Cubans living on the island and those in the diaspora.[23] But as the Cuban-American writer and artist Coco Fusco has observed, "As usual, the politicians on both sides still lag behind, evincing unfailing rigidity. Complain, joke, or speculate as we may, the Cuban-American National Foundation on the one hand, and Fidel and the Central Committee on the other, still call the shots" (1995, 212).

Despite growing discontent inside Cuba, however, the first independent poll conducted on the island in more than thirty years revealed that "58 percent of Cubans think the revolution had more achievements than failures and 69 percent of those polled say they still closely identify themselves with the revolution" (Levinson 1995, 9). The poll was conducted by a Costa Rican firm associated with the Gallup organization, in November 1994.[24] It is important to remember that before the Revolution there were enormous differences between the living conditions of the minority of white, middle-and upper-class educated women and those of the majority of mostly peasant, black, mulatto, and poor white women, who were often illiterate and subjected to conditions of extreme poverty. Following the Revolution, the gap between these social sectors narrowed significantly.

Yet although Castro has preached an official policy of women's equality and referred to the challenge of creating a truly egalitarian society in which women participate fully in every aspect of Cuba's economic, social, political, and cultural life as a "revolution within a revolution," a look at statistics proves that it is men who really control the island and make all the important decisions.[25] The small circle of the power elite is almost exclusively male, and there is, of course, only *one man* who has the final say on the most fundamental issues affecting daily life. This lack of power sharing is one of the principal contradictions and most widely criticized aspects of the Cuban socialist experiment. Many Cubans as well as non-Cubans are critical of Fidel's monopoly of power; his enemies consider him an "evil dictator," a *caudillo*, or else a power-hungry megalomaniac whose compulsion for grandeur blinds him to what is in the best interest of the people.

Although women in Cuba benefited socially and economically because women's advancement was of interest to the patriarch, it is important to note that Castro made use of women's voluntary, or unpaid, labor in support of the regime and its predetermined policies. As Smith and Padula point out, "The constant mobilizations of women . . . from the workforce to the agricultural and health brigades to the organs of social vigilance to the militias," and the use of the FMC as a tool for the promotion of progressive legislation for women such as the maternity law, sex education, and the Family Code, were strategies of the central government to promote an ideal of Cuban womanhood (1996, 183). This monolithic image, however, is not an accurate depiction of the diversity of ideologies existing among Cuban women. Many women fled Cuba, and through the years significant numbers of women were imprisoned for opposing the revolution.

The most well-publicized example is the Cuban poet María Elena Varela, who was sentenced to two years in prison for an open letter she wrote to Fidel Castro protesting the lack of democracy and human rights in Cuba (Smith and Padula 1996, 183-85). Varela was cofounder of a human rights group called Criterio Alternativo (Alternative Criteria) and had been outspoken against the regime for years. According to one source, "Varela had signed a declaration of principles that was to become the constitution of a coalition of human rights groups. Rapid Response Brigades (groups organized by the government) staged a two-day sit-in at her home, beat her, dragged her downstairs, and forced her to literally eat her declaration" (Rivero y Méndez 1993, 16).

Smith and Padula argue that "Cuban women were isolated by the very ideology that purported to liberate them. All ideas that did not encourage women to march as commanded by the great patriarch, the *comandante*, were deemed 'diversionary,' enemy propaganda" (1996, 183). The revolutionary ideal of all Cuban women united in loyalty to the regime was not an accurate, honest protrayal of the wide spectrum of women's public opinions about socialist Cuba. The views of Castro revealed by the testimonies in this book range from starry-eyed support to strong criticism. Nevertheless, they all show support of some form of socialism in post-Castro Cuba. Thus, the interviews here do not reflect the entire range of diverse points of view among Cuban women but concentrate on perspectives that are sympathetic to (although not uncritical of) the Revolution.

The centralized government does not provide any functioning mechanisms for ordinary citizens to influence the state; therefore, no real democracy is allowed to exist in Cuba. National policies and decisions affecting women's lives continue to be made primarily by men. As Smith and Padula observe:

This absence—even exclusion—of women from decision-making positions is reflected in rules that barred housewives from party membership for nearly thirty years. It is suggested also by the fact that abortion was disallowed for a number of years after the revolution, and that only recently was there public access to information on the potential side effects of certain birth control devices. It is evidenced in the militaristic and patriarchal bent of Cuban education. It is evidenced in the chronic underfunding of support services for working women while millions were spent to maintain tens of thousands of Cuban troops in Africa for more than ten years. It is suggested by the great official silence on domestic violence and rape. [1996, 182]

When the Communist Party of Cuba was established in 1965, there were no women on the eight-member Political Bureau or the six-member Secretariat, and only five of the hundred members of the Central Committee were women. Juan del Aguila has observed that "the interlocking membership by the Castro brothers in top party, state, administration, and military roles emerged as a permanent characteristic of Cuba's structure of political power, with additional key positions occupied by loyal revolutionaries from the ranks of the July 26th Movement" (1994, 65-72). That scheme has carried over into the 1990s. In fact, there is a gross underrepresentation not only of women but of peasants and workers in top-ranking positions of political power in the PCC, National Assembly, Council of State, and the military.

As Vilma Espín pointed out in 1988 that only "thirteen percent of the Central Committee of the PCC members are women. In the Political Bureau 13.6 percent are women. Of the total membership 21.5 percent are female" (qtd. in Shnookal 1991, 21). These statistics suggest that women's status in Cuban society, though somewhat enhanced, has not been transformed into real political power. Women do not exert much direct political influence; consequently, most of their concerns, especially peasant and working women's issues, are not adequately represented within the present distribution of power. Margaret Randall, who lived in Cuba from 1969 through 1980, is critical of the failure of the Cuban Revolution to develop a feminist agenda: in the 1970s, "Castro's exhortation that women lead the struggle for our own equality faced the contradiction implicit in the Cuban revolutionary model. Its failure to develop a genuine and popular critical process greatly reduced the possibility that women—or anyone else—might question official assumptions" (1992, 146). This observation still rings true.

Naty Revuelta

CULTURAL WORKER

Naty Revuelta (1992) with portrait of José Martí.

Naty Revuelta, who is now in her sixties, was an active participant in the the Martí Women's Civic Front (FCMM). Although she has reached retirement age, she is currently director of international relations, at the Ministry of Culture. An elegant, slim, attractive woman with penetrating green eyes and silver hair, she is independent and strong-willed, and has a keen sense of humor. (She told me several jokes about Fidel but made me promise not to include them.) By Cuban standards, Naty Revuelta is upper-middle class; she lives in the once posh neighborhood of Nuevo Vedado with her aging mother. Before the Revolution her family was wealthy, and she was married to a physician—a marriage that did not survive the triumph of the Cuban Revolution.

That Naty Revuelta was an intimate friend of Fidel Castro during the 1950s is public knowledge; their daughter—whom Castro never publicly recognized—recently defected to the United States, creating a scandal in Cuba. In recounting her involvement in the revolutionary struggle, Revuelta speaks with nostalgia about the night she met the young leader before the failed attack on the Moncada Barracks.

My memories of my childhood are varied, as you can imagine. For the most part, I was a rather happy kid. I'm from a family of mostly professionals. We lived a comfortable life, without too many problems. My parents got divorced when I was only three or four years old. My mother remarried a man who worked as the finance director of a transportation company, and we had a relatively high standard of living. I remember feeling very proud of my uncles, who had all completed university degrees and had become professionals.

I remember my maternal grandfather with special affection. He was English and came to Cuba at the end of the nineteenth century, in 1893. My grandfather made some close friendships with Cubans, and shortly after he arrived he joined the *mambises*, as the fighters for Cuba's independence were called back then. He fought for three years in the war, from 1895 to 1898, and rapidly rose in rank to the level of a lieutenant colonel. Although he died when I was six or seven years old, I still remember the stories he told me about Cuba's second war for independence [1895-98]. My mother's father was a wonderful grandfather to me, and he had an important early influence on my life; I was very fond of him.

My father lived in the interior of the island and would only come to visit me in Havana about once a year. Each time he came to see me, he would find me more lovely and more grown up. Of course, it was natural that he would think I was beautiful because he was my father. Actually, I didn't have much of a relationship with him until after I got married.

By then, he was living in Havana, and we were able to see each other frequently.

From a very young age, I was sent to boarding schools. But it wasn't so bad; at least my parents sent me to good schools. I attended a school named Sepúlveda in El Vedado for the first three grades. Then I went to an all-girl bilingual school, an American school run by the Protestant church, called Colegio Buena Vista. The liberal arts education I received had an important impact on my personal development and on the formation of my thinking and values. I think that, generally speaking, the Protestant religion is liberal and healthy; it teaches tolerance and introspection, unlike the Catholic religion, which is more dogmatic and teaches you to feel guilty. After graduating from Buena Vista I went to Philadelphia, Pennsylvania, where I was supposed to complete high school.[1] But I became ill after one year and had to return to Havana. I continued my high school education at an excellent North American high school here.

After that, I was sent to Washington, D.C., for a course in business administration. I completed the two-year program in just one year. This was during the Second World War. In general, I loved art, literature, music, and dance, but I didn't have any clearly defined vocation in any of those areas. (I've always said that I have a lot of undeveloped talent. In a way, I'm like a pressure cooker with the lid on it. I've never let out any of the steam, any of the vapor trapped inside.) So when I returned from D.C., I got a job right away. First, I worked at a Canadian bank, then for the American Embassy at the Office of Immigration until in 1950 I landed a job at the international office of a large oil company, Esso Standard (now Exxon). I worked there until the triumph of the Revolution. After that, my life changed drastically.

I come from an apolitical family. Most of my family members distrust all politicians. In Cuba, the traditional political parties were always very corrupt. Politics were associated with becoming wealthy illegally, with robbery, hypocrisy, and demagoguery. As Martí once said, "These are the political *lacras* [sores] of the traditional political system in Cuba."

I became interested in politics in the 1950s, around the time Eduardo Chibás formed the Orthodox Party. This was a liberal, reformist, middle-class party that suited me and my thinking at that time in my life. Although I wasn't aware of having any particular political ideology, I was sensitive to and acutely aware of my country's problems. I would ask myself, "Why are some people so wealthy while others are so poor?" "Why is there a large middle class without any economic security here in Cuba?" Each time there were elections and the government changed, so did all the public employees; every four years all government employees were laid off. There were few hospitals and constant shortages of medicine. I remember Chibás's last speech: before he killed himself, he called on the Cuban people to wake up, to wake up to all the corruption and social injustices in our country. I became more and more politically and socially conscious and began to support the Orthodox Party's line that continued after Chibás's death on August 16, 1951.

Then on March 10, 1952, there was the coup d'état led by Fulgencio Batista. We, the Cuban people, resented being governed by the force of cannons, bayonets, and rifles. We resisted being told what to do by the paternalistic U.S. administration that supported Batista. We began to organize an opposition force immediately after the coup. I remember attending a symbolic burial of the Cuban Constitution [of 1940], organized as a sign of protest. I started to attend the meetings of some of the student organizations at the University of Havana. I was married and already had a baby daughter at the time. I remember going to all of the student demonstrations following Batista's seizure of power.

I was happy at my job during this period of my life. I liked my coworkers, I was well paid, and I found my work satisfying. But my husband, who was a doctor, didn't like for me to work outside the home. He had a sister-in-law who was a housewife, whom he considered to be the ideal wife and mother. She was concerned only about the daily menu and the running of the home—giving orders to the gardener, to the chauffeur, to the domestic servants, and so on. I didn't feel that I needed to be firmly in command at home for things to run smoothly. Of course, my mother helped me out a lot with the domestic chores, and that made it possible for me to continue working. My husband had to resign himself to the fact that I was very politically active and needed to work outside the house. When I was nine months pregnant with our daughter, I was still driving. My husband had to hide the car keys in order to keep me off the streets. I couldn't stay cooped up in the house; I needed to go out, to work and to be with people.

I remember that following the Batista coup there was a huge demonstration near the steps of the university on November 21, 1952. My husband and I both went to this demonstration to protest the coup d'état. That night the police surrounded the university, where several thousand demonstrators had gathered, and cut off the electricity so that we couldn't continue giving speeches with the microphone.

That night was special for me, because it was then that I first met Fidel Castro. One of my husband's patients, Boris, who was already a political activist, introduced me to Fidel that evening. We met there in the dark. But our association had started even before that night: on March 10 I had three new sets of house keys made. One was for the president of the Orthodox Party, another for the Orthodox candidate for the presidency, and the third for Fidel Castro. I had sent the key to Fidel with a note telling him that if they needed a safe hiding place for themselves or their families, they could count on us. It would be a safe refuge because, although I had developed a political consciousness, our family didn't have any tradition of political participation, any ties to politicians or political parties. I found out later that Fidel had appreciated my small gesture of offering him a key to our home.

Throughout this period I kept my close ties with the leaders of the Orthodox Party. As I just said, I didn't meet Fidel until November 1952. Then in February 1953 a young man came to our house to ask whether Fidel could stop by for a visit. I responded, "Of course, I am usually at home anytime after 5:00 P.M." One evening Fidel showed up, and we talked until my husband came home from work. We invited him to stay for dinner and stayed up very late that night talking with Fidel. He explained to us many details about the organization of the revolutionary movement, and about how he was raising money to buy weapons. I was very interested and my husband gave him some money he had in his wallet. But when I saw Fidel to the door later that evening, I told him, "Listen, Fidel, Orlando gave you what he felt he could afford, but you can count on me to help in any way I can. We can contribute more money, and you can use the house whenever you want to. Please let me know however I can be of help to you."

Fidel and some of his comrades began to meet frequently at our home, sometimes for an hour or an hour and a half, or maybe just half an hour. From that moment on I became fully incorporated in the planning stage of the attack on the Moncada Barracks in Santiago de Cuba and participated actively in the July 26 Movement (the M-26-7). I didn't become involved in the Martí Women's Civic Front (FCMM) until 1956. I worked with them through 1959 while, of course, continuing my work with the M-26-7. For all practical purposes, the FCMM was the women's front of the July 26 Movement, although we also worked closely with all of the other revolutionary groups in the country.

The FCMM comprised women from many different parties—the Orthodox Party, the Authentic Party, the socialists, the communists, the M-26-7, and other revolutionary organizations—as well as women with no party affiliations. Most were students, others were workers or housewives. Many of us risked everything by participating in the organized resistance to Batista. At that time, people, especially young people, were being killed right and left. You could be killed just for possessing leaflets or perhaps even for having the telephone number of a "subversive" *compañero*. I recall two young women, the Girol sisters from Cienfuegos, who were living in Havana and belonged to the FCMM as well as to the July 26 Movement. The military raided their home looking for someone else, and brutally raped and murdered these young women. There were many terrible incidents of political assassinations and all forms of repression during that dark period of Cuban history.

Before the attack on the Moncada, Fidel asked me to make photocopies of the July 26th Manifesto. When he stopped by my house to pick up the copies, before leaving for Santiago, he told me that he was going to send Haydée [Santamaría] and Melba [Hernández] back to Havana to help me distribute the manifesto to certain important people—well-known politicians, news reporters and journalists, and other opposition leaders. Fidel told me that if Haydée and Melba didn't make it to Havana, I should go ahead and distribute the manifesto myself to people whom I trusted not to denounce me. He foresaw that after the attack on the Moncada the system of communications between Oriente Province and the rest of the island would be cut off, and there would be no way for people to know what was happening at the military headquarters in Santiago de Cuba and Bayamo. He told me not to leave the house before 5:15 A.M., so as to coordinate the timing of the distribution of the manifesto with the assault on the military barracks.

I got up early the morning of July 26 and told my husband that I had a special mission to perform and that I would explain everything to him later. I left the house at exactly 5:15 A.M. and I gave the manifesto to about eight different people I visited that day. I saw Chibás's brother, Coronel Cosme de la Torriente, the editors of the newspaper *Prensa Libre* and the magazine *Bohemia*. I gave the manifesto to people in key positions who I knew were against the Batista dictatorship. When I realized that I had been followed by secret service officers all morning, I waited until they stopped following me, at about 11:30 A.M., and then returned home. I was very frightened. Melba and Haydée never made it back to Havana, so I had to distribute the manifesto all by myself. And it would be a lie if I told you I wasn't afraid! I was. You'd better believe it. But I continued to participate in the resistance. It was a personal decision that required some courage on my part. I feel very satisfied that Fidel trusted me and counted on me to carry out this task, and that I was capable of responding to that trust.

I was very active in the FCMM. Carmen Castro, a talented organizer with a sharp mind and experience in the newspaper business, edited a clandestine bulletin. It was a concise summary of all the news about the revolutionary movement that could possibly fit on one page, headed with a maxim by Martí and closed, perhaps, with an anecdote about him or a comment on his thought. I was involved in reproducing and distributing about three to five hundred copies of this bulletin. It didn't last for many months, but it did appear at a very crucial moment in the struggle against Batista. These bulletins were easy to reproduce and were copied four or five times each by many other individuals, who in turn distributed them to an even wider public. After that we started to get news on the radio, directly from Radio Rebelde in the Sierra Maestra. We would type out this news and send it to others to print and distribute, creating a network of news distribution during this period of strict censorship.

I remember the palace assault when the military killed many young people who were part of the resistance leadership. Several close friends of the FCMM were assassinated. I remember taking flowers to the funeral home where the corpses of some of these victims, Pelayo Cuervo, Menelao Mora, and José Antonio Echeverría, were being kept. Pelayo was a close friend of my family. I remember that José Antonio's corpse was in a separate chapel upstairs, where he was lying naked and all alone; I placed the flowers on top of him to cover him. These are some of the memories that always accompany me. These memories form a central part of my life. They represent something of who I am as a person.

Aída Pelayo can tell you many extraordinary stories about the clandestine activities of the FCMM. She was the general coordinator of the *martianas* and is gifted with a sharp mind and an outstanding memory. I don't consider myself to have done anything heroic, but Aída, yes, *she* is a very heroic woman. She carried out numerous heroic acts and can tell you many anecdotes about her personal involvement in the Revolution as well as about the clandestine activities of the FCMM.

After the triumph of the Revolution I was, of course, filled with joy. It was a splendid moment of victory. It meant total liberation for those of us who had formed part of the revolutionary struggle. At the beginning of the new government I didn't hold any leadership position. I was eventually laid off from my position at Esso, because most of the managers had already left the country, and after that all the foreign oil companies were nationalized, and there was no need for our office. I found myself unemployed for about six months.

I also got divorced right after the 1959 triumph. I needed to be available to continue to defend the Revolution, but my husband wasn't as committed as I was to the revolutionary process. He was a professional who loved his career as a doctor. He had worked very hard to develop his practice and to achieve success; I could understand that. He had tolerated my revolutionary "adventure" at first because he thought I was young, passionate, and idealistic and that it was just a stage I would eventually outgrow. After the triumph in 1959, Orlando expected me to renounce politics and give up my revolutionary activities, but this would have been impossible for me. I suffered a terrible crisis of conscience; I knew that I could not renounce my commitment to the Revolution. I had already devoted my life to this cause, and I needed to be true to myself, to my principles. I had begun as a wealthy housewife, but I had already been transformed into a revolutionary!

Although I had two daughters, I decided to get divorced. About a year and a half after the triumph of the Revolution, my ex-husband left the country. I had been unemployed for about six months, but eventually a *compañera* called to offer me a job at the National Hospital. I worked there for about a year, then as a radio broadcaster for Radio Cubana at the international station. After that, I worked at the Cuban Embassy in France for about two years. When I returned to the island, I began to work at the National Center for Scientific Research in the area of history. My job was to unearth and gather information about the many Cuban martyrs who lost their lives fighting during the Revolution. And finally, I went to work at the Ministry of Foreign Trade, where I stayed until I retired. I petitioned to continue working after retirement, and I was offered a position at the Ministry of Culture, where I am currently employed as the director of the office of international relations.

Right now, Cuba is enduring the most difficult period in its history, in my opinion, since it became a republic, not just since the Revolution. I still closely identify myself with the revolutionary process, and I'm doing everything I can to confront all the obstacles that make daily life so difficult. For example, sometimes I want to cook and find that there isn't any gas. Or without gasoline, it's impossible for me to drive to work. I live too far to walk, and the bus schedules have been greatly reduced because of the fuel shortages. Often the phones don't work. These are the kinds of daily frustrations that all Cubans must suffer. I often tell myself, if ten million Cubans can survive this, so can I. It is very difficult to get food. One must wait in long lines for vegetables and fruit and bread. All of us are going through hard times and nobody knows how long this so-called Special Period is going to last.

I can't tell you whether we are going to be able to solve this economic crisis. I am not an economist, and I don't know what the answer is. I feel very Cuban and I love my country. I'm proud to say that I am Cuban, and it hurts me very much to see so much hostility directed toward us. All the hatred the United States directed at the entire socialist camp during the Cold War is now aimed exclusively at Cuba. We are the only enemy. We are a small island nation of only ten million people, the size of the state of Pennsylvania. Can you imagine what would happen if the United States decided to impose an economic blockade on Pennsylvania and spend millions of dollars annually in a covert war to overthrow Pennsylvania? How would that state possibly survive?

We are an underdeveloped nation that had the possibility to achieve a higher standard of living than other Third World countries because of our trade relations with the former USSR and other socialist-bloc countries. We traded sugar for oil and many other supplies that we needed to develop our agriculture, our small industry, and other areas of our economy. Cuba doesn't have large rivers, oil, or the other natural resources necessary to develop heavy industry. As you know, though, and are probably tired of hearing, Cuba has an educational system, medical care system, and biotechnology industry that are more sophisticated than those of any other developing country. Sometimes during this crisis we Cubans forget that we still have a higher standard of living than millions of people living in the underdeveloped Third World nations. Those are the countries that we should compare ourselves with, not the highly advanced, industrialized nations of the world. Cubans are very creative people with a lot of imagination. Now it's time for us collectively to come up with some kind of solution to this economic crisis. We can't leave it to one man, or five or ten leaders, to get us out of this crisis; all of us, as Cubans, are people with great creative potential and resources. We all need to play a part in finding the solutions to our many problems.

Before the Revolution I had everything I needed and desired. I went to good schools, had well-paying jobs, and lived very comfortably. I never felt the need to take major trips or to buy expensive clothing or jewelry. At home I always had domestic workers and didn't lack for anything. Therefore, I can't tell you that my life was personally improved by the Revolution. In fact, since then my life has been nothing except incessant hard work; I feel as if all I have done is work. That is to say, I've devoted most of my time and energy to working for socialist Cuba. And definitely, my standard of living decreased drastically after the triumph of the Revolution. But I always knew that happiness does not depend on material possessions; rather, it is a state of mind and has to do with being true to one's own beliefs and principles.

So I can't say that the revolution *gave* me opportunities, because I was among the privileged minority that lived very well in prerevolutionary Cuba. But I can speak for tens of thousands of marginal Cuban women whose lives *were* greatly improved by the social reforms brought about after the Revolution. Many of these women became professionals or technicians and were able to develop themselves personally and professionally in ways they could never have dreamed of before. For thousands of black women who suffered double discrimination, the Revolution opened up many doors of opportunity. They can tell you about their own experiences. This is the cause I have devoted all my adult life to fighting for and defending.

Education has always been a priority of the revolutionary government. In recent years, universities have been built in different provinces throughout the island so that more and more young people would have access to a college education. Also, when the Ministry of Culture was established in 1976, one of its goals was to organize cultural centers in every town, so that each town would have its own movie theater, chorus, dance hall, theater troupe, library, art gallery, and handicraft store. This has made life in the interior of the island less boring and has improved the access of people living in the provinces to cultural activities and entertainment.

One of the problems we are facing today is prostitution, especially in Havana and at the beach resorts, even though there is no need for any young woman to turn to prostitution as a means of survival, as there was before the Revolution. There are no parents who sell their children in order for the family to eat, just as there are no beggars or homeless people on the streets in Cuba. I think that many of today's prostitutes are just lazy or cannot resist the temptation of making so much quick money. What worries me most is that they aren't thinking about the health risks or the dangers involved in this sort of activity. Perhaps if we had been more concerned about the spiritual, emotional, and moral development of our youth, this wouldn't be happening now. But unfortunately, prostitution does exist in Cuba, and it is a serious problem that we need to address collectively.

There is definitely a need for us to provide more entertainment for our young people. We need to have more outdoor concerts and open more nightclubs where they can dance. Cubans love to dance. One of our failures during this period of crisis has been to offer the best live entertainment in Cuba to tourists and not to our own people, especially the young people who need an opportunity to socialize and to dance in order to feel satisfied.

Nowadays in Cuba many men and women have decided not to get married or even live together. Since women no longer depend economically on their husbands, many will tell you, "Why marry? To have to cook for some man and wash his dirty underwear? No, not me. I prefer to have an affair, to have a relationship, but with him in his house and me in mine. We can get together to have a good time, go to the movies, make love, but without sharing the same house. I don't want any man living in my home." This is what a lot of Cuban women will tell you. Likewise, many Cuban men will say, "Me, get married? Why? So I have to run home at a certain time and help out with the grocery shopping and all the other domestic chores? I prefer to have a relationship without getting married." Gradually, Cuban men are becoming less sexist, but it is a long, slow process. You can't change centuries of patriarchal attitudes overnight. There are still many vestiges of our colonial and macho past.

Since my divorce, I have not remarried. It's not that I haven't had opportunities, but as one grows older and more experienced, one becomes more selective. I've been alone for about thirty-six years, but I've had a full, rich life. I'm mentally and emotionally healthy; I'm optimistic but also realistic; and my family responsibilities have compensated for the loneliness I might otherwise have felt. I'm not saying that an intimate relationship is not important to me. Of course it is. I recognize that all human beings need emotional and physical closeness. It's not that I'm against the idea of a romantic, intimate relationship, but it just hasn't happened. What doesn't happen simply doesn't happen.

I have a few select, close friends whom I can always count on. We love each other and enjoy one another's company. I have taken on a lot of family responsibilities. Our family was divided by the revolution; all my mother's brothers left the country, and one of my daughters is also living outside of Cuba. My mother is now ninety-one years old and lives here with me, but she is still in good health and very independent. It helps me a lot to know that I can count on my friends. When I need help, they are always there for me. And when I don't need help, they are also there.

Likewise, several coworkers have become like family to me. A coworker isn't exactly a friend but can be someone with whom one feels a special affinity and can talk to about many things. Of my twenty or so coworkers there are perhaps two who have become like part of my family—like a cousin or a brother or an uncle.

During the organization of the attack on the Moncada I had a close personal relationship with Fidel. But after that, as you know, he was sent to jail, went into exile in Mexico, and then finally returned to the Sierra Maestra to lead the Revolution. We were still in close contact and maintained a friendship, but after the triumph of the revolution we went our separate ways. He became the principal political leader of the country, the commander in chief, and I was merely a loyal rank-and-file soldier, so to speak. This naturally created a lot of distance between us.

But at one time we were very close, and I can honestly tell you that I still have very fond memories of that period of my life and of my relationship with Fidel. I know that I was there for him during an important period in his life, during an important period in both our lives. I was able to help him when he needed me, during a time of anguish in his life. When Fidel was a prisoner, when he was in exile, and during the war, I offered him my support and friendship. After that, as I already said, he took his road and I took mine.

And finally, I want to reiterate something I said earlier. I feel that I've lived a full, rich life and that I've been true to myself and true to my convictions. Even now, during this dark period of crisis in Cuba, I feel full of life and full of possibility. I still have contributions to make, and I'm not just talking about work or professional contributions. I believe that I still have a lot to offer as a human being. As for my personal and spiritual development, I am happy to say that I'm still growing, learning, and evolving.

Aída Pelayo

SCHOOL TEACHER AND REVOLUTIONARY

Aída Pelayo (1992).

Aída Pelayo was born in 1913 to a white, middle-class family and became an elementary school teacher, choosing one of the few professions available to women of her social class before the revolution. Although petite in stature, at eighty-four she is still a strong, independent woman with incredible energy and zeal. Pelayo defines herself as a feminist; she participated in the drafting of the Constitution of 1940 that gave Cuban women the right to vote and promoted women's equality.

Aída Pelayo took part in the struggle against Gerardo Machado, the dicta-tor who ruled Cuba in the early 1930s. She had become an active member of the Young Communists at the age of fifteen; a few years later she joined the Student Left Wing at the university. She was a major actor on Cuba's political stage fol-lowing the 1952 coup d'état in which Batista seized power. She played a leading role in the organized resistance to this dictator, actively participating in the clan-destine movement in Havana. She also was a founder and the general coordinator of the Martí Women's Civic Front.

I interviewed Aída Pelayo at her home in one of Havana's formerly upper-class neighborhoods called Miramar. That same afternoon I had the opportunity to meet Olga Román, Maruja Iglesias, and Mercedes Blanco Mesa, who were also active in the FCMM in the 1950s. Maria Antonia Carrillo accompanied me be-cause she wanted to meet these women. We drank demitasses of strong Cuban coffee as the women reminisced about their forty-year-long friendship and revolu-tionary activity. Pelayo's testimony details her political militancy, which is a cen-tral part of her life history.

When I think of my childhood, I think of my parents, grandparents, uncles, and cousins. We Cubans are rather tribal in that we've always lived close to our extended families, and we still do. I had a pretty normal child-hood, with the usual ups and downs of growing up. At first I attended pri-vate schools in the town where I was born, but after we moved to Havana when I was in the second grade, I began to study in public schools. It was then that I started to become aware of my Cuban identity. At this public school, I first learned about the people who had fought for Cuba's inde-pendence. At that time in my young life José Martí was born in me, and he has never left me. Martí is still with me today; he accompanies me every-where I go. His teachings and his words are etched in my memory forever. I can honestly say that José Martí has been the most important influence on my life.

I was always a strong defender of the public school system in Cuba. Before the revolution perhaps we didn't have enough classrooms, school supplies or books, but that wasn't the teachers' fault. In fact, many teachers bought books and supplies themselves and brought them to school, be-cause they knew the government was corrupt and didn't care if the chil-dren didn't have books or pens and paper. Before the revolution, teachers in Cuba were poorly paid and had to make great sacrifices. During the economic crisis of 1930-33 people used to say, "He or she's more hungry than a school teacher."

From the time I was very young, I began to develop social consciousness and a strong sense of justice. I remember the coup led by Machado [1928] took place when I was only fifteen years old. I joined the struggle against this brutal dictator and experienced my first battles. At this time, my parents were separated; I was living with my mother and depended solely on her. My mom was very understanding, and when she realized that I was firm in my convictions and that there was no turning back for me, she came to accept my political involvement. She remained supportive and proud of me. Each time I was arrested, she was the first person to visit me in jail; she would bring my toothbrush, a comb, and a clean towel and would demand to see her daughter.

Since I was poor, I studied at the Teacher's College in Havana where young people of the lower-middle class could get a professional degree that would enable them to earn a living. I am rather bossy and like to give orders; perhaps that is why teaching was an appropriate vocation for me. But I would have loved to study law. I think I would have been a good lawyer, because I like to give passionate speeches. My dream was to stand up in court and defend my client. But that wasn't within my possibilities, so I became a school teacher.

My first political experience was with the Young Communists when I was still in high school. During this stage we would break windows, shout slogans in the streets, get arrested, make banners, throw Molotov cocktails; we were still just kids and not able to accomplish much. We would throw small bombs that would make a little noise and let off some smoke. That's about all we did at this stage. We were still too young to participate in more important kinds of militancy against Machado.

It was while studying at the Teacher's College that I joined the Student Left Wing of the university student movement and began my serious commitment to the revolutionary cause. Historically, Havana University students were at the forefront of the resistance. Julio Antonio Mello was the main leader of the student movement in 1923, 1925, and 1927; in 1930 we began our struggle against the Machado dictatorship. Secondary school and college students joined forces. I met Carmen Castro soon after I became involved in the Student Left Wing; she was working at the International Red Cross for Workers' Defense.

Carmen Castro and I started to work together, helping those who were underground or in jail, denouncing the assassinations and repressive tactics of the fascist dictator, "the Butcher," as Machado was called. We were very active in showing our solidarity with the Republicans during the

Spanish Civil War [1936-39]. We also worked for the release of political prisoners in many Latin American countries—in Brazil, Puerto Rico, the Dominican Republic, and wherever else people were being persecuted by fascist regimes.

In March 1935 there was a large general strike to protest Batista's first rise to power. Following the strike there was severe repression by the newly installed military government. Many Cubans were taken as political prisoners, others were killed, or disappeared, or were forced into exile. At this point, we lacked the weapons needed to confront the armed violence of Batista's repression. Following this strike, I participated in a newly formed committee demanding a general amnesty for all political prisoners here in Cuba.

As I became more and more involved in political activities, I decided to leave the university for a while; I never did finish my university degree in education. I landed a job working for the International Red Cross which took me all over the world: I was sent to Brazil to work for the release of Luís Carlos Preste, to El Salvador to defend those activists who had been sentenced to death, to Venezuela and other parts of Latin America and Europe. There were Cubans who had fought in the Spanish Civil War and were being detained as political prisoners in France; we were actively engaged in the battle to bring them back home to Cuba. All this work prevented me from beginning my career as a school teacher, though I did eventually make it to the classroom.

During this period I began to participate in the demand for women's equal legal rights in the new Constitution of 1940. Women did not have access to well-paying jobs, nor did we have the right to vote or to be elected to public office. As women, all we could do was accept the sad fact that it was men who ruled. I remember several of the Women's Congresses. I was a delegate at the 1939 Women's Congress, where there were some good discussions. Women finally got the right to vote. But our demands as revolutionary women went beyond those of the Cuban middle-class feminist movement, which fought only for women's rights to vote and to inherit wealth. We did, of course, and still do consider ourselves feminists, but our struggle was also a revolutionary, political struggle for the full participation of women and the underprivileged in all levels of society, including politics.

I decided that I wanted to have a baby. So I got pregnant and had a son. My marriage lasted only one day, because we never really understood each other. My husband was a Spaniard who had to go back to Spain to fight in the Civil War and I was not going to leave my country to follow this man. I raised my son by myself as a single mom. He is now a merchant marine and travels a lot. Right now, he is in Turkey. I had only one child, and all my female friends are like his aunts. He is a Party militant and was a combatant in the Revolution. He became a wonderful husband and father, and as you can see, I'm very proud of him. He gave me two grand-daughters and one great-granddaughter.

One of my first teaching jobs, around 1948, was at a school for indigent children in Havana. These kids were so poor that most of them had only rags to wear and had never owned a pair of shoes. In addition to teaching them how to read and write, we taught them proper table manners and some basic social skills. For example, we had to teach them not to spit on the classroom floor and the proper use of the bathroom facilities. Since most of them had grown up without indoor plumbing, they had never used a toilet before coming to school. This work was very rewarding. For the first time, I had direct contact with the conditions of extreme poverty in prerevolutionary Cuba. I learned from this firsthand experience about how difficult life was for tens of thousands of disadvantaged Cubans.

In 1952, shortly after Batista pulled off his bloody coup d'état, Carmen Castro and I decided that the time was right to launch an organized resistance, an all-women's group, to fight against the dictatorship. In order to pay homage to the great Cuban leader José Martí on the hundredth anniversary of his birth, we named our organization the Martí Women's Civic Front. We convoked an assembly of about forty women affiliated with different political parties—socialists, communists, and the more moderate, centrist Authentic and Orthodox Parties—but certainly not anyone from the ranks of the political sellouts or collaborators. Some of the women had no political affiliation; the women who came together to establish the Front had varying degrees of political experience and militancy. We wanted to set an example of unity for other revolutionary groups that were splintered and divided at that time.

The purpose of this meeting was to constitute our organization formally. The women who gathered that day named me the general coordinator of the Front. Our platform was very simple: we demanded Batista's ouster and the establishment of a government responsive to our needs, not one run by political hacks and corrupt politicians. We wanted to follow the path outlined by Fidel Castro, the leader of the July 26 Movement. The organization grew to include thousands of women throughout the island, although those whose names were actually registered as members numbered somewhere between six and seven hundred.

We had two different methods of operation. One was in the open, within the law, and allowed us to visit newspapers and television and radio stations, to print and circulate manifestos and documents, and even to publish a small newspaper. We visited political prisoners in jail and offered support to the families of revolutionaries who had been murdered by the regime. All of this work was legal and was done openly. But some members, including me, were active in the clandestine movement: mainly trafficking in weapons, taking care of the wounded, moving people to different hideouts, and burying some of those who had died (we would also notify the families of these victims so that they could be given a proper burial). Those of us who were working clandestinely would sometimes have to carry a bomb under our skirts or plant a bomb at a certain place. These are things I remember very well. I think that during the 1950s I spent more time in jail or in hiding than out in the streets organizing. Every time I was released, the secret police would find me and arrest me again.

I also have a vivid memory of finding corpses that had been buried in some obscure place and were already beginning to deteriorate. One of the worst memories of my life is when I discovered the corpse of a young man whose father was my close friend. We found him eight days after the military had brutally tortured and murdered him. His body was so swollen that I could hardly recognize him. He had swelled up like an elephant. It was a horrifying sight that I've never, ever forgotten. His image still haunts me; it is engraved in my memory forever. I would often think about how much the family of this young man suffered because of this tragic loss. They were in agony, just like the families of so many other young martyrs of our Revolution.

Most of the members of our Front were students at the Teacher's College in Havana, the Business School, or the Institute in Havana and also the one in Marianao. A large group of high school students as well joined our organization. But working-class women were also active in the Front. Many of them worked at the textile plants, or were housewives or domestic servants. The FCMM was all-inclusive, made up of all kinds of women from different walks of life, and with different religious beliefs—Catholics, Protestants, *espiritistas*, and nonbelievers too. The only requirement was to be sincere and committed to Martí's thinking and to the revolutionary struggle to overthrow the fascist dictatorship. There was a membership card and, as I already said, we followed the teachings and ideology of José Martí. All our propaganda included passages taken from Martí's writings. We worked closely with the July 26 Movement and with all of the other revolutionary groups in the country at that time. Martí understood the important role of propaganda in his revolutionary struggle for Cuba's independence. This is one of the main lessons that our Front learned from the Apostle [Martí]. We were convinced that the distribution of propaganda was essential in rallying support to overthrow Batista.

I was arrested following the assault on the Moncada Barracks on July 26, 1953. Even though I didn't participate directly in the attack in Santiago de Cuba, because of my history of revolutionary activities I had already been identified by the Batista regime as an enemy, so they came to my house and they took me away. The military government held me in prison until after the trial ended in October. I was forced to witness the trial. I have been to many of my comrades' trials throughout my life, but this one was particularly painful to watch. I saw how, one by one, each of these young rebels was forced to testify and then convicted and sentenced to prison. I was certain that I, too, would be convicted, but when they asked the defendants about my involvement, all of them denied it. I remember that Fidel spoke out, "Why is Aída Pelayo here? Why is she always arrested every time a gunshot goes off in this country?" Everyone laughed. He insisted that I had nothing to do with the attack on the Moncada Barracks, and I was finally released on the last day of the trial. I remember Raúl Castro, Fidel's brother, hugged me and told me, "Please don't forget about the twenty of us who are still imprisoned." I assured him that we would visit them, write to them, and make sure that nobody forgot about these heroic rebels.

Another major event I recall vividly was the General Strike on April 9, 1958. The FCMM participated in the organization of this strike. The call for this offensive came from the leadership of the July 26 Movement. It seemed to them the time was right for a General Strike that would continue until Batista was finally defeated. The level of revolutionary fervor had increased throughout the island, especially in the cities; the opposition to Batista was so pervasive and strong that the following announcement was sent out to all Cubans on the radio stations on April 9: "Attention Cubans! Today is the day for liberation. The July 26 Movement is calling for the final revolutionary general strike that will not end until the dictatorship is overthrown."

From the time we got wind of the plans for this strike early in March, the FCMM worked incessantly to mobilize the masses of workers and to unify urban activists. On April 9 the revolutionary sector of the urban militias occupied parts of Old Havana, converting it into a stronghold; they took over the Military Museum on Mercaderes Street, where they confiscated some weapons. Other urban guerrillas bombed the record offices of the electric company. The bus drivers refused to operate their buses and took over some streets.

Throughout the island, however, the General Strike was violently repressed by the tyrannical military forces. Hundreds of people were left dead in the wake of this unsuccessful effort. I remember that on the morning of April 9, after a meeting with some workers, I was on my way back to the Front's clandestine refuge, an apartment on 18th Street in Vedado. A group of *martianas* surrounded the neighborhood; they met me in the street and warned me not to go to our apartment. These women informed me that the soldiers had already raided our apartment twice. They had broken all of the furniture, windows, and doors, and stolen our documents, books, and belongings. These soldiers would probably be back to arrest me. My *compañeras* had probably saved my life with this warning, for which I was very grateful.

Many urban guerrillas were brutally murdered that day. The repression continued on April 10, and the jails were full of young activists and workers. The corpses mounted. I remember that we went to some of the funerals of fallen comrades. The *martianas* tried to offer support and to help out the families of a number of young people massacred during the strike. Among the July 26th Movement combatants killed in Havana were Marcelo Salado, Juan Oscar Alvarado, Adolfo Cacau, and others.

After the triumph of the Revolution, the Martí Women's Civic Front disbanded as a functioning organization on January 28, 1959. A core group of us has maintained close personal ties throughout all these years. These friendships have lasted more than forty-three years. We still get together several times a week to chat, go to the movies, or see a play. We care for each other deeply and look out for one another. As I already said earlier, Olga, Maruja, and Carmen were like aunts to my son when he was growing up. We have been through many difficult times together and this has created some deep, lasting bonds.

After our 1959 victory, I went back to the classroom. I also took part in the literacy campaign and was active in the organization of the militias, the Committees for the Defense of the Revolution (CDRs), and the Federation of Cuban Women (FMC). I was awarded two medals for my participation in the literacy campaign. The FMC gave me a medal for my role as a combatant in the Revolution. Among my many postrevolutionary activities, I used to work closely with the Young Pioneers. I am often invited by them, and by other groups, to give my testimony about my role in the Revolution, to speak about the July 26 Movement and about the urban revolutionary groups in Havana.

Of course, this Special Period is difficult for me as it is for everyone. It's hard to cook without cooking oil. Sometimes I would give anything for a piece of cheese or for some flan—I used to make delicious flan! I've already eaten a lot of delicious food throughout my lifetime, but I feel bad for the kids. If they are over seven years old, they don't get any fresh milk and have to make do with Cerelac. The children complain that this cereal, which is a protein substitute for milk, tastes terrible. Although these are tough times, I trust that the Cuban people will find a way to endure and to resist. My dream is that although we are all crying and hurting now, we will be able to learn from this crisis, to rise up once again, and start a new fire of freedom—freedom of conscience and of the hope of creating a better life for the Cuban people!

María Antonia Carrillo

AFRO-CUBAN DANCE TROUPE DIRECTOR AND ARTIST

María Antonia Carrillo (1992).

María Antonia Carrillo is a fifty-six-year-old Afro-Cuban woman whom I met by chance. Shortly after my arrival in Havana in July 1992, I was taking a stroll along the Malecón (a broad seaside boulevard that is a favorite meeting place for Cubans) when Roberto, a teenage boy who was selling cigars on the black market, approached me. I told him about my project on Cuban revolutionary women, and he offered to introduce me to María Antonia Carrillo, who joined the Mariana Grajales Platoon when she was nineteen years old. She is now an artist and the director of an Afro-Cuban dance troupe that recently toured Brazil and Mexico. That same afternoon we stopped by her home in a part of town called Centro Habana. She was enthusiastic about my project and not only accompanied me on several other interviews but offered me her friendship and hospitality throughout my one-month stay in Cuba that summer. She was a terrific "tour guide," sharing countless anecdotes about "what life is really like" in Cuba as we walked up and down the streets of Old Havana, Central Havana, and Nuevo Vedado.

One afternoon we took a ferry across the bay to Regla to visit an old Catholic Church and its patron saint, the Virgin of Regla, the protectress of sailors. This Catholic saint has been syncretized or fused with the African goddess Yemayá, the mother of all life, represented by the ocean. Carrillo shared with me much of her knowledge about the Afro-Cuban religion Santería; she showed me her own altar at home and invited me to ceremonies where someone's initiation into this religion was celebrated and a saint assigned to protect the new member.[1]

María Antonia Carrillo proudly showed me her paintings (mostly bright-colored abstracts with Afro-centric icons) and also invited me to take pictures of the dance troupe she coordinates. During our many hours of conversation, she talked about how the black market and the dual economy functioned during this period of crisis. Carrillo, herself a beneficiary of the educational programs sponsored by the Revolution, has spent most of her adult life involved in the revolutionary process; she has contributed to the goal of creating a "new society" based on racial, class, and gender equality. She now lives with her husband of more than twenty years and with their only daughter and granddaughter.

I was born in 1939 in the province of Cienfuegos. Before the Revolution this province was called Las Villas. I don't know if I can even say I had a childhood. It wasn't much of a childhood. During the early years of my life everything was such a struggle. My family was very poor, and we were struggling to survive. There were so many ups and downs. My grandparents lived here in Havana. My father worked cutting sugarcane in season, and during the off season he would come to Havana and work with my grandfather at the Cuatro Caminos market. He worked very hard to earn enough money so we could at least subsist. My mother worked too, as a domestic servant. This is how my three brothers and sisters and I grew up, just barely getting by.

Since the time I was a young child I was drawn to the Afro-Cuban religion Santería and to the practice of spiritualism (*espiritismo*). I grew up surrounded by many people who practiced this religion of African origin and who believed in the *orishas*, or African gods. My mother had an altar at home devoted to the *orishas*, and she taught me a lot about this religion. At an early age I began attending ceremonies and dances, and I'm still involved in this practice today. I have my little altar with my saints. I'm also very interested in everything related to my Afro-Cuban heritage, all the so-called "folklore," our traditional dances and music, the art, handicrafts, and other forms of popular culture. When I was a little girl I learned Afro-Cuban dances and songs, with African rhythms and lyrics.

Since my family was so poor, I was able to attend school only through the sixth grade. I went to school in a small town that's so small I don't even know if you can call it a town. I lived near enough to walk there, barefoot, together with my siblings. This region was so destitute that most of the kids didn't have any shoes to wear to school. It wasn't until after the Revolution that I was able to continue my education. I completed my high school degree at one of the schools in Havana started by the Federation of Cuban Women. It was part of the FMC's project to incorporate peasant and poor women into the work force.

In the region I came from everybody supported the Revolution. Many peasants and workers on small farms in the area rose up and fought in the armed struggle against Batista. When I was still a teenager, I had a boyfriend who was a combatant. His name was José Chacón. He would send me letters, and I would go to see him and take messages for other fighters from friends and families who lived nearby. I became more and more committed to the Revolution without really understanding why. Perhaps it was love—I loved José, I loved life, and I loved the Revolution. I didn't really have much political awareness or fully comprehend what the war was all about, but I was becoming increasingly involved. By the time I was eighteen, José had died in combat. The military had searched our home twice, and they took the only pair of shoes I owned. This is the story about how I got involved in the Revolution.

I was one of the women who fought in the all-woman platoon called Mariana Grajales. It was a beautiful experience. We were all so united and so in love with the Revolution. There weren't any bad feelings of rivalry or jealousy among us. I had to learn how to use a weapon; I didn't think I would be able to, but I did. The sense of revolutionary fervor that enveloped us was so strong that fighting back seemed like the only thing to do. It was the only way to get rid of the tyrannical dictator who was torturing and murdering so many of our *compañeros*. The only thing we cared about was to keep moving forward and to keep fighting. We fought in a number of battles near the end of the Revolution, during the last months of 1958. I will always carry with me, in my heart, the memories of this experience, and of the celebration and joy of our victory!

After the triumph of the Revolution I worked with the Federation of Cuban Women. One of our first tasks was to go out into the countryside and try to persuade peasant women to come to the new schools established to teach them how to read and write. It wasn't easy, but I remember doing this work with such enthusiasm. It was a very difficult period for us because of the counterrevolutionaries, but I recall doing all of this work with a lot of love.

For me, personally, as a black woman in Cuba, the Revolution brought opportunities that I'd never even dreamed were possible. In prerevolutionary Cuba the only option for a black woman was to work as a domestic servant in the home of some wealthy white woman who lived in Miramar or some other fancy neighborhood, or maybe get a job as a waitress at a third- or fourth- or fifth-class joint. Most of the first-class restaurants and nightclubs preferred to hire white women. Because of racial discrimination in this country, very few blacks were able to get a university education before the Revolution. Even in my small town the whites strolled in the center of the park and expected us to stay on the edges—that is actually outside the park. I think racism was one of the main reasons why so many of us black Cubans joined the revolutionary forces. The rebels were fighting for a new society based on racial equality and on the equality of women.

In my opinion, there still isn't full racial equality in Cuba, but I don't think it's the fault of the government that there are so few black leaders in high positions of power. I am a militant in the PCC and our platform is one of racial and gender equality, but it's difficult to change racist attitudes that have existed for many generations. We still have a long way to go. Even Fidel asked in one of his speeches, "What has happened here? Why are there so few blacks and women elected to high-level Party positions?" I think the commander in chief was asking, "Why do racism and sexism still exist in Cuba?"

So let me tell you, because of this new revolutionary government, I was able to get an education and to become who I am today. I am now directing an Afro-Cuban dance troupe. We just got back from a tour of Mexico! Do you think I could have even dreamed about traveling to Mexico before the Revolution? Or showing my paintings at art exhibitions? No way! I could never even have finished high school if it hadn't been for the new government. I think that the problems of racial discrimination and machismo still haven't been eradicated in the popular, grassroots sectors of Cuban society, but I don't think it's the government's fault.

I've been directing an Afro-Cuban dance troupe since 1985. It is very rewarding work. I love working with young people and teaching them about their heritage through dance. The government has been very supportive of the promotion of Afro-Cuban dance, music, and popular culture, which are seen primarily as part of our national folklore, not as related to any religious cult. Our dance troupe has performed at many hotels and convention and tourist centers, in addition to national festivals of popular culture. As I said, we were invited to Mexico City. I'm hoping we will be invited on another international tour.

As for gender equality, I've had a happy marriage that has lasted more than twenty years, something that is rare today in Cuba. My husband, Oscar, is also black. He was a combatant in the clandestine movement, and since the triumph of the Revolution he has always had important leadership roles in areas related to the militias and to the defense of the Revolution. Because of all his responsibility, Oscar never spent much time at home. He would leave early in the morning and usually come home late at night; he often had to attend Party meetings in the evenings. But now that he is retired, we spend a lot more time together. My partner is very good about helping out at home. Actually, we get along very well regarding the running of the house. He is understanding, and if he has to go shopping for food, he goes. Oscar does most of the cooking, since he gets home before I do. He washes the dishes and helps out with most of the domestic chores.

In addition to my dance troupe activities, I paint. I began painting sometime around 1976, when I was already middle-aged, in my forties. I had my first exhibition in 1980, and I recently showed some of my work in Mexico City. I had the honor of participating in the Association of Cuban Artists and Artisans when it was first organized. Many important Cuban artists belonged to this group, William Sotomayor and others. I've always felt inspired to paint Afro-Cuban folk themes, mostly *orisha* motifs, although some of my early work is landscapes. I paint with both acrylics and watercolors.

As well as the strides made towards racial and sexual equality, recently there has been more tolerance and acceptance of all types of religious expression here in Cuba. Freedom of religion was discussed a lot at the last Party Congress. Not only *espiritistas* but people from many different religions are now allowed to worship openly. Before, it wasn't like they would put you in prison or break into your home to see if you were praying, but there was little tolerance of religion, of any religion. All good Marxists were supposed to be atheists. Fortunately, those attitudes and government policies have changed. Now it is possible to be a Party militant *and* openly express one's religious beliefs.

Now that there is more freedom of religious expression, an increasing number of young people have been initiated into Santería. And since they no longer fear losing their jobs or facing other hassles because of their religion, you can see people on the streets wearing colored, beaded necklaces that correspond to their particular saint. Until recently, most people practiced their religion at home, secretly, and would never discuss their beliefs openly. But this is changing. I believe, just as my African ancestors believed, that the gods are everywhere—in nature, in the air, in the trees, in the sun, and in the moon. Human beings may disappear, but the universe is everlasting. For me, this is my religion; this is my idea of God, and this is everything to me!

I also want to tell you that if the gringos invade our island, I, María Antonia Carrillo, will be among the first to take up arms and fight in the trenches. There is no way I want to return to the prerevolutionary Cuba of misery and racial discrimination. I will die fighting for the ideals of our Revolution before submitting to a return to Yankee imperialism on the island. Sure, we have serious problems. It would be a lie not to admit that we have problems. There are shortages of lard and cooking oil and lots of things. But we need to be able to endure and to resist. Nobody is dying of hunger in Cuba. Our soil is fertile, and it gives us fruits and vegetables, and we have sugar. So we can survive. As you know, if you get sick or need an operation, it is free. You don't have to pay anything. Of course, I hate our policy of tourism, just as a lot of Cubans hate it. I don't think it's fair that everything in Cuba is for the tourists and nothing is for us, the Cubans. I can still be a revolutionary and not like everything about my country. But I do think the Cuban people are very creative, and we need to come together to find solutions to our problems. This is the only way we can survive this economic crisis, and the only way the Revolution can survive.

Zoila Elisa Alfonso González

Tobacco Worker and Union Organizer

Zoila Elisa Alfonso González (1992) with her husband.

Zoila Elisa Alfonso González is a petite, spry, fiery woman who wears her eighty-one years with dignity. Born in Havana of a Spanish father and a Cuban mother, Alfonso González has spent her entire life, since she was a little girl, working at to-bacco factories and defending the rights of Cuban women, especially women tobacco workers. Traditionally, tobacco has been Cuba's second largest export, after sugar. In her testimony, Alfonso González tells us about her firsthand experience with poverty, deplorable working conditions, and the repression prior to the Revolution.

As a lifelong activist in the struggle for women's and workers' rights, this retired tobacco worker proudly enumerates the accomplishments achieved by the Confederation of Cuban Workers (CTC) and the Federation of Cuban Women (FMC).

I met Zoila Elisa Alfonso González at a birthday celebration attended by about fifty people in a mostly black working-class neighborhood in Centro Habana.[1] I overheard her arguing with a tall man almost twice her size. This young man, named Juan, was a Marielito (one of those who left Cuba from Port Mariel during the exodus in the early 1980s) who had returned to Havana after becoming disappointed with life in Miami, where he failed to find work, suffered from racial discrimination, and felt trapped in a violent, gang-infested slum. When Juan, angry with Fidel Castro, blamed him for Cuba's problems, Alfonso González became furious; she yelled at this man and called him a "counter-revolutionary," a "delinquent," a "good for nothing." In her own words, "it was Fidel who gave me and hundreds of thousands of working-class women decent wages, benefits, day-care, dignity, and respect denied them in prerevolutionary Cuba."[2]

At this neighborhood gathering I had been struck by what seemed a major contradiction: how was it possible that so many little girls had brand-new party dresses, shiny patent leather shoes, lace-trimmed socks, colorful bows in their hair, and cute little parasols when most of the shelves at the government-run stores in Cuba were completely empty? At this party in a working-class neighborhood there was a hired clown, a photographer taking pictures, balloons, birthday cake, and sandwiches and soda for everyone. Observing this relative opulence during a period of economic crisis and severe shortages, I started to understand how the black market functions as a major source of goods and services in Cuba.

When I approached Alfonso González and introduced myself, she was eager to tell me her story. She began to reminisce about how she had fought alongside Lázaro Peña, the well-known leader of Cuban tobacco workers, in the Revolution. With nostalgia and admiration she spoke of her militant parents as her most important role models in the struggle for social justice; she referred modestly to her own leadership in the Tobacco Workers' Union. At her home in Centro Habana we continued our conversation and I met her husband. Later, we visited the headquarters of the Tobacco Workers' local, where she is still active as a volunteer, working with and organizing events for retired members.

My name is Zoila Elisa Alfonso González. I was born in 1915 here in Havana. My father was a Spaniard from Madrid, a Communist who had been imprisoned in Spain for his beliefs. Upon his release from prison, he moved to Cuba. Although my dad was Spanish, he hated the repressive colonial regime here, and even took up arms and fought alongside the

The finery displayed at a birthday party in a working-class Cuban neighborhood in 1992 could have been obtained only through the black market.

Cubans in the second war for independence. He admired José Martí and used to teach us all about the life and writings of this national hero. My father also explained to us a lot about Communism, socialism, class struggle, imperialism, and these sorts of things. He was a very intelligent man who understood so much about life, politics, and the world. My dad was a worker in a tobacco factory and also a union leader. I remember every time he organized a strike or planned a demonstration, the police would come and arrest him. Papi was always in and out of jail. He taught us to be respectful to others, but also to defend ourselves and never let anyone step all over us. Both my parents were activists who taught us to fight back, to stand tall and have dignity, to stand up for our beliefs. Unfortunately, neither of them lived long enough to see the triumph of the Cuban Revolution.

My mother, Victoria Alfonso, was from a Cuban family of tobacco workers. Her parents and grandparents too had toiled at making Cuban cigars, and Mom spent her entire life as a struggling tobacco worker. She was one of the pioneers in the women's movement here in Cuba. I'm so proud of her; she taught us, her daughters, to fight for women's equality. Victoria fought long and hard for women's liberation in Cuba; she organized women tobacco workers, demanded a salary hike of a few pesos, and campaigned for an eight-hour work day. In 1935 there was a huge strike and we were all arrested and hauled away to jail. Just like my dad, my mom was arrested all the time when I was growing up. I remember my brothers and sisters and I would sit on the steps outside the police station waiting for her release each time they locked her up. When my mother died there were so many people at her funeral that they didn't all fit in the church. She was loved by everybody—especially the women. I remember at the funeral there were women waiting in a long line to sign their names and express their sympathy. Many of them were weeping at the loss of this great woman who had spent her whole life defending them against cruel, abusive factory owners. My parents were my best teachers in the struggle for social justice; I tried to follow in their footsteps and to teach my children these same values.

Anyway, returning to the story about my childhood: I was very, very poor growing up. My mom labored cutting stems at a tobacco factory owned by a Spaniard. Stemming was the worst job. The women who rolled earned a little bit more. But the best-paying jobs at the factory, especially slicing, went to the men. Before the Revolution, women in the tobacco factories had to fight, fight, and fight to get paid just a few cents more. It wasn't like it is now, with the Party and the CTC [Organization of Cuban Trade Unions] to look out for our interests and defend our rights.

My mother was so active in organizing the women tobacco workers that the owners of these factories, who were really greedy S.O.B.'s, used to say, "We don't want the daughters of that troublemaker, Victoria Alfonso, working here at our plant." My mom had a reputation for being a fighter; she was a strong, combative woman and the factory owners hated her! As I already told you, I remember my mom was taken prisoner many, many times when we were still small children. The owners of these tobacco factories were Spanish families (Menéndez, Cifuentes, and others) who really exploited the workers, especially the women.

I remember I had to start working at the factory when I was just a little girl. I was only twelve years old, but this wasn't uncommon back then. My parents had eight children, although only five of us survived. We didn't have the opportunity to go to school beyond the sixth grade. Wages were so low that we all had to work, just so we could eat. We would all get up at 5:00 A.M. in order to be at work by 6:00 A.M., and then it was nonstop work until 6:00 P.M.—twelve-hour days, six days a week, for only a pittance! Often, all we would get to eat in an entire day was a roll that we would buy from a stand near the factory. As you can imagine, we used to get really hungry.

Before the Revolution many children were forced to work, just so the family could barely subsist. On the other hand, the owners were filthy rich. They would go to Miami for vacations and to all the nice places in Havana. Yet we couldn't go anywhere, and we didn't have anything. I remember feeling hungry almost all the time when I was a kid. We never had enough to eat. The exploitation was terrible! I'm telling you, that Menéndez family from Galicia really exploited the Cuban women and children. They were so selfish and mean-spirited! When Cuba was capitalist, the stores were all full of imported products and luxury items, but most of the Cuban people were starving. Only the wealthy could afford to buy these things, while we lived in abject misery.

I became involved in the tobacco workers' struggle from the time I was about twelve, when I first started working. The bosses weren't supposed to hire anyone under fifteen, because it was against child labor laws. But they would hire young kids to work sitting on the floor, and when the Health Department would come for routine inspections, the manager would hide all the underage children up on the rooftop.

Before the Revolution, I worked as a militant in the Communist party organizing women. We would go to the *solares*, which were multiple dwelling units for families, where entire families were cramped into small rooms, and talk with the women. We would hold classes on women's equality, on machismo, and on the need for us as female workers to organize and fight for our rights. We had a tremendous outreach campaign in the marginal *barrios* and all the poor neighborhoods. Many of the men were angry about our demands for equality. They wanted to dominate us and keep us locked up inside the house. They didn't want us to have the same freedoms they had, or to enjoy the same things they enjoyed.

I was put in jail many times because of this work for women's liberation. Before the Revolution I worked with an organization called the Confederation of Women. (I also worked with the Federation of Cuban Women, but that was after the Revolution). I attended the Women's Congress in 1939. We passed laws giving women the right to vote and other legal rights as the result of the new Constitution of 1940.

I got married and had five children. Rafael and I have been married for forty-five years. We get along very well, and in spite of many economic difficulties we've had a happy life together. My *compañero* worked at the National Packaging Company making cigar boxes and was also very active in the workers' movement.

I was already in my forties—actually, I was forty-four—when Batista fell and Castro came to power in 1959. Throughout the 1950s I had worked closely with Lázaro Peña, the most important leader of the tobacco workers; we all loved him. After the Revolution he became general secretary of the CTC. In a book about the history of the tobacco workers' movement, I'm referred to as "the blonde who fought in the Revolution with Lázaro Peña." He and I got arrested often, and we would do time together. Lázaro Peña used to say, "There is strength in unity." This is exactly what is needed now, during the Special Period—the unity of the Cuban family, and the unity of the Cuban people. This is the only way that the Revolution can survive.

But let me tell you something: for us, as working-class women, even the Special Period is better than what we endured when Cuba was a capitalist country. If you come to visit me now, I can at least offer you a *batido* [a drink made of banana, water, and sugar]. When the capitalists were in power—that is, when the Spaniards and then the gringos ran our country—we were so poor we couldn't even drink a *batido* ourselves. Forget about being able to offer something to eat or drink to our guests. No, even the Special Period is magnificent in comparison to the misery we lived through before the Revolution.

Here is an example of how the bosses used to exploit the female tobacco workers. They would always give the stem cutters three or four more pounds of tobacco than we were getting paid to stem. So we had to buy our own scales, weigh the tobacco, and then put all of the extra in another basket. These bosses were always trying to take advantage of us, so we had to protect ourselves.

We used to work very hard during the months when there was a high international demand for Cuban cigars. Then, if there wasn't any more stemming to do, the bosses would often lay us off. And if you weren't able to pay your rent, the landlords would just throw you out onto the streets. They would take all your furniture and belongings and leave them outside the door, in front of the building. I remember, as a form of protest, we would go to help these evicted people; we would break down the door and put all the furniture back inside. Then we would just stay there with them. We would occupy these dwellings as a way of fighting back.

Once I was taken prisoner because a group of us broke into a store and distributed all the milk to the families living in the neighborhood. The storeowner was such a thief. He was active in the black market and used to hoard food to sell at inflated prices that the workers couldn't afford. So we got together, and we decided to break in and give the milk to the children who needed it.

Another time, I was imprisoned for supporting the candidacy of Castellanos, who was running against a corrupt *bandolero* [bandit]. We went throughout the neighborhood carrying the ballot box and getting people to vote for Castellanos, a popular candidate who was for justice. Also, during a demonstration against the Korean War the police hauled me off to jail again. That time they kept me there for three or four days.

My grandchildren had the opportunity to go to school, since they were born after the Revolution, and none of them work in the tobacco sector. They all studied, and several of them became professionals. I have a granddaughter who is a family doctor. I never had the opportunity to study, neither did my children—who could afford to, during capitalism? None of us. Only the wealthy. Things are much better now. A lot of the children of tobacco workers are able to study and get technical or professional jobs. And even tobacco workers are well paid, and we have free health care, retirement, paid maternity leave, and other benefits. There are day-care centers for our kids and community dining halls where we eat lunch.

Both my husband and I are retired, but we still work on a voluntary basis. Right now I'm putting in three or four hours each day at a tobacco factory (Rey del Mundo) that has fallen behind in its quotas. I enjoy helping out. When the factories are in a pinch, I like to go there and help them. I'm also directing the Association of Retired Tobacco Workers. We plan social and recreational activities for the retired workers. Right now I'm in the middle of organizing a big party we're going to throw at the Tobacco Workers' Union.

The situation for women has improved greatly since the Revolution. Many women now have leadership positions in the unions and in government (though we need still more women in these high-level jobs). There are still some macho men who abuse women, get drunk and beat up their wives; some of them have extramarital affairs. But there is no reason for women in Cuba to tolerate this kind of behavior now. They don't have to be afraid of their husbands or to be treated badly. If a woman lets herself be abused, then as far as I am concerned, it is her fault! Because today in Cuba no woman should put up with an abusive husband. Cuban women don't need to depend on men for financial support or for anything anymore. Things have changed, and women *are* liberated now! If a woman is unhappy in her marriage, she can easily get a divorce. Women must be free and never tolerate machismo! No, no, no . . .

I have very good memories of Che Guevara, who was always a defender of women's rights.[3] I remember talking with him a lot when he came to the CTC; he used to spend a lot of time there, talking with the workers and asking us questions. El Che was so intelligent and a man of such great ideas, a real visionary. He was always in a good mood; he would joke with us and make us laugh. The tobacco workers loved Che Guevara; we were all devastated when they killed him in Bolivia. It was such a terrible loss for all of Latin America!

I am proud of the life I have lived. I am proud to be a revolutionary who has fought for women's rights and has been active in the Tobacco Workers' Union most of my life. My only wish for the future is for the Cuban people to be able to unite so we can save the Revolution. Because a return to imperialism would be a major catastrophe!

Nancy Morejón

AFRO-CUBAN POET AND JOURNALIST

Nancy Morejón (1992).

I interviewed Nancy Morejón, one of Cuba's most prominent poets, on July 3, 1992, at Casa de las Américas, in Havana.[1] *Morejón was born in Havana in*

*1944. She studied French language and literature at the University of Havana,
from where she graduated in 1966. She has worked as a teacher and translator at
the Instituto del Libro and has published cultural criticism in many journals and
newspapers, including* La Gaceta de Cuba *and* Cuba Internacional. *Most of
her translations are from French and English-language poetry. This Afro-Cuban
poet has held important positions at the National Union of Cuban Writers and
Artists (UNEAC), Casa de las Américas, and until recently was working as the
director of "Ediciones PM," the publishing arm of the Pablo Milanés Foundation.*

*Nancy Morejón is the author of seven collections of poetry, the most recent
book of which,* Paisaje Célebre *[Famed landscape] (1993), received a finalist
award in an international poetry competition.[2] Morejón's works of literary
criticism include texts on Nicolás Guillén, the Afro-Cuban Revolutionary poet;
and* Fundación de la imagen *(1988), a collection of essays about Cuban culture
and on writers such as Mirta Aguirre, José Lezama Lima, Gioconda Belli, Carlos
Pellicer, Langston Hughes, Jacques Romain, and Edward Brathwaite.*

*Nancy Morejón has traveled widely in Europe, Africa, the Caribbean, Latin
America, and the United States as a sort of cultural ambassador for Cuba. Her
poetry has been translated into many languages. She has never married or had
children; she told me that she has only a small number of close friends and that she
enjoys spending most of her free time at home, reading and writing.*

Like everyone, I have many childhood memories. I have even been
tempted to write about these memories because I think that my childhood
was a very special stage of my life. It was not only a time when my personality was formed (just as it is for everyone) but an area full of mystery, full
of magical things. I was born and raised in Havana. During my childhood
and throughout all my life the city of Havana has been very important to
me. The city has always had a central place in my memories. My family
and Havana, resonant Havana, and the sounds of the city form an important part of my psychological landscape.

I am from a neighborhood in Havana called Los Sitios—a neighborhood that has a lot of folklore surrounding it. Los Sitios is a neighborhood
that produced great *rumberos* [rumba players]. I want to share with you
some of what I consider interesting memories about events that took place
in that neighborhood. I have written some stories, some poems, and some
other pieces about my childhood experiences, but I believe that now is the
time to sit down and reflect, to record my childhood memories in a systematic manner and try to publish a book about those years of my life.
This is an unfinished project that I have not yet had the chance to complete. I simply haven't had time to do it.

Generally speaking, I must confess that I had a peaceful childhood. It was a childhood full of love. In fact, I am a warm, affectionate person, and I think the reason is that my parents were always loving and affectionate with me. I am an only child. I remember clearly and distinctly the love my parents had for me. They took great care of me and gave me a lot of attention. This love and caring provided me with a sense of security and self-confidence. (Psychologists say that 95 percent of the security one feels as an adult comes from one's early childhood experiences.)

I was the only daughter in a very humble, modest home. My mother stopped working when she married my father. She had been a dressmaker, and before that a tobacco stemmer. Before marrying my mother, my father was a sailor. After I was born, my father settled down. He didn't want to travel any more; he never sailed again. He would say, "I am not going to sail any more, because my daughter was born and I want to be with her, to raise her, and to watch her grow up." So, my dad became a stevedore and worked on the docks.

I was a shy, introverted little girl who was prone to daydreaming and to drifting into deep thought. This was not because I had suffered but because I had a rich imagination. For example, I remember watching ants for hours and hours, and imagining what it must be like to be an ant. I recall my early fascination with books. I used to like to pick up books and hold them and look at the pictures when I was still a toddler, before I learned how to read. My father had a small library at home. It was a very modest collection. But I do remember how much my father loved literature. He had a great respect for learning and for books. Among the books in his library were several collections of poems by Nicolás Guillén, books that had been published in Argentina where Guillén was living in exile at that time. My father was definitely one of the most important influences in my life. He transmitted to me his love for books, for knowledge, for literature, for words. (When my father died in 1987, I was filled with grief and sorrow. Fortunately, my mother is still alive.)

Both my parents were trade unionists and belonged to the Communist Party in Cuba. That political involvement gave them their education, the little education that they were able to acquire. They were honest, hard-working people who struggled to defend their rights as members of the working class. They used to read a lot; they were completely self-taught. I feel proud of them because of the level of education that they achieved all by themselves, without having had the opportunity to attend high schools or universities. I really believe that they achieved an enviable cultural refinement that is worthy of praise. My parents were born into a Cuba where the opportunity for a formal education did not exist for black people, nor did it exist for poor, working-class sectors of society. Access to education was not a right granted them. Only white people with money could get a formal education in prerevolutionary Cuba. This made my parents' cultural refinement no small feat and something that I always admired and respected. They were people of great awareness who understood the importance of knowledge. My education was a central concern to them; they always encouraged my studies and intellectual development.

My parents weren't at all religious. I was raised in a very secular atmosphere. Although we declared ourselves to be Roman Catholic, just as almost everyone in Cuba did, religion didn't play much of a role in our everyday lives. My parents did have me baptized and I received my first Holy Communion, but religion didn't have any impact on me when I was growing up. My father was a Communist and an atheist; he cursed religion and believed that it contributed to oppressed people's attitude that they must be resigned to suffering on earth in order to receive their reward in heaven. Actually, I grew up completely removed from both the Catholic religion and the Afro-Cuban religion (Santería), which were practiced on the island by large percentages of the Cuban population. My parents raised me with the social taboos that existed at that time in relation to Santería and African spirituality, though nevertheless, I do remember that these beliefs and practices were commonplace in my neighborhood. Santería was, and still is, a form of cultural as well as spiritual expression in Cuba.

Back on the subject of my early interest in books and what I told you about being prone to deep thought and daydreaming. I liked to look at the pages of books, to imitate my father a bit, and before I started talking I would wait for the arrival of the magazine *Bohemia* on Fridays. My parents told me that "Bohemia" was one of the first words I uttered, but I said it poorly: "Gohemia." I would say "Gohemia," and if it didn't arrive as I was sitting waiting for it, I would start to cry.

Later, I learned to read at home, with my mother. She taught me the alphabet and how to form simple words phonetically. My parents discovered that I was a gifted child with a rich imagination, a good memory, and a lot of curiosity. Before I started school, I would wait by the window each morning until a group of students and their teacher would pass by the house on their way to the school that I would attend a few years later. I would follow them and my mother would run after me and bring me back home.

I remember very well a teacher named Beba. She was one of my favorite teachers. I don't know whether she is still alive or not; I think she left the country. Beba was my kindergarten teacher. I entered kindergarten when I was only two years old. When I was two, I talked a lot; even before that age I talked a lot. Words were always important to me. I recall how Beba loved me. I remember that she invited me to her house one time, and my mother took me there. I used to spend some days with her and her family. Beba was from a white family, a very distinguished, wealthy family that lived in the exclusive neighborhood of El Vedado. The first time Beba invited me to her home was my first trip to El Vedado, and I'll never forget how enjoyable it was. I was really nervous because this experience was something so different from what I was used to. It was my first journey into the world of the wealthy, and I was struck by how differently they lived than we working-class Cuban people lived.

Thus, I can say that race and class consciousness awoke in me when I was still a very young child. There was an episode in my childhood that made me very aware of interracial relations and racism. I was an outstanding student; I always won awards for having the best grades in my class. I attended a private school called Academia de la Plaza, and for the most part I have very good memories of that school; however, I do remember an incident of racial discrimination that occurred there. I was in either first or second grade, and we were going to perform a play for the graduation ceremony. Well, this play was based on some children's story about a hen and some chicks. It was a story whose argument I don't exactly remember, but I do remember that there was a bad chick and the evil chick was a black chick. So the teacher chose me to play the part of the black chick. But the behavior of the black chick was like that of a black sheep, and I was traumatized. I remember asking my father, "Why, Papi, should they think of me for the part of the bad chicken if I'm such a good student, with so many awards and such good grades? Why was I the bad chick?"

When I told my parents what had happened, they went to the school and complained to the principal. I was born into a household with a lot of awareness, a lot of sensitivity for racial problems and interracial tensions. The director of the school understood the error that my teacher had made; she had been carried away by the color and because I was one of the few little black girls who attended this school. But after that incident, and after my parents complained to the principal, the teachers at that school were always very careful not to discriminate; they became tremendously aware and sensitive to the issue of my racial difference.

In my school there were very few blacks; I remember only two or three other girls in the entire school. And the other black children were the daughters and sons of doctors and other middle-class professionals. It cost my father a lot of effort to pay the tuition; in fact, my parents sacrificed every spare penny to be able to send me to that private elementary school. Even so, it was a modest school in the neighborhood. There were other private schools at the time in Cuba for the children of the wealthy and the elite ruling class. For example, the Instituto Edison and the Colegio-Academia Pitman were among the most exclusive—schools that only the rich people could afford.

I don't remember any other specific incidents of racism when I was growing up, but interracial relations in Cuba are very complex. I didn't feel discriminated against as a child, because my friends were still children who had not yet been corrupted by society's racist attitudes. Children are children; they are not society. They have not yet learned to be prejudiced or to hate other people because of the color of their skin. I had wonderful friends and classmates and I would often go with them to their homes. Yet I do remember that I almost always felt a strong sense of isolation. I *was* isolated! I was alienated because there were not many black children at the school I attended, not even mulattos.

In my neighborhood, of course, there were lots of other black children. It was a working-class neighborhood full of blacks, mulattos, and also whites. In recent years here the theory of Afro-Cuban marginality has been developed. I consider this theory flawed and inaccurate; in my opinion, it is an opportunistic interpretation of the past that doesn't correspond to the reality of life in Cuba before the Revolution. If I were to outline a theory of marginality in prerevolutionary Cuba, you would likely believe it because you didn't live through that experience, and there is no one who can prove the contrary to you. But the truth is that I grew up in an essentially working-class world, composed of many whites as well as blacks and mulattos. One can't say that only the lumpen [marginal] or poor workers lived in those neighborhoods. My mother was a worker, but it is false to say that she formed part of the lumpenproletariat. These Marxist classifications are valuable, but sometimes they respond to abstract notions and conceptions and don't really describe the diversity and complexity of social reality. I don't believe that the lumpenproletariat who served Marx in creating his theory had much to do with what I lived and observed here in Cuba in the 1940s. Back then, it wasn't only the Afro-Cuban population that was poor and marginal; many white people too had economic difficulties. And many of these poor whites had an awareness of being exploited, as well as a feeling of belonging to the neighborhood.

I met many persons of different races active in the trade unions and in the struggle for life. Blacks, whites, and mulattos were all engaged in the struggle to change our unjust and racist society. Also, because my parents were such exceptional people with respect to their active engagement in the struggle to change society, my own personal history and perceptions of reality are colored by their consciousness of class and race and by their commitment to fighting for social justice. They were very committed politically; I remember that they went to meetings regularly and attended political events. Therefore, I was raised in a world with a social and political consciousness. My parents taught me to be sensitive to these issues and not to adopt a conformist position. In any case, I have very beautiful memories, and I feel nostalgia for those early years of my life.

I'll tell you something, one of the things that I have already written about is the important role of music in the formation of my identity. When I evoke those years I realize that what springs forth most in those memories is resonance, sounds, Afro-Cuban rhythms and melodies. I have many memories of music, especially of the *guaracha* [salsa-dance music]. Actually, I grew up in a neighborhood full of extremely talented musicians. In fact, my book *Richard trajo su flauta y otros argumentos* [Richard brought his flute, and other stories] pays homage to a great musician who accompanied me during my childhood. Richard Egues, then the flutist in the Orquesta Aragón, forms an essential part of my literary and musical family. I wrote this collection of poetry as an homage to the families of those great musicians and to the entire neighborhood that loved them.

My mother tried to get me to take piano lessons, and I did go to a few classes, but I didn't like them. I remember saying, "This is limiting me." So I rebelled against piano lessons. This was too bad for me because now, with hindsight, I think that I might have been a talented musician. I have a very good ear for music. Perhaps I would have achieved more as a musician than as a writer and poet. Perhaps? Often, if I'm unable to sleep, or sometimes when I'm sleepy, the songs that I used to listen to when I was a young girl come to me in the middle of the night. I lie in bed remembering precious conga rhythms, and rumbas without drums, rumbas played on the bodies of people. Everyone would be out in the streets, partying, and then, suddenly, a group of people would improvise a rumba at two in the morning. Each person would make the sound of beating drums, and there were choruses and the people would dance. Ay, how I remember that! What fond, happy memories!

I should tell you, to be frank, that because my parents were interested in politics and social life, they were very aware that a lumpen world, a delinquent underworld, also existed in Havana. They tried to raise me, with the best of intentions, removed from this world of night life and the criminal elements of society. They didn't want me to be exposed to drinking, crime, prostitution, or any of that. I understand it, I really do understand it, but I also think that their desire to protect and shelter me created a lot of cultural limitations for me. I harbored many feelings deep inside me that the Revolution set free, much later in my life.

For example, let me share with you this marvelous anecdote about my uncle, my soul uncle, Juan, the uncle I most loved, who people say was a marvelous *rumbero*. I saw him dance once, and this changed my life forever! One day when I was three or four years old he said to me, "Let's go, Nancy, let's go for a walk." So I went for a walk with my uncle. And suddenly, I was in the middle of an enormous party. It was so incredible and amazing for me. I had never seen a house so full of people! It was one big party, the most sonorous and tremendous party that I remember from my childhood. I remember that I was both thrilled and also a bit frightened. This party was overwhelming for me, because as a little girl I had always lived inside the protected, tranquil world of my parents' home. It wasn't a noisy world. My folks never had big parties with music and dancing. In our house one didn't do such things; at our house, one read books or listened to the radio or to records on the phonograph. I recall sitting there at this party and suddenly I started to cry, not because I rejected it but because sometimes children communicate by crying. And I said, "Uncle, Uncle, get me out of here, get me out of here, take me home!" When we arrived at my house, I told my mother: "Mami, Mami, Uncle took me to a party for blacks!" It made a great impression on me. It marked me for the rest of my life in a very positive way because, for me the rumba is an expression of Afro-Cuban identity, of my own identity. It is a really powerful thing and I know that I inherited my love for salsa music and dancing from my mother's family, especially from my Uncle Juan, that marvelous *rumbero*. At the time I didn't understand why this event had such a profound impact on me, but later I realized that I loved salsa and other Afro-Cuban cultural practices, and that this feeling was rooted in my childhood. Especially late at night, when I could hear the people improvising percussions with the palms of their hands. All of this shaped me.

I remember the sounds of the conga and how everyone would dance the conga, forming winding lines of dancers in the streets. I loved the rhythm of the conga. I recall how the dancers would form a long line during carnival, and everyone would join in and dance. The street vendors, the women who sold pottery, the gardeners—many people would wait for the conga dancers to pass by, and they would all join in. In fact, in my neighborhood in Havana there was always a great tradition of carnivals and processions. I remember how, as a child, I longed to join in the conga; deep within me, I felt a need to participate in the carnival.

After 1959 all the popular Afro-Cuban dances and music entered into the category of folklore. As Sarita Gómez, the folk singer—who was so intelligent and so sweet—would say: "Well, that which for the blacks is backward, that is to say, that which white folks say that for the blacks is backward and primitive, when the whites themselves become interested in it, then it's not backward, but instead, it's called "folklore." If *we* do it, it isn't folklore. It's simply backward."

Anyway, the main point I wanted to make is that these early memories about the sounds of the rumba and the conga and about the popular culture of my neighborhood are a fundamental chapter in my evolution as a writer. I came to understand these Afro-Cuban cultural practices much better after the Revolution, which dismantled all the prejudices against such practices and provided a legitimate space for the exploration of the African roots of our culture. Santería and the "folklore" of my neighborhood were no longer devalued or considered taboo; on the contrary, these practices were to be celebrated as a central part of our Cuban heritage.

I enjoy writing essays about Afro-Cuban music and musicians. I just wrote an article about José Antonio Méndez, the great *bolero* [ballad] singer. His recent death, which was very sudden, affected me profoundly. The article was also an expression of sincere condolence for Richard, his brother. I think this particular essay turned out quite well. Sometimes when I'm most hurt by a particular situation or event, it moves me and inspires me to write better than usual, or else it doesn't work out at all. I write about music in many of my essays as well as in much of my poetry; it's a fundamental part of my creative life as a writer. Afro-Cuban music, in particular, has a central place in much of my writing.

At the same time, North American music, especially jazz and rock 'n' roll, were also very important influences during the formative years of my adolescence. As a teenager, I loved rock 'n' roll. I wasn't just a fan; I was a true rocker—well, a rocker of the Elvis Presley, Bill Haley, and Little Richard kind. These two important manifestations of Afro-America—jazz and rock—were always central in my cultural formation and in my personal life. I believe that in some way I am going to continue to develop these musical influences in a more systematic and deeper way in my writing and in my work.

This music definitely helped to shape my sensibility. My father studied the trumpet and also the bass; he never became a musician, but during his years as a sailor he established many ties with North American jazz groups. My father didn't talk much; he was a quiet, contemplative man. He was a marvelous person, but he just didn't talk much. He was always observing things around him and reflecting on life, rather than talking or telling stories. Sometimes when he was navigating (he always used the word "navigate"), I would go with him. I remember once when I had gone with him to Louisiana, we went to the place where Louis Armstrong used to rehearse. I actually met the great Louis Armstrong! I loved to go watch him jam! I knew all of the hours, the practice schedules, and I would go to listen to him. I remember that this music reminded me of the sonority of the rumba, of the black world of the *barrios* in Havana that I was familiar with. I felt an affinity for the world of jazz, black jazz, North American jazz.

In my house we listened to a lot of jazz records. When I was a small child we had an RCA Victor record player, which had an enormous figure of a dog on it. It was a phonograph that is now a collector's item. We would play many records and listen to music for hours and hours. He had a collection of jazz records. Papi had the first collection of the Nat King Cole Trio. (My father, who was a generous man, lent those albums to some Nat King Cole fan who unfortunately never returned them.) Through my father's collection of music, I became acquainted with many of the great orchestras of the period: Glenn Miller during the years of the Second World War, Benny Goodman—well, all of them, Armstrong, Frank Sinatra, Nat King Cole, the greats, Count Basie, even Billie Holliday, everyone. I was very lucky to have had this opportunity to listen to the great contemporary jazz musicians.

I was fourteen years old when the Revolution triumphed. I was just leaving childhood and entering adolescence. I can honestly say that what I witnessed as a result of the Cuban Revolution was an extraordinary change of values! Among the things that most attracted me—apart from the agrarian reform, the urban reform, the new health care and educational programs, and so forth—were Fidel's speeches regarding the racial question. It was very moving for me to hear him defend the rights of *all* Cubans, including blacks, to equal access to Cuba's resources. Fidel spoke about the need to open up all the beaches and clubs to everyone and not to discriminate on the basis of race. Following the triumph of the Revolution there were many complaints about blacks being allowed to enter into such and such a beach, or such and such a restaurant or club. And finally, Fidel declared all the beaches to be public beaches, and everyone was given free access to beaches and clubs that had previously been private resorts (and were later converted to syndicate vacation spots and so forth). This was a really beautiful period in Cuban history when my intellectual life was being formed.

I entered the university in 1962. The Revolution had succeeded, and a series of social reforms had already been implemented, including the right to a free college education; my father never had to pay university tuition for me. At this time the humanistic tradition was very solid and strong in Cuban universities. It was a great tradition—one must recognize that— even though it was, in my opinion, much too Eurocentric. During the postcolonial period in which the Europeans began to question their own history, we began to discover the Third World: Africa, Latin America, and Asian cultural traditions. This was the time when Che Guevara published Spanish translations of important anticolonialist texts such as *The Wretched of the Earth* and *Black Skin, White Masks,* both by the Algerian writer Frantz Fanon. A tricontinental conference was held, in which leaders and intellectuals from Asia, Latin America, and Africa came together to discuss issues of imperialism and plans for a postcolonial future. I remember how these ideas completely consumed me. I believe that these were really very beautiful years, years of great hope and promise for a better future here in Cuba and in the developing world.

My first encounter with machismo wasn't at home, because my father was a very liberal man who believed in equality between the sexes. He didn't raise me to be a prim, proper, prissy *señorita,* or "little lady." My father would chat with my friends, and they all thought he was very "cool" because he respected me and trusted me so much. He was interested in listening to me tell him many details of my life; I was eager to share my experiences with him. I would even tell him, "Papi, I have a boyfriend." I felt as though he really understood me. He also encouraged me to pursue my literary vocation. He wasn't just my father; he was also my friend. He didn't impose a lot of rules or strict moral standards of behavior on me. For example, one night I got home very late—I was a student leader at the university and we had a meeting with Armando Hart, Cuba's current Minister of Culture, who at that time was the Minister of Education, the youngest high-level official in the revolutionary government. Anyway, as I was telling you, we went to a meeting with him, and I got home at four in the morning. I remember vividly the image of my mother in her bathrobe, desperate, yelling at me: "Listen, girl, where have you been? I've been worried sick about you!" And on the other hand, my father? He was sound asleep. He really trusted me and gave me so much freedom. (Of course, there was almost no crime in Cuba at that time, and it was safe for me to be out late at night with a group of friends. I suppose that it's very different in the United States, where there is so much crime on the streets.)

My parents supported me in my political work and also as a writer. They were both extremely honored by my chosen profession as a writer and poet. I began writing at the age of nine. I had an extraordinarily rich imaginary world. When there were things I couldn't talk about to my father or mother, I would go to my room and write and write. I would spend hours alone writing. It was my vocation, which was something that they didn't understand as such at that time. But they sacrificed much to give me a good education. I was very fortunate to have parents who were so supportive of me. I didn't have to fight at home in order to become a writer, like those proverbial cases of men and women alike who suffered hostility from their families because of their aspirations. Their parents would constantly nag at them: "And why be a writer? This isn't good for anything. You can't make a decent living as a writer." In my house, as I already told you, there was always a unique sensitivity, a refinement, and an appreciation for culture and for learning. My parents both read the newspaper daily, and they also read magazines and books. They insisted that I have a formal education and that I become a professional. For example, at one time Mami wanted me to study to become a nurse and I told her, "No, medicine doesn't interest me." (I have some photos of myself when I was eight years old, dressed up as a nurse. But it would have been a disaster for me to have a sick person in my hands to care for and give injections to; I'm so clumsy with manual things.) But they always supported my interest in literature and my desire to write.

I didn't incorporate myself into the Revolution; rather, I was immersed in the revolutionary process. I began my political education within that process, and I believe that I have been part of it because of my family tradition. I didn't receive it passively. We, as Afro-Cubans, formed part of something that was our right. I believe that my fundamental contribution to the life of my country is tied to literature. I think the first duty of any writer is to write well. It is very important. If you aren't a good writer, it is impossible for your ideas, whatever they are, to make sense to people or touch them. Words lose meaning if they aren't used precisely and carefully. The best causes can lose meaning through bad literature. Sometimes an author has a civic vocation to fight to change society, or wants to share ideas concerning socialism, Communism, whatever—but when we look at his or her writing, we are disappointed, because literature really cannot be, nor has it ever been, a summary of slogans, of dogma, or of abstract notions.

I believe that my writing is characterized by my sense of belonging to a particular place, to my country. I strongly identify with the culture of my people, especially with the culture of Afro-Cuban people. This is something that can't slip away from me and that is always present in my writing. I feel that this element is central in my writing (and in my life) because my parents contributed to the formation of my values and way of thinking with their exemplary lives, with their ideals and their sacrifices. And in some way I have been able and I have always tried to reciprocate in this process. But I have done it in other spheres, as a journalist, writer, poet, and producer of cultural knowledge. Of course, literature is something very complex and very difficult to define. The process is even somewhat irrational. Many times people have asked me why I write, and I say that I don't know. All I know is that I have a need to write, and that is enough. It is difficult to tell you why I write. I write because I want to. No, I write because I write, because it is a necessity. I do believe in inspiration. What I write is something that visits me; it comes and I write. I never force it. It is born of a mystery, a mystery that later became a habit. If the outcome of my literary endeavors is to provide service to a good cause, this is magnificent for me. I feel satisfied. And if it isn't—well, I can't do anything to change that. I am not going to regret my literature nor the things that I do, because I do them with passion and with love.

My vocation awoke in me at a very young age; as I already told you, at the age of nine I began to write, in 1962, when I was only seventeen, I published my first book. I have always enjoyed translating. French poetry has always been for me a great oasis, Spanish poetry as well. Of course, I can't do anything with the latter except read it, enjoy it; you can't translate the poets of your own language! There are so many poets to whom I owe so much. I'm indebted to Nicolás Guillén, to Emilio Vallagas, to Roberto Fernández Retamar, and to many others. I'm also indebted to Paul Eluard, to Aimé Césaire, to Pablo Neruda, to César Vallejo, to Efraín Huerta. My debt to them is extraordinary. Another poet who influenced my own writing is an Argentine poet from Buenos Aires, named Enrique Molina. I also owe much to Mario Benedetti, and even Nicanor Parra in some way. And finally among many influences, I'm indebted to the lyrics of many *boleros* and many rumbas. I believe that the poetry of the writers I've mentioned has left the most visible traces in my own work.

I have written two books of literary criticism about Nicolás Guillén, analyzing the themes of identity, miscegenation, Afro-Cuban popular culture, and Cuban religious syncretism in the work of Guillén. I have had the privilege to know, discuss, and study his poetry as something very close to me. His verse, clear and simple, as Martí suggested, has served to awaken the consciousness of the worker and resolutely denounce the most subtle or direct expressions of racial prejudice. In my opinion, the poetry of Guillén is a voice that expresses the purest social, political, and artistic aspirations of the Cuban people. He belongs not only to Cuba but also to the Caribbean and to all of Latin America. Guillén knew how to create an image of the national soul through a poetics of the legitimate pillars of our landscape and culture: the green and the blue of the Antilles, the guitar, the palm tree, the precious woods of the mountains, the lizard, the rose bush, the little paper bird, and the like.

In my 1988 collection of essays, *Fundación de la imagen*, I wrote about the process of Cuban transculturation. I quoted Fernando Ortiz, who affirmed in his book *Contrapunteo cubano del tobaco y el azucar* [Cuban counterpoint of tobacco and sugar] (1940): "The true history of Cuba is the history of its extremely intricate transculturations." In my opinion, "transculturation" means constant interaction, the transmutation between two or more cultural components whose unconscious finality creates a third new and independent cultural whole, even though its bases, its roots, rest over the preceding elements. The reciprocal influence of each component is determinative.[3] Our culture is none other than that—a new culture created as the consequence of an irreversible racial and cultural transculturation.[4]

In Cuba today we are going through very difficult times. This is a period of great isolation in spite of all our efforts at joint business ventures with other countries. Everyone knows about the collapse of the socialist countries, the fall of the Berlin Wall, and the world events that have occurred since 1989. The world has changed, and the Cuban Revolution has been profoundly affected by those changes in Eastern Europe. As a consequence of our loss of former trading partners and subsidized prices for our sugar exports, Cuba is in a severe economic crisis. Nevertheless, I believe that those of us who are a little bit older are able to see that the situation we are in today—even though it is very critical—isn't an entirely new situation for us, as Cubans. The truth is that we have been struggling for many years. Naturally, we struggled in the 1960s and the 1970s against the biggest imperial power in the world. As you recall, the U.S. administration invaded our shores at the Bay of Pigs, and we defeated them. Formerly, we had allies in socialist East European countries. We have been abandoned by those former allies and trading partners. Therefore, this moment, the so-called Special Period, is truly critical and difficult.

But I believe that this moment is not a time for self-pity. It's a moment to act, to contribute our talents, and to try to overcome these circumstances through our own efforts, through our own work. We need to keep moving forward and to make progress in our business ventures with other countries and to continue to develop our biotechnology, which is very advanced and sophisticated. I'm not an economist, but it seems to me that we need to continue to make great strides in the diversification of our agricultural production. I think that these are some of the areas where we need to continue to develop and to work toward greater self-determination. I believe that we have been working, we are still working, and I hope we will always continue to work to defend the achievements of our Revolution.

As a writer, I find the question more difficult. Because the immediate situation is so tense, other urgent matters may not come to light until many years later. I wouldn't dare, for example, write anything that is directly about the Special Period, because I believe that sometimes reality is only an appearance; it can deceive us. I think that one should respect someone's writing to the extent that that person communicates the urgency of the times. And I think that a person feels such urgency through his or her condition as a citizen of a country. That is my interpretation of the role of the writer in society.

In my everyday life, I am affected like all Cubans by this Special Period we are living through. As a writer, I am affected mostly by the power blackouts. Most writers, whether they are good or bad writers, usually spend a good amount of time reading, and all these power blackouts have interrupted my reading. From a technological point of view, most writers here in Cuba don't have access to a personal computer. At work we still use old-fashioned typewriters, and very few of us own a computer that we can use at home. I still haven't entered the information age of computing. I regret this, because obviously computers can be very useful tools for research and for many other purposes. But we are a poor island nation and our priority right now is surviving this economic crisis without sacrificing the advances we have achieved such as health care and education for everyone. And besides, I still believe that you don't need a computer in order to write a poem. Sure, writing with a word processor is faster and more efficient—you don't have to keep writing more and more drafts—but it isn't essential. I am trying to find solutions like those of my *cimarrón* [runaway slave] ancestors, solutions that are engendered by a culture of resistance. But I believe that even in the midst of this battle to survive, we must preserve the right to beauty and the right to cultural refinement. In my opinion, this is tremendously important.

In these times of so many economic difficulties, there are many prejudices regarding culture, because some old-fashioned people think there's no room for culture during times like these. This seems to me to be a dreadfully dangerous conclusion. I firmly believe that culture should always play an important role in any society. I think that it is our right as long as we live to create and to enjoy culture; it is a very beautiful way to resist and to express our struggle for survival.

We have done a lot at Casa de las Américas to promote Caribbean culture and unity among the islands of the Caribbean. Casa de las Américas is considered by many to be a house of friendship. As people of the Caribbean, whether we speak English, Spanish, French, or Creole, we share a common historical experience of colonialism and of slavery. We have tried to make Casa de las Américas a gateway through which to translate all the Caribbean literatures and cultures into Spanish. That is one of our fundamental tasks, and for me, it has been a wonderful experience. It has enriched me personally because I feel that I am a talented translator, and I've been able to work on projects that are meaningful to me. I'm not a professional writer, able to make a living strictly through my writing, but working there at Casa de las Américas is a job that isn't alienating. On the contrary, it is satisfying work that enables me to grow and develop; it gives me great joy. I have worked there since January of 1986, and that has given me the opportunity to travel throughout the Caribbean. I have also traveled widely in Latin America, the United States, Canada, Eastern and Western Europe, and Africa. One place I haven't been that fascinates me is Asia. I would very much like to visit some Asian country. I would really love to travel to Vietnam someday.

My main aspirations for the future are to continue writing poetry, short stories, and critical essays and to keep developing my thoughts and ideas. I hope to continue contributing to my country through my cultural and literary production. I still write regularly for a number of journals and newspapers. Of course, during this period of crisis there aren't as many publications in Cuba as there used to be—because of paper shortages and the lack of other resources—but even so, I continue to send out my articles, poems, and short stories. After all, writing is my vocation.

Belkis Vega

DOCUMENTARY FILM MAKER

Belkis Vega (1992).

Belkis Vega, now forty-seven years old, is one of very few Latin American women cinematographers to achieve a successful career in a field still dominated by men. Several of her films deal specifically with women's issues in Cuba. In our interview, conducted on July 5, 1992, at her home in Nuevo Vedado in Havana, Vega highlighted her passion for making documentaries that focus on what she calls the "human dimension" of political realities and world events: the civil war in Lebanon, the plight of the Palestinians, the participation of Cubans in Angola, the nuclear disaster at Chernobyl.

Belkis Vega was among the privileged class before the Revolution and afterward experienced a decline in her standard of living as a consequence of the radical socioeconomic changes in Cuban society. The values by which she measures her success and well-being, however, are not the consumer-oriented, materialistic values that prevail in capitalist countries. The filmmaker has had job offers in foreign countries and could live much more comfortably in exile; nevertheless, she is dedicated to making films in Cuba, despite the scarcity of resources, power shortages, lack of equipment, and day-to-day difficulties of the Special Period.

I was born near the end of 1951, and by the time of the triumph of the Cuban Revolution, I had just turned seven. Therefore I don't remember much from before the Revolution, except for some very strong memories about how my family was divided and torn apart. I come from a middle-class family; my parents were professionals, and I never lacked for anything during the imperialist years. My family was very close; I have fond and happy memories of my childhood. I remember the Revolution as something very beautiful and even romantic. But of course I was too young to understand what it was all about.

My mother's side of the family was not in favor of the Revolution. Members of a small family that had come from Spain around the beginning of this century, they had achieved a certain economic status and had become quite wealthy—they owned stores, factories, and other buildings. As a result of the Revolution they lost many of these properties, and most of them left Cuba, migrating to Venezuela, Spain, Puerto Rico, and the United States.

My father's side of the family was different. Although most of his relatives had studied at the university, they weren't as wealthy. Most of them had put themselves through college by working, and some of them had fought against Batista. Two of my uncles were involved in clandestine fighting against the dictatorship, and they and two other uncles were members of the July 26 Movement. All of my father's family strongly supported the Revolution and stayed here in Cuba to work toward its success.

Thus, the Revolution caused a division in the very heart of my family, and this was very hard on me, because I was quite close to those on my mother's side, and I gradually lost touch with them. No one left Cuba right away, but during the 1960s they all left except my grandparents, my mother, and one uncle.

Aside from this sadness, however, I remember the Revolution as something very lovely; I recall everyone celebrating joyfully in the streets the day Fidel Castro seized power. And in 1959 I even met Fidel; he was visiting a journalist who lived in the same building as I did. I remember him as if he were a legend. I also met Camilo Torres before he died.[1] I met him on the beach where he was reading, relaxing beneath the pine trees. When Camilo died in a car accident, I cried. In general, I would say I had a very happy childhood. It was very difficult for me when my parents divorced; but overall, I had a happy childhood filled with pleasant memories, and I lacked nothing.

When I was fourteen, some of my friends tried to recruit me to become a youth militant in the Cuban Communist Party. I still believed in God at that time, and I believed that to be a youth militant one had to be a Marxist, and Marxists couldn't be Catholics. (Catholics didn't join the revolutionary groups then; it's different now. In any case, no one could make up my mind for me, and I decided then that I would continue believing in God and not join the youth organization. Now, however, I don't believe in God anymore; it's been many years since I stopped believing. After studying philosophy and especially the history of philosophy and other nonreligious thinking, I decided that I really didn't believe the world was created by a god. But I never lost my respect for religion, and I have no ill feelings about having been raised as a Catholic.

I was always interested in cinema as a spectator, but for years I never considered the possibility of becoming a filmmaker because during my high school years, when I started to think about my future career, for a Cuban woman to think about becoming a film director was like thinking about being a pilot or an astronaut. There just weren't any concrete ways for a woman to achieve such a goal. One reason was that cinema wasn't studied at all in Cuba until very recently. Another reason was that there was only one female cinematographer, Sara Gomez, in Cuba; and she wasn't widely known outside the country, only among specialists in Latin American film.

So when I got to the university, I began to study graphic design and publicity. Within this field we spent some time studying mass media—television, cinema, and radio—so for my first-year thesis I decided to make a didactic documentary with visual materials for the school of design. From then on I was fascinated with film much more than I ever had been as a spectator. It was like a good cancer that had possessed me and taken over my existence. From then on I decided to make cinema my career.

When I began directing, many films were made on commission, at the request of someone else. Years ago, almost all films in Cuba were made this way. Then things changed a bit; directors could propose films but still had to do some work on commission. Commissions were still the standard when I started, but I decided to work within them to give my films a different nuance, a personal viewpoint. For example, I was commissioned to make a documentary about the time the militias were formed, a general film about all members of territorial troop militias. I was interested in two types of members: the old people that should not have been in the militia, from a practical standpoint, and the very young people in the militia. From a human interest perspective it seemed to me to be very interesting that old people, sometimes into their eighties, would even think of entering the militia. And the young members were as young as sixteen—they looked like babies. These two groups were at opposite poles.

When I made this documentary there were people with ideas different from mine. Some comrades, including my boss, thought that it promoted the participation of old people in the militia, which they didn't want. It seemed to me that if there was a voluntary militia in a country, then everyone who wanted to join, including the youngest and the oldest citizens, should be able to and that that was good for Cuba. In other words, my film demonstrated that everyone supported the militia, if these extremes supported it. In the end I won, and the documentary was released, even though some had wanted to change it. This is an example of what it was like to work on commission but still put in my own touches and fight to express my own point of view against the opposing viewpoints of some of my coworkers and superiors.[2]

The films I made in Angola about Cuban collaboration there were also commissioned. I had asked permission to travel to Angola to look it over before writing and submitting my proposal. I was very fortunate to go as a member of a political group that at that moment was directly offering assistance to Angola. This made it possible for me to travel all over the country in a short period of time. With all that I learned during this journey, I was able to write my proposal when I returned: to make one documentary that would cover Cuban military collaboration, and another that would cover the collaboration of Cuban civilians in Angola. I felt it would be impossible to cover the entire history of Cuban participation in the conflict in a single documentary. I wanted to focus on climactic moments of that participation.

I felt that the best way to document the military participation was from a cinematographic point of view. I started with Che's visit to Africa at the beginning of the African liberation movement. Then I jumped to 1975 and from event to event during this period. In the civilian collaboration film, for example, I focused on the health campaign and the literacy campaign. Another moment that I thought was important was the first cutting of the sugarcane by the people, especially in light of the importance of sugarcane in Cuba.

I made three other documentaries in Angola, as well. One was about the Cubans who were cutting trees in the Mayombá jungle in conditions very different from those in Cuba. They were cutting down both slender pines and trees that measured thirty meters in diameter. I thought they were just as heroic as those Cubans who were fighting in the war. Another film was about a boy who was born on December 31; he and his mother were close to death. A Cuban doctor left a New Year's Eve party in order to save them, and the family named the child Fidelito. The third was called *Guambo, crónica de un crimen* [Guambo, chronicle of a crime] and was about a civilian building bombed by UNITA [the National Union for the Total Independence of Angola]. I was particularly interested in this story. The building housed Cuban teachers, builders, and health personnel, and the bomb was very strong; it immediately killed twenty-five people, wounded many others, and shattered windows up to the tenth floor. Officially, according to UNITA, the bomb hit a military building housing Cuban and Soviet military personnel, killing two Soviet lieutenant colonels and several Cuban officers. This was misinformation; it was a lie. So I made a documentary based on both accounts—from UNITA and Cuban sources—and tried to reconstruct the event as it had really happened. Thus, out of original commissions for two, I was able to make five documentaries.

In 1982 I started making films that were much closer to my heart, truer to what I really wanted to do. The first that I proposed on my own was called *España en el corazón* [Spain in the heart]. I controlled the use of cinematographic techniques and the content and organization of the script. This film documented the participation of Cubans in the Spanish Civil War.

This war has always affected me a lot. My maternal grandparents were Spanish, and my memory of my grandfather is vivid. He was very opinionated, yet quite brilliant. He was difficult and contradictory; he loved to argue and had his own ideas about things, but he was very refined as well. He was like an encyclopedia—any time I didn't know something or was unsure about it, I would consult my grandfather. To me, whatever he said was the truth, and that was that. And he would tell me about the Spanish Civil War. He was an old Communist. This war always seemed monstrous to me, despite the international solidarity that it produced. No other event in contemporary history has mobilized 34,000 men the way the Spanish Civil War did. It was quite epic—a thousand Cubans went there to fight with the Republicans, despite the situation here at the time; they organized themselves clandestinely, raising money and recruiting others. From this thousand, seventeen became commanders, some in the popular army— that is, the Republican army itself—and some in the international brigades.

So in 1982 I decided to make a documentary of this participation in order to analyze it from the human interest viewpoint. I wanted to examine what made these people leave everything and go fight for another country, risking their own lives. I was able to interview thirteen Cubans who had participated in the war: one woman and twelve men. I named the film *España en el corazón* after a book of poems with that title, written by Pablo Neruda. All those I interviewed had a very sentimental connection to that war. I also feel a strong sentimental connection to it.

This film won several awards. In a national film festival sponsored by UNEAC it won the Caracol Award. In a European film festival it won for best documentary about the fight against fascism. The film also won a journalism award.

I think that after the documentary on the Spanish Civil War, my most important work was *Corresponsal de guerra* [War correspondent]. I was a war correspondent in Lebanon for three months, working as an assistant director of film in a small group that comprised a director, a cameraman, a sound man, and me. I also served as a photographer. I learned on this trip that one's values and principles change after such a violent experience. Things like human feelings, friends, family, and the like became extremely valuable and important to me.

When you go to a country like Lebanon and you see a family outside of a hospital with someone dying wrapped in a rug, collecting money in order to get medical treatment for this person, then you appreciate what you have. Or perhaps you see someone who died after a car accident, and even though the hospital was unable to save him or her, the family has to pay for the unsuccessful operation in order to be able to claim the body. You change when you see children in Angola with their bellies swollen from amebic dysentery, and the Cuban doctor tells you there is no way to cure them, that they will die in a few months. When you see such things in other countries, you value what you have much more.

I identify very much with Palestinians. In my opinion, one of the most serious injustices of the century was the theft of the Palestinian homeland, and I will do anything in my power to help them. Therefore, I made the film *El Corresponsal de guerra* in an effort to clarify the historical background of the Palestinian question—its origin, why Israel exists today but not Palestine, how Israel was able to occupy Palestine, and so forth—and to denounce what the Israelis have done to the Palestinians. I wanted to denounce Zionism. This is the way I felt I could help the Palestinian people. No one asked me to go to Lebanon; I requested to go there. While I was working there as a war correspondent, we were subjected to an Israeli bombing raid. We were in the middle of a Palestinian armed incursion inside of Beirut, in enemy territory. We filmed all these things.

Such experiences cause contradictory feelings. On the one hand you fear for your life, but on the other you feel that you have achieved something that cannot be repeated. For example, we felt this way when we were filming the bombing raid, which occurred in the Castle of Beaufort, a very symbolic place for the Palestinians: Saladin climbed down from this castle when he recovered Jerusalem, which had been lost in the Crusades. This castle, much attacked by the Israeli Air Force, was buried, and its defenders were underground. It was so dangerous the Palestinians didn't want us to go there, but we kept to the sidelines and were able finally to film the bombing. Perhaps one is actually in more danger during a ground artillery attack, but the lack of visible protection during an air raid makes one feel more vulnerable. Nevertheless, although we were quite frightened, we felt that we were capturing an irrefutable image and thereby making a strong denunciation. We were doing what we could and that was more important than the fear. Having a purpose like that allows one to overcome the fear.

In Lebanon we interviewed Major Saad Haddad.[3] We requested the interview through UN troops, and he sent back a message back telling us when and where it would be. At that point I felt more afraid than I had through the whole visit until then—not afraid of being killed so much as of being tortured. The Irish representatives of the UN that we had spoken to told us that Haddad was a fascist, because he had taken two Irish UN soldiers hostage and had split them open. Moreover, he would announce on the radio that he was going to bomb such and such a city in order to create terror, and in fact he would carry through his threats. We were in a Palestinian camp called Rashidie. Haddad bombed the cemetery a few times, with the sole intention of removing the dead from the graves; certainly no military advantage was gained from doing that. In Rashidie life was a living hell. The women and children slept in the air-raid shelters while the men operated the antiaircraft guns.

One part of my film synthesizes my experience in Lebanon in the person of one five-year-old Palestinian boy. He was born in a refugee camp in Lebanon, and we asked him why he was in Rashidie. He responded with a maturity beyond his age, "Because we want to wake up the world." He was five years old. Like so many other Palestinian children, he had lived through one too many hangings, deaths, raids, and tank advances. His tragic answer made me think of all the other people I had met there. I remember an orphanage of child survivors of the massacre of a Palestinian camp: out of this camp of nineteen thousand persons, only eight thousand survived. A person would have to be made of steel not to feel something after seeing such a thing. Unfortunately, the world has become very insensitive to such injustices.

When you film events as a war correspondent, you can film from only one angle, in one location. Your movements are confined. In addition, you are living a part of what you are filming, and it is impossible to represent all of that experience on film. I have realized that if you can unite the image with the history of that image, your film takes on another dimension and perhaps comes closer to representing the lived event.

At the request of the BBC, I added a fourth chapter to the three original chapters of *El corresponsal de guerra*. This fundamental work is very much tied to my personal experience and feelings; it is also the work that has gained me the most recognition.

I recall with great fondness two documentaries that I made in relation to the nuclear accident in Chernobyl. One was filmed in 1990 with one of the children, a ten-year-old named Victor Morchenko, who fell victim to the electronuclear explosion there. Many of those children came to Cuba afterward to receive medical treatment. I was commissioned in Cuba to make an informative documentary about these children for the Soviet Union. I agreed to do so, provided I could do it my way. What intrigued me most was Victor's inner thoughts. He had been exposed to nuclear radiation and was fully aware of the implications. He remembered what had happened to him at Chernobyl and all that he had lost, including his city, his friends, everything that was connected to his childhood. Moreover, it was very clear to him that his future was changed by the accident. He doesn't know what will happen to his children or his grandchildren from his exposure to the radiation. From all of this, Victor reasoned that the accident, when compared to what could happen in a nuclear war, was just a drop in the ocean. Therefore I called the film *Una gota en el mar o un viaje al interior de Victor Morchenko* [A drop in the ocean, or A trip inside Victor Morchenko].

I chose Victor after looking for just the right child, one who had personally experienced the accident and who was a bit older, an adolescent. But Victor, although only ten, was very sensitive. He would say such things as "My dreams fell apart." He had wanted to be a pilot, and now he couldn't be one. Victor came to Cuba with a movie camera, and he was enrolled in a music school, playing the trumpet; in addition, he liked to draw. Thus he was able not only to talk about Chernobyl but also to share the things he loved about life and people. I really identified with Victor and wondered what his future would be like.

Therefore in the documentary, I tried to show what was at the heart of this child—all the feelings of loneliness, uprootedness, and loss. I didn't want to use the Chernobyl archives in this film, as I did in the other one; instead, I used some photographs by a friend of mine who had done an exposition called *La guerra del tiempo* [The war of time] about the destruction of things over time. Chernobyl was not the sort of disaster that simultaneously destroys everything; instead, the explosion and the resulting nuclear reactions that caused the evacuation of the city affected its people bit by bit. Thus time was a fundamental element in the event. I wanted to show time as a sense of loss. Through the pictures and the feelings of the child Victor, the film shows the most intimate feelings of people. I think it is one of the most significant of my recent films.

My latest film is called *Siempre esperanza* [Forever hope], the story of a Cuban man who participated in the Angolan war not as a military officer or soldier but as a gasoline truck driver. He was ambushed when alone and held prisoner for six and a half years. In the beginning his captors did not acknowledge his existence, and Cuba was unable to get any information about him. He was never given a trial. He didn't know how long he would be held. He had no contact with his family, couldn't read a book, couldn't listen to music. In other words, they isolated him completely from the world, from everything that makes a man a man. Many times he contemplated suicide. He couldn't talk with anyone either; if he wanted something, he had to ask for it with gestures. I wondered what happens to a man in such circumstances? What keeps his hope alive that this will end someday, that he will be able to live? What enables him to withstand such adversity and self-estrangement? How does he keep his memory alive? This is what I wanted to explore in my film, not the events but the inner feelings and what kept him going, by showing his fantasies and imagination.

At the moment I am working on a documentary about three artists who have been in African countries. One was in Angola, another was in Angola and Ethiopia, and the third in the three Guineas, Angola, Ethiopia, and Uganda. One is a musician, another a cinematographer and poet, and the third a painter. For all of them the time in Africa influenced their work, their lives, and the way they see the world and their work. The painter has been to the United States and exhibited his work in New York. Now he is preparing an exhibition in Mexico. After his experience in Africa his painting changed completely. He is black and says that everything he did was an effort to get back to his African roots. (One of the other artists is mulatto and one is white.)

In the long term, I am planning two films of fiction. One will be based on the story of the prisoner in Angola but with many fictional elements— all the things he imagined while in jail—mixed with reality, as well as past events, real and imagined, in his life. I'm doing it as a series for television, with six episodes. My other fictional film is related to the first in that it is based on a true story. The protagonist is a person confined to a psychiatric hospital. We still have to visit there; we are now reviewing all the clinical history. Even though we are going to incorporate fictional elements, we want to start from a solid base of fact.

I also have several documentary film projects in the planning stages. One will be about Che Guevara, but not the public figure everyone knows. Instead, it will portray his family life, particularly in relation to his children. From what I have learned in conversations with them, they had a wonderful relationship with their father. I would like to restore the man of legendary stature to a more human state. I have submitted proposals for two films about the Palestinians to the Palestinians themselves. I would also like to make a documentary about Sabra and Shatila ten years after the 1982 massacre.[4] I have to find out if they will authorize it. If they don't, it will be more complicated, but I'd still like to do it.

The current economic crisis in Cuba, the Special Period, hasn't affected my work much, but I know other filmmakers who have gone without working for over a year. Unemployment is very depressing and contributes to a general sense of frustration and disillusionment in Cuban society as a whole. One of the accomplishments of the Revolution in Cuba had been full employment; but now there is much underemployment and professionals working as waiters and taxi drivers. There have been substantial cuts in funding in the Cuban film industry because everything we need for our work must be bought outside of the country with dollars. Nothing is produced in Cuba. A lot of the equipment is old. Right now it's really difficult. But since videotape is much cheaper than film, we have been able to continue producing pieces on video. Of the current projects I mentioned, both the television series and the documentary on Che Guevara are on video. Times are tough right now.

In personal terms, the crisis has affected me the same as everyone else. There are restrictions on the normal food quotas. There are fewer possibilities to go to restaurants and to eat certain things—like burgers and pastries—in the street. There are also restrictions on gasoline and car parts. Without question, these things are more difficult than ever—the national situation, the international situation, all the changes—everything.

I have made two documentary films on the theme of Cuban women. One was about the first Cuban woman to be a heroine of the *zafra*, that is, the first female cutter of sugarcane. As a girl she sold charcoal, because capitalism was very hard on her. She is a very lovely, friendly woman. The other film was about the same woman that I interviewed for *España en el corazón*, an old fighter from the time of Machado. She started fighting then and stopped when the Revolution started. Moreover, this woman had a wonderful marriage. Many women who dedicated their lives to the Revolution stayed single. This woman dedicated a great amount of her time to the struggle but nevertheless married and had a son. She was a very good-looking woman. She had a beautiful relationship with her husband until he died. I interviewed him as well.

The documentary begins with how they met. He had been placed in hiding in her house, since she was a member of the struggle. I found it very funny that to get her to fall in love with him, he got her drunk at a party. She didn't like it when he told me this; she blushed with embarrassment. This was all caught on film. She called me ten times to tell me that we couldn't keep that segment in the documentary. So I filmed other things—the two of them holding hands and so forth. In addition, I used many photographs. It is a work of photomontage. She had been in Spain during the Civil War, had worked with Che creating committees to aid the Cuban Revolution, had traveled to many Latin American countries. She was in Nicaragua when Somoza was still in power, during Cuba's first assistance effort. I have a poet friend who had been her student. I wanted someone who knew her independently of me to write a poem about her. He wrote a beautiful poem without her knowing, which I put at the end of the documentary. When I showed her the finished documentary I told her, "No protests or opinions or anything until it's over." When she heard the poem, she started to cry, hugged me, and left. Her husband was still alive to see the film; she was very happy. This film was shown in Germany and

Switzerland in translation, and the people enjoyed it a lot, laughing and applauding because it was so human. There was nothing cardboard about it; she was a true revolutionary but viewed in terms of her family life and not in terms of history or ideology. These are the only films I have done about women; I haven't done any others.

I have a ten-year-old son. I was married for nine years. It was a good marriage for many years, but one day it started to change; we began to have differences and we decided to separate. My son is very important to me, as I'm sure all children are very important to their mothers. In this profession it is very difficult to have children, unless you have someone available unconditionally to help you. For example, my mother is a professional, a math professor; she has her own life, so I couldn't decide to go off and film somewhere and leave my son with her for two months. When I was married, my husband took care of our son when I was gone. He knew when we met that I was a cinematographer, and he married me knowing that I was going to continue to be a filmmaker. His mother, who lived with us, helped as well. I went to Lebanon before I had my son, but when I went to Angola he was already two years old. Without my husband's help it would have been impossible for me to go to Angola. I worried more about the danger in Angola than I had in Lebanon. I had no desire to die in Lebanon, but if I had, I wouldn't have left anyone behind, whereas if I had died in Angola, my son would have had to grow up without his mother. Nevertheless, despite the difficulties of juggling my career and my responsibilities as a mother, I would never have decided not to have children. I think it is very important for a woman to have a child. For me, motherhood has been and continues to be one of the most rewarding and vital experiences of my life.

My son and I have a great relationship. He understands me; I talk with him a lot. When I get an award, he is the first person I tell. I have taken him with me to film sessions, editing sessions, music recording sessions, everywhere. I think that the more he learns about my work, the more he will understand and respect it. He likes it that his mother is a cinematographer. He's very proud of me when they give me an award; he goes with me to the ceremonies, and sometimes he holds the award and they photograph us together. Sometimes he memorizes fragments from my films. The other day it was funny because I played a Pink Floyd cassette that contains a song I used a fragment of in one of my films. He recognized it and said, "Mami, listen, that's the music from your documentary." It wasn't a whole song, just a fragment, but he recognized it nonetheless. This made me feel very good and very proud of him.

I want my son to be what he wants to be in the future, and I want to prepare him for it. For example, he likes to draw, so I found him a painting instructor to give him lessons. Later I want him to go to the alternative high school of fine arts because he likes art. It makes me very happy that he has an artistic sensibility. Also, I want him to learn English. I learned English as a child. I was in an English school before the triumph of the Revolution, and I think it is very important to know the English language, especially in our changing world with the globalization of the world economy. Already my son studies English with a private tutor. I try to prepare him for the future, but I also try to help him face the realities of life in Cuba. For example, he loves milk, but I don't have milk to give him because of the economic crisis during this Special Period. I have explained the situation to him, and he understands that instead of milk I can give him something called Cerelac, which has all the proteins and nutrients of milk. Although it hurts me not to be able to give my growing son milk every day, I don't deceive him. I want him to learn things about our reality, especially the things that are appropriate for him to understand according to his age and maturity.

There are some people who try to hide our economic reality from their children. There are people who are overprotective of their children. Even among devoted revolutionaries I know people like that. For example, some of them get a medical certification so that their children don't have to go to the school in the country.[5] I'm not going to be happy while my child is in the country; I'm going to be very worried. But when it is my child's turn to go, he is going to go. And he will stay the forty-five days that all Cuban children in Cuba are required to stay. I had this experience, and so will he. He must learn to accept reality so that he can be a good person and successful in what he decides to do, whether that is to direct films or to drive taxis.

Che Guevara died when I was fifteen years old. His death shocked me and made me think about what I really wanted to do in the future and how I was going to live my life. I wasn't so interested in whether Che was right about its being Latin America's moment for revolution as much as that he lived and died according to his own very high ideals. That is, he knew what he wanted to do with his life, in his work and in his personal life. I have a friend who was in Bolivia a little while back writing a book about Che's last days. His theory is that Che could have saved himself from dying, from being ambushed, but that ambush was the final consequence of his actions. It's a complicated story. Anyway, he is an important figure in my life and I plan to do various cinematographic projects about his life—the one of Che as family man, and another about his first trip through Latin America, when he was twenty-three years old. That trip determined for him what he was going to do with his life. I would like very much to make that film; it would be a way to repay some of my debt to him I also feel I can repay some of that debt by living according to my principles. But whether cinematographically or artistically, I haven't yet been able to repay him. Che's death, which I remember very clearly—I think all of my generation does—was very violent, but it inspired many people of my generation to take a revolutionary stand in life.

((((((((((((**8**))))))))))))

Toward an Interpretation of Cuban Testimonies

María Antonia Carrillo (standing, left), with some founding members of the Martí Women's Civic Front: standing, Olga Román and Mercedes Blanco Mesa; seated, Maruja Iglesias and Aída Pelayo, at whose home these old friends gathered in 1992.

It is important to note that the tone of these Cuban texts is for the most part triumphant. The Cuban Revolution, although beseiged, was successful; all these women participated in one way or another in that struggle. Some of them (Pelayo, Revuelta, Carrillo, and Alfonso González) were directly involved in the rebellion against Batista; others (Morejón and Vega) took part afterward, as artists in support of the revolution's goals. All of them are still committed to continuing the Revolution, though not un-willing to be critical of some aspects of it. These Cuban testimonies, how-ever, are not uniform. The interviews of the older women read like long-congealed narratives of revolutionary triumph mixed with a certain kind of reticence; they reiterate the official Party line with little deviation. Those of the younger women, both internationally recognized artists, are far less single-minded.

The interviews reveal only a partial picture of these Cuban women's complex and contradictory views regarding the successes and the failures of the socialist project in Cuba. Generally speaking, they used the inter-view situation to reiterate the official take on life in Cuba; most tended to be less critical of the regime during the recorded interviews than in our more lively, spontaneous discussions. Only when the tape recorder was turned off did any of them express anger toward Fidel Castro and many of his economic policies. The tape recorder seemed to take on a life of its own, like a third party in the room. But why this gap between the women's official narrations for a North American public and their seemingly more honest off-the-record discussions? Why this reluctance to record the truth?

One may speculate that during almost forty years of limited free speech on the island, all Cubans have become conditioned to offer an offi-cial account to foreign tourists, reporters, and outsiders, whereas they tend to be more candid and spontaneous among themselves, constantly telling jokes about Fidel and the economic crisis and speaking their minds. Per-haps it is fear of reprisals from the regime? Or is there a general suspicion that all U.S. foreigners are CIA agents and potential Cuba bashers who come to the island to gather information about discontent and contribute to an already widespread anti-Cuban sentiment in the United States?

This defensiveness might also be explained as the long-term psycho-logical effect of isolation and blockade: a feeling of being attacked, ag-gressively demeaned, and economically strangled by U.S. imperialism, accompanied by a feeling of being abandoned and betrayed by trading partners from the former socialist-bloc nations. Added to this is the frus-tration of limited freedom of the press in Cuba and lack of access to global information, the Internet, and the new books and research coming out all over the planet. (CNN has opened its first office in Havana, but most Cubans are not allowed to watch or are denied access to the cable news channel.) The island is in many ways isolated and removed from the global entry into the twenty-first century. Thus the testimonies of the older women point to a state of denial that is typical of many staunch

Cuban revolutionaries: they continue to function as cheerleaders for a revolution that is in serious danger of collapse.

It is interesting to note the silences in Naty Revuelta's testimony, those zones of her private life which she chooses not to discuss, especially regarding her intimate relationship with Fidel Castro. What is not explicitly revealed but only alluded to can be as telling as what is actually said. Out of respect for her privacy, I did not probe much into this area of her past. When I did ask directly about her affair with Fidel, she neither confirmed nor denied that they had been lovers, though it is public knowledge that Fidel fathered her daughter, who defected to Miami several years ago.

It is possible to read between the lines of this narrative a sense of frustration at having been abandoned by Fidel after the triumph of the Revolution. There is a tinge of resentment in Revuelta's voice when she recalls finding herself unemployed; despite her loyalty and willingness to risk everything for Fidel and the revolution, Castro did not offer her a position in the new revolutionary government. She uses the interview situation to draw attention to this painful memory, suggesting an understandable bitterness toward her former lover. Nevertheless, she remains committed to the ideals of the Revolution in spite of her personal betrayal by its leader. Outside the formal interview situation, Revuelta poked fun at Fidel for his machismo and stubborn, unyielding positions.

Another key feature in her testimony is the way Naty Revuelta persistently defines herself as hard-working and as willing to sacrifice material well-being for the collective good of her country—very much an echo of the Cuban official line about exemplary revolutionary behavior. Unlike her ex-husband and many others of her social class, she chose not to defect but to remain on the island and to devote her energy to the creation of a new socialist society. This choice, which meant giving up her privileges as a wealthy, white, educated woman, illustrates the ways in which the political and the personal overlap. She describes herself as fulfilled and at peace because of having lived her life in accordance with her political beliefs: putting human values and socialist principles above materialistic, consumer-oriented individualism. Naty Revuelta says that she fiercely rejected the subservient role of women in prerevolutionary Cuba; she describes herself as a woman who refused to become a traditional wife and rebelled against the stultifying conventions of a bourgeois marriage. She fashions herself as a strong, independent woman who has overcome personal tragedy and remains hopeful and cheerful despite the everyday economic hardships of living in Cuba. One of her simple pleasures (a luxury by Cuban standards) is the powdered milk that her son sends to her from the United States.

Significantly, Revuelta underscores the fact that it was *she*, and not her husband, who initiated contact with Fidel by sending him a key to her house. She emphasizes that she took charge of the situation, offering her home, financial support, solidarity, and other services to the young revolutionary leader of the July 26 Movement. Although Naty Revuelta does not define herself as a feminist, there is no doubt that she represents herself as a strong, independent, assertive woman who has lived her life according to egalitarian principles and fought steadily for gender equality in Cuba.

Aída Pelayo describes herself as a loyal disciple of José Martí, whom she regards as her teacher in the cause of Cuba's freedom. Evoking this central icon in the national imagination, the man who embodies the ideal of Cuban identity and independence, she claims that Martí has been the driving force in her life of political militancy. Pelayo recalls learning about Martí in Cuba's struggle against colonial rule when she was only in grade school. She declares that from that moment on she became proud of her Cuban heritage and continued to find strength and inspiration in Martí's words and deeds. In her narrative, conflating Cuban identity and a love for Martí, her language is propagandistic and resonates with dogmatic phrases and clichés typical of the official discourse of the Cuban regime.

Pelayo's testimony comes across as overly optimistic and celebratory in its tone and content. Her analysis of current events in Cuba is not fresh; nor is it in tune with recent major transformations and crises. On the contrary, it reads as if frozen in the past; Pelayo seems to be repeating the same speech that she may have recited by rote hundreds of times to the youth at Cuban schools and summer camps. Still, as a valuable social document recounting her participation in the Revolution, it does contribute to the inscription of women in the history of Cuba.

Aspects of Pelayo's feminism are suggested by her repeated references to her strong sense of solidarity with other women, especially with her lifelong friends and comrades. In spending an entire afternoon with Pelayo and several friends who had been active in the Martí Women's Civic Front during the 1950s, I was impressed by what appeared to be their genuine affection for one another. All these women, now in their seventies and eighties, still closely identify with the revolutionary project, although they openly expressed their criticism of Fidel and some of his controversial economic policies. Each one freely offered her opinions regarding the current crisis and the direction she felt the leadership should take. Generally speaking, they all agreed that Castro should step down (though they thought it unlikely, given his inflexible, *caudillo*-like nature), but none of them wish to see the Miami exile community intervene in a postsocialist Cuba. All of them expressed concern about the future for Cuban women, fearing that a neoconservative regime in post-Castro Cuba could drive women back to the kitchen and to a position of dependency on men for their economic survival.

Aída Pelayo highlights the overlapping in her life of the personal and the political. She defines herself in terms of her political militancy and structures her oral narrative around a chronology that testifies to her direct participation in major political events in contemporary Cuban history: her early opposition to Machado's dictatorship, her role as a witness in the trial of the young rebels arrested following the attack on the Moncada Barracks, the founding of the FCMM, the General Strike on April 9, 1958, her defense of political prisoners as a member of the International Red Cross, the triumph of the Revolution, and her role in the Federation of Cuban Women, the literacy campaigns, and so on.

The link between memory and identity can be observed in this testimony. Pelayo recalls with a sense of pride, dignity, and nostalgia the many times she was sent to jail because of her militancy; she repeatedly asserts that she refused to submit to a traditional female role and defines herself as a political activist and as a rebel; she represents herself as a strong-willed, independent woman who courageously engaged in traditional male activities such as planting bombs, trafficking in weapons, giving political speeches, and organizing strikes. She tends to idealize her revolutionary past and focuses on having survived some dangerous situations during her political participation. Pelayo appears to be living in a nostalgic past. She seems less interested in the present-day crisis of socialism in general, and the collapse of the traditional left in Latin American politics, than in narrating her role as a revolutionary heroine. In this sense, her testimony is marked by an evocation of a utopian, idealized past.

Another important feature in Pelayo's story is her assertion that she defiantly refused (and continues to refuse) to depend on a relationship with a man for her sense of self-worth. Pelayo boasts that she chose to have a child without being married and decided to raise her son as a single mother, even though this was still considered taboo in prerevolutionary Cuba. Unlike several of the other women, she is not ashamed to call herself a feminist; on the contrary, she proudly considers herself to be a pioneer of the present-day feminist movement in her country.

María Antonia Carrillo's narrative highlights her improved standard of living since the Revolution. Like most Afro-Cuban women, Carrillo suffered the double oppression of being a poor woman *and* being black in prerevolutionary Cuba. She had been denied educational and cultural opportunities that the Revolution would provide future generations of black children in Cuba. This is the crux of her testimony.

During the tape-recorded interview Carrillo repeated clichés regarding education and health reform, yet I sensed in her a great frustration and anger with the status quo, coupled with a fervent desire to defend the triumphs of the revolution for poor, black women like herself. This tension was present throughout all my conversations with this particular informant. It became more and more apparent to me that many Cubans have contradictory, mixed feelings about their revolutionary past and about the direction Cuba should take in the future. In this regard, Carrillo's ambivalence might be considered the norm, rather than an exception, especially among Afro-Cuban women who were beneficiaries of revolutionary social reforms.

Central to Carrillo's self-fashioning is her pride in her African heritage. This is revealed in her religious beliefs and the practice of Santería, her choice of African icons in her paintings, and her work with an Afro-Cuban dance troupe. She attributes her self-expression as a black artist to the opportunities granted her by the Revolution.

Zoila Elisa Alfonso González's testimony is structured around the binary opposition of before versus after the Revolution, dividing Cuba's capitalist past from its socialist present. A recurring theme is the brutal oppression on the basis of social class and gender prior to 1959. The relationship between her childhood memories of the harsh exploitation of tobacco workers in prerevolutionary Cuba and her self-representation as a staunch defender of the Revolution is made visible in this narrative.

Alfonso González's personal account provides an important recording of significant aspects of Cuba's social history—especially of the standard of living of Cuban tobacco workers, before and after the Revolution, from the insider perspective of a white, female tobacco worker. According to the standards of the industrialized world, Alfonso González still lives very poorly, but the recollection of her family's miserable life before the triumph of the Revolution is the main explanation she gives for her unwavering defense of Fidel and of the socialist regime. And again, compared with that of working-class women in the developing world, her standard of living is quite high. Unlike the younger generation of Cubans who grew up with the Revolution, she remembers what it was like as a young child to work in a tobacco factory from dawn to dusk without any dreams for a better future. Her identity as a revolutionary woman is shaped and determined by these childhood recollections of extreme poverty and of organized, collective resistance.

Proudly affirming that her militancy began at the age of twelve, Alfonso González defines herself in terms of her commitment to the cause of gender equality and to the defense of the rights of Cuban tobacco workers. She presents herself as an exemplary revolutionary who even volunteers her time to help the younger generation of tobacco rollers meet their quotas. Despite her somewhat stale revolutionary rhetoric and her simplistic analysis of Cuban society in the limited terms of rich versus poor, capitalist versus socialist, good revolutionaries versus bad traitors, I was deeply touched by her strong commitment to the continuation of the Revolution. I was also moved by the generosity with which, despite food shortages and rationing, she offered me a *batido*, a drink made with bananas, cold water, and sugar, and told me that before the Revolution her family was so poor that she could never have offered a guest anything to eat or drink.

Nancy Morejón is a self-reflective and eloquent writer, who expressed herself fluently despite the usual awkwardness of the interview situation. Before our "official" interview she had already elaborated quite extensively on her theories regarding the link between the creative process and her childhood memories of the sights and sounds—especially those of the Afro-Cuban popular culture—of her neighborhood. Morejón chose to share her thoughts regarding the fundamental role of the collective memory of Cuban music in the shaping of her Afro-Cuban cultural identity, an identity that is reflected in her poetry and critical essays. In structuring her oral testimony, she drew attention to the significance of specific childhood memories in the formation of her identity as a working-class black person growing up in Cuba during the 1940s.

Considering music a major, powerful force in the constitution of her subjectivity, Morejón selects and highlights what she considers some of the most significant memories of sounds from her childhood: the sounds of a rumba, or a *guaracha*, or of her neighbors dancing in the streets to the rhythm of a conga. She underscores the crucial ways in which she and, consequently, her writing were influenced by the sonorous world of her neighborhood, especially late at night, when she would listen to the percussion improvisations practiced by her neighbors with the palms of their hands. These memories—as well as those of hearing African American jazz legends such as Louis Armstrong and rock 'n' rollers such as Little Richard—formed the early chapters of Nancy Morejon's evolution as an Afro-Cuban writer, who is (like Carrillo) proud of the African roots of her cultural heritage. Interestingly, the issues of race and ethnicity highlighted by these two black women were not mentioned by any of the white Cuban women I interviewed.

Belkis Vega welcomed me into her home, offered a cup of dark Cuban coffee, and was very open in discussing her views about politics, her work, and her life as a divorced single mother. We talked all afternoon and well into the evening until it was time for me to catch the last bus back to my hotel.

One of the most striking features of Belkis Vega's story is her affirmation of dedication to the socialist project in her country and her evocation of the legendary Che Guevara as the main source of inspiration in her life. I consider her testimony an important source of information for us, as North Americans, who, because of a decades-long anti-Castro propaganda campaign, find it difficult to imagine living well in Communist Cuba or choosing not to defect if given the opportunity. Vega's articulation of a point of view that is seldom voiced in the United States, where the dominant perspective is that of the anti-Castro Cuban exiles, can help dismantle some American misconceptions about life in Cuba and contribute to the formation of a more balanced, informed opinion.

These testimonies sample the variety of ways in which Cuban revolutionary women appropriate certain aspects of the Revolution and translate it into their own terms. Each interpretation is shaped by the particular social class and ethnicity of the speaking subject as she constructs the story of her own intervention in the making of Cuban history. For each of these women, the Cuban Revolution represents an intersection between the personal and the political, between the quotidian and the historical, between the private and the collective. For all of them the Revolution has a profound, personal significance and suggests a complexity that foreigners are distanced from and have difficulty comprehending. Their testimonies offer a small window into a political economy and way of life quite different from the consumer-oriented U.S. society.

Nevertheless, all the Cuban women I spoke with on the streets of Havana and along the Malecón, as well as those I interviewed, seem to long for an end to the economic blockade and an opening up of the Cuban economy.

One of their main complaints was the unavailability of the variety of foods they had enjoyed during the 1980s; having no meat or chicken or fish, being limited a mere four eggs per week. Other frequent complaints were the drastically reduced bus schedules resulting from fuel shortages, blackouts, the lack of medicines, the limited freedom of the press, and the lack of freedom to travel. And everyone was unhappy with the social inequities brought about by the recent rise in tourism. Many young Cubans who have known only the reality of Cuban socialism spoke of their desire for material comforts and luxury items: new cars, designer clothing, athletic shoes, expensive perfumes, compact discs, and so on. Some expressed

A crowded bus (1992) and one of the many bicycles that have replaced much of the motorized transportation in Havana during the Special Period.

feelings of having been deprived of the high standard of living represented by the images of prosperity in Hollywood films and on North American television. For many of them, this sense of deprivation of material things is the root cause of their discontent with the present regime.

Most of the testimonies included here, however, represent a sector of older Cuban women who remember the social inequities before 1959. These women still support the ideals of the Revolution, whatever their dissatisfation with Castro. They are modest in their desires; they may long for such simple things as fresh milk, cheese, fish, and an end to the fuel shortages, but they are not seduced by the status symbols of consumer society. Although these women want a more open economy, with some forms of market capitalism, they are wary of anything that suggests a return to U.S. imperialism on the island or the life they knew before the Revolution.

Chile:
SEVEN VOICES OF OPPOSITION

(((((((((((((*9*)))))))))))))
Chilean Women and Human Rights

There are five thousand of us here
prisoners in this stadium . . .
here alone are ten thousand hands
that plant seeds and make the factories run. . . .
Let the world cry out against this atrocity!
We are ten thousand hands that can produce nothing. . . .
How hard it is to sing when I must sing of horror
                                                    —Víctor Jara, fragment of song smuggled out of the
                                                                            Chile Stadium, September 1973

Although there are few records tracing women's political activities during the period of Chile's industrialization, beginning in the 1900s, some Chilean women were politically involved early in the century. Patricia Chuchryk observes, "As early as 1913, in the northern mining regions of Chile, working-class women organized the Centros de Belén de Zárraga to address the exploitation of women workers" (1989, 150).[1] Meanwhile, Luis Emilio Recabarren, the founder in 1912 of the Socialist Workers Party (Partido Obrero Socialista)—which would later become the Communist Party—was writing newspaper articles calling for women's liberation and women's suffrage. And throughout the 1920s, women formed numerous organizations dedicated to the expansion of their legal and economic rights.

By 1917 a number of women's groups focusing on education had also emerged. Among their leaders were the Chilean poet and later Nobel Prize winner Gabriela Mistral and the writer and poet Amanda Labarca. Both these women began their careers as teachers and were involved in the formation of reading groups, such as the Women's Reading Circle, which gave many Chilean women their first educational experience (Agosín 1993, 1).

In 1919 the Chilean Women's Party was established. This organization of mostly upper-class women called for suffrage and human rights for women, reform of legislation for the protection of women and children, and women's rights to be independent citizens (Kirkwood 1986, 24). It was also committed to education for women and formed centers to raise women's consciousness about exploitation in the workplace. The Chilean Women's Party was only partially successful in meeting its goals, however. According to Chilean sociologist Julieta Kirkwood, it failed to mobilize masses of women primarily because it was unable to incorporate poor and working-class women into its ranks (1986, 114).

Although Chilean women did not achieve the right to vote in national elections until 1949, they were granted the right to vote in municipal elections in 1931. By the mid-1930s three different women's groups had been established: the Movement for the Emancipation of Chilean Women (MEMCH), Feminine Action (associated with the Chilean Women's Party), and the Movement of Chilean Women. Margorie Agosín has observed that "the goals of the last two groups were conservative and focused on traditional women's issues such as child care, health care, and maternity law. The MEMCH, in contrast, drew its vision from the political left" (1993, 2). This organization viewed the emancipation of women as inseparable from the emancipation of the working class. It also fought for women's suffrage and the diffusion of birth control methods to the poor. All three groups, despite unresolved differences, managed to unite in the effort to win suffrage; once this goal was achieved, however, these women's organizations did not remain politically active.

Julieta Kirkwood, who has studied Chilean women's political activity, maintains that women's participation in politics did increase during the 1950s and 1960s: individual women began to vote regularly and to participate in political parties. But no group emerged to unite women of different social classes in dialogue or coordinated action. The only contact that existed between wealthy women and poor women was either in the context of charity or as employers and domestic employees. Most working-class women organized not separately but through labor unions and political parties of the left.

Salvador Allende and his Unidad Popular (Popular Unity) coalition came to power in 1970. As the first Marxist to be elected by popular vote in Latin America, he hoped to increase state control over industry and agriculture and to raise the living standards of the nation's poor. Allende took bold steps in efforts to transform the socioeconomic structures of Chile.[2] He nationalized the copper industry, implemented new agrarian reform laws, raised the minimum wage, encouraged the organization of labor unions and the political participation of the poor, and initiated plans to improve public education. Life for working-class Chileans improved greatly during the brief period of the UP coalition government.

During the Allende presidency the political arena was opened up to women, especially urban middle- and upper-class women. But Allende did not promote women as political actors; there were few in high administrative positions during his brief presidency. As Agosín points out, although he "made frequent allusions to the importance of women and their contributions to social and cultural change, he did not nominate a woman to his Cabinet until he had been in office for two years" (1993, 4).

Moreover, Allende articulated a view of women that confined them, generally speaking, to the domestic sphere and their traditional roles as wives and mothers. For example: "When I speak of women I always think of the wife/mother. When I speak of women I refer to their function within the nuclear family. Children are the prolongation of the woman who is essentially born to be a mother" (qtd. in Chaney 1974, 54). Allende's conventional, bourgeois, male-oriented view of the nuclear family as the central axis of society was similar to the ideology of gender of the more conservative political parties. Although he contended that he wanted to incorporate women into his political agenda, the programs he supported, such as the Mothers' Centers, "taught women stereotypical skills such as sewing and knitting" (Agosín 1993, 4), confining women to traditional domestic roles.

In all fairness, though, it is important not to underestimate the severe financial constraints on the projects and social reforms that Popular Unity was able to carry out. There was a strong antigovernment campaign to destabilize the economy, to create shortages, and eventually to overthrow Allende. Neither foreign imperialists nor the Chilean elite (mainly the bourgeoisie, the military, right-wing political parties, and conservative elements within the Catholic Church) were willing to sit back and allow Allende's radical economic measures to unsettle a socioeconomic and political status quo that had served their own economic and political interests. Thus, with external funding from the United States and covert political intervention, this ruling group, fearful of losing its power and privilege, "created a conspiratorial 'Comando Gremialista' which incorporated truckers, merchants, retailers, industrialists, agricultural landowners, white collar professionals, and women's groups" (Loveman 1988, 17).

Middle-class and upper-class women were instrumental in the campaign to overthrow Allende's Popular Unity coalition. As Jo Fisher has pointed out, "Ideas about women and the family were . . . manipulated by right-wing parties and provided the justification for one of the first large-scale opposition movements to Allende's government. '*El Poder Femenino*' ('Female Power') was the name of a middle- and upper-class housewives' movement, founded in 1971, which organized 'empty pot' marches in protest at food shortages and the 'threat of communism' in Chile" (1993, 178).[3]

These women formed part of the larger organized opposition, composed mostly of rightist political parties and commercial entrepreneurial groups, which moved aggressively to destablize the economy and unleashed an explosive media campaign to portray the Allende government in a negative light. The ideological underpinning of this propaganda against the Popular Unity was the invented "threat of Soviet penetration" in the hemisphere. Right-wing groups, with the support of the Church hierarchy, falsely accused the Marxist president of leading the country away from God and of advocating the destruction of traditional family values.

The Nixon administration and the CIA played a significant role in the covert funding of this discrediting of Allende and in the systematic undermining of the Chilean economy—mainly through an economic blockade and by refusing to buy Chilean products. It is important to keep in mind, however, the many internal factors that made the coup in Chile possible; the complex socioeconomic and political conditions leading to the military takeover were the result of a decades- long class struggle.[4]

It was a chilly, overcast morning on September 11, 1973, when the Chilean military staged its bloody coup d'état in Santiago.[5] The Chilean armed forces attacked Salvador Allende's home in an upper-class district on Tomás Moro Street. He broadcast his poignant farewell speech to the nation, a speech in which he defended the socialist principles of his Popular Unity coalition government, shortly before he was killed.[6] The military bombed the presidential palace, which went up in flames.

In the following hours tens of thousands of Chileans were forced from their homes in the *poblaciones* (urban slums and shantytowns) of Santiago and other regions of the country and taken away to detention centers that served as torture chambers.

> I'd never seen anything like it in my life. In the first raid they took away all the men. At six in the morning, when it was still dark, we woke up with the noise of the helicopters which sounded like they were landing on the houses. They were calling out over the loudspeakers that all the men between the ages of 18 and 60 had to go out into the streets. When we went outside we saw that everything was surrounded by the military, police, tanks and soldiers. They led the men off to a nearby football stadium, hitting them with sticks. The women followed behind. The streets were full of women and we were

Cerro Monjas, a *poblacíon* (shantytown) in Valparaiso (1993).

all shouting "murderers!'"They kept the men in the stadiums for days without food and some never came back. It went on for a week, the neighborhood surrounded, police and army everywhere, the shooting. We couldn't go outside because they were firing bullets from the main road into the neighborhood. They raided many houses, went through everything, did whatever they wanted. They said they were looking for weapons and for leaders. ["Olga," qtd. in Fischer 1993, 20-21]

The military surrounded the *poblaciones* associated with left-wing political parties.[7] "Day and night we heard shooting, and saw helicopters overhead with search lights. It was unbearable. We couldn't get out, we couldn't fight. Then people started to disappear. Some they killed right here. I remember them shooting a woman and her three children here on the street." ("Rosa," qtd. in Schneider 1995, 75). Killing residents "almost indiscriminately," they "scattered the bodies . . . as both a symbol and a warning to potential opposition" (Schneider 1994, 75). As one woman from the shantytown of La Victoria remembers, "Every day new bodies arrived, nude and headless. They floated in the river. We were stunned. It wasn't possible. We cried, please no more. They took my husband on the twelfth. A police patrol arrived. My youngest son was only thirteen years old. The wife of my older son was six months pregnant. She was disappeared. Her son still goes to sleep under the bed. In this way we learned that anything was possible" (qtd. in Schneider 1994, 75).[8]

The bloodbath in the wake of this coup was probably the worst in all of Latin American history. In the days and weeks after General Augusto Pinochet seized power, Chile's main soccer stadium became one of the nation's makeshift detention centers. Formerly the site of cheering fans, it was converted into a site of mass murder and torture, as some 3,000 people were rounded up, interrogated, and slaughtered or "disappeared." A North American journalist named Charles Horman, who had been living in Chile, also disappeared; Constantin Costa Gavras's film *Missing* (1982) documents the complicity of the U.S. government in the cover-up of his murder.[9]

Among the thousands of victims was the well-known folk singer Víctor Jara, who had been one of the founders of the Chilean New Song Movement and a symbol of hope for tens of thousands of Latin American youth. According to eyewitness accounts of survivors who had been detained at the stadium with Jara, the soldiers made him play his guitar and sing, while they tortured and murdered those around him and finally shattered his wrists. And he kept on singing. Then they shot him.[10] This horrifying slaughter of innocent civilians provoked a wave of international condemnation.

Military rule in Chile brought an abrupt halt to some four decades of stable parliamentary government.[11] In the aftermath of the takeover, Pinochet imposed a state of siege. Political parties and trade unions were declared illegal. It was prohibited by law for more than two or three people to gather or hold meetings. The repression was especially severe in the shantytowns where popular support for Allende had been the strongest. In these working-class neighborhoods many residents had participated in trade unions, leftist political parties, and grassroots social organizations under the Popular Unity government. During the first two years of authoritarian rule, military tanks continued to roll into the impoverished *poblaciones*, and soldiers raided homes in search of "subversives": that is to say, anyone whom the military deemed a potential enemy of the regime. There was strict censorship: the soldiers burned books and any political pamphlets and documents they were able to dig up; the government maintained absolute control over the radio, TV, newspapers—all the means of communication. Tens of thousands of Chileans were forced into exile, and the lives of many others were shattered. Fear and distrust were pervasive throughout the country.

Following the coup, the military regime launched a restructuring of the economy, based on the neoliberal policies of Milton Friedman and others of the Chicago School. These policies included "austerity measures" that led to widespread unemployment, poverty, and unprecedented hunger and misery for large sectors of the Chilean population. Those most affected by this economic onslaught were the working class and the poor—the slum dwellers living on the outskirts of Santiago and other urban centers. Over two million people, half of Santiago's population, now live in the *poblaciones*. In the words of Chilean sociologist Teresa Valdés, "as a result of economic policy and a desire for tight police control of the populace, a kind of socio-spatial segregation has been put into effect that has south-africanized the city of Santiago, turning it into a Latin American version of 'apartheid'" (1988, 101).

The monetary policies of Pinochet's authoritarian regime served the interests of transnational companies and foreign creditors, especially the International Monetary Fund and the World Bank. The opening-up to external markets left Chilean national industries unprotected. Neoliberal policies emphasized the production of raw materials (especially copper and fruit) and Chilean wines for export, free enterprise, increase in foreign investments, privatization of national industry, increasing privatization of health and education services, and massive cutbacks in welfare and social services. The ensuing economic crisis, according to Valdés, "was interrupted only by a brief, successful interval that was the outcome of massive infusions of foreign capital"; it brought "real unemployment to levels as high as 25% and 30% (1981-82) . . . concentrated in the working-class sectors and in the country's youth. This resulted in an increasing deterioration of living standards and purchasing power for the majority of the population (per capita consumption fell by 76% between 1973 and 1986)" (1988, 100).

Pinochet maintained absolute control over the Chilean people by creating a reign of terror throughout the country. According to the Ad Hoc Working Group of the United Nations, "by mid-1975 the military had detained between forty and fifty thousand civilians, brutally torturing many of them" (1975, 50). Few dared to express opinions about politics or the economy or to protest the violence and repression for fear of being themselves detained and disappeared. The state of siege and the threat of death or violence against the family members of anyone who spoke out was a powerful weapon of control over the civilian population. The military seemed to be invincible.

Many of the middle-and upper-class women who opposed Allende became supporters of Pinochet's regime. They were influenced by the military government's close alliance with members of the Catholic hierarchy and applauded Pinochet's rhetoric regarding women's role as mothers who must uphold traditional family values. Nevertheless, immediately following the 1973 seizure of power, small groups of the families of the victims of the repression—mostly wives and mothers of the disappeared and of the political prisoners—began to organize and to denounce the human rights abuses in Chile. Less than three weeks after the coup, on October 1, 1973, the Agrupación de Mujeres Democráticas (Association of Democratic Women) was formed (Chuchryk 1989, 156).

In May 1980, however, Pinochet held a plebiscite on a new constitution, institutionalizing his rule, and won overwhelmingly. Then, following the severe economic crisis of 1982, a storm of protest swept through Chile in May 1983. Public protests, strikes, and demonstrations were met with equally strong repression, arrests, tear gas, and military abuses of power, but the growing opposition movement led to the October 1988 plebiscite in which Pinochet was defeated. And finally, after seventeen years of bloody terror, in March 1990 a democratically elected civilian president, Patricio Aylwin, took office.

Following the end of the military regime in 1990, the civilian, democratically elected administrations of Aylwin and (after March 1994) Eduardo Frei were committed to making the alleviation of poverty a top priority. According to David Hojman, the Chilean model, with its combination of democratic politics and neoliberal, free-market economics, has been "extremely good for the upper-middle quintile." He goes on to explain that this model has stimulated rapid economic growth combined with external stability and no inflation; therefore, it has "proved beneficial, though to a lesser degree, to the poorest quintile (and to everyone else)." But even though there is less poverty in Chile, given to the growth of the economy and the appreciation of the peso, Hojman notes that "the distribution of income became more unequal between 1989 and 1992 as those in the lowest income quintile saw their share decrease, while those in the middle sectors saw their shares increase" (1996, 88-89). Since trickle-down toward the bottom of the income pyramid is minimal, there is still a need to redistribute social expenditures in primary education, youth training, and other long-term social investments that will contribute to the alleviation of poverty and income inequities in the future.

And whatever the benefits of the long-awaited transition to democracy, the 1980 constitution remains in effect, and General Augusto Pinochet is still the commander in chief of the Armed Forces. An amnesty law passed by the new government allows notorious, high-level military officers and secret service agents who were involved in planning and carrying out torture and murder to walk free, without having been tried or punished for their crimes.[12] Many families of the victims of the repression continue to demand that justice be done, and that the corrupt generals and security agents of the DINA (Directorate of National Intelligence) and CNI (National Center of Information), with the blood of innocent civilians on their hands, pay for their horrendous crimes.

As many of the testimonies in this book reveal, the transition to democracy has not significantly improved the lives of subaltern populations that continue to live in poverty or, in particular, the lives of Chilean women. Chile is a country with a long patriarchal tradition in which men and women were ascribed different social roles. The majority of Chilean girls were brought up to believe that it was their natural role in life to become a mother and to serve their husbands and families inside the home.

Patricia Chuchryk notes that women's participation in the labor force "has steadily increased from 25.2 percent of all women ages 15 and over in 1976 to 28.2 percent in 1985" (1989, 153). According to *Women's International Network News*, "Forty-five percent of university students are women and roughly half the graduates of medicine, dentistry and other professional programs are female. But women's earnings average 30 percent less than men's and they head a disproportionate number of Chile's poorest families. . . . One area of the work force dominated by women is the export fruit industry. In packing plants and orchards, about 500,000 temporary workers, mostly women, work 12 to 16 hours, six or seven days a week" (*WINN* 1994, 74).

Teresa Valdés points out that the "equality of the sexes proclaimed in numerous legal documents does not correspond to the reality of domination suffered by women. . . . Married life treats a woman as if she were a minor, comparable to people who are not responsible for their behavior, and . . . the law still prevents a mother from traveling outside the country with her children without first obtaining her husband's permission" (1988, 102). In some sectors of Chilean society men are still expected to protect their wives, and women are expected to obey their husbands.

This is not to say that there is not a professional class of well-educated, middle-class Chilean women who have been active members of the work force and have contributed to Chilean society for several generations. In fact, during the 1960s and early 1970s there were proportionately more active professional women in Chile and Argentina than in the United States.[13] Until the 1970s, however, only a small number of educated, professional women participated or were leaders in political organizations. There were some women in parliament throughout the 1960s and early 1970s, but it is important to note that most leadership roles in the traditional political parties, even those of the left, were still held by men.

As the Chilean sociologist Julieta Kirkwood convincingly argues, the traditional leftist parties tended to be authoritarian in their structure and did not specifically address issues related to gender. They aimed at the integration of women but did not provide an analysis of authoritarian culture and women's oppression in Chilean society. Kirkwood rightly points out that although authoritarian discourse emerges from the military and the bourgeoisie, "it can also be found in the middle classes, including professionals and intellectuals, and even among workers and peasants. In reality, it can be found throughout society" (1983, 5). In her feminist analysis of society, Kirkwood claims that the root of authoritarian culture lies in the patriarchal structure of the family. She also suggests that one of the consequences of military rule was that Chilean women began to make connections between state repression and oppression in the home, becoming more aware of their subordination: "People have begun to say that the family is authoritarian; that the socialization of children is authoritarian and rigid in its assignment of gender roles; that education, factory work, social organizations, and political parties have been constituted in an authoritarian manner" (1986, 180).

Another Chilean sociologist, María Elena Valenzuela, also argues that there are similarities between the military's control over civil society and male domination over women. She asserts that the Chilean military state is the quintessential expression of patriarchy, a common theme among Chilean feminists: "Both the military and patriarchy are structured in terms of authoritarianism and hierarchies. Just as military institutions are based on the principles of obedience and respect for authority and hierarchical structures, so is the traditional family structured around the figure of the father as the head of the family, who by law and by custom, has power over the rest of the group" (1987, 63).

The feminist political project is grounded on the notion of the negation of authoritarianism. Patricia Chuchryk explains that, according to Chilean feminists, this project also "involves the negation of the separation of existence into two spheres of activity, the public and the private; the negation of women's work being treated as nonwork; and the negation of women's condition of political, economic, social, legal, psychological, and sexual dependence" (1989, 171). In general, Latin American feminists tend to be class conscious and to view gender oppression as connected to other forms of class oppression. Kirkwood has argued that there is a need for feminists to merge class struggle with gender issues in their analysis; a single focus on class oppression in the public sphere leaves machismo in the home too often unchallenged. This only perpetuates the distinction between public and private life, and ignores the fact that men also have private lives.

As the feminist movement grew in Chile during the 1970s, one of the most significant groups to emerge was the Círculo de Estudios de la Mujer (The Women's Studies Circle) in 1977, which "focused on generating knowledge about women and generating consciousness about women's oppression. In addition to a core group of feminist researchers, there were grassroots activists, ongoing consciousness groups, a feminist theatre group, courses on women's history, a documentation center, and public forums on a wide variety of issues" (Chuchryk 1989, 165). Later, the group broke up into two separate organizations: the Centro de Estudios de la Mujer (CEM), a feminist research organization; and the Centro de Análisis y Difusión de la Condición de la Mujer, known as La Morada (home, dwelling place), which continues to offer workshops and other consciousness-raising activities.[14]

Many members of these feminist groups were middle- and upper-class women, whose concerns were sometimes far removed from those of poor and working-class women. In fact, women in the *poblaciones* were often suspicious of "academic" feminists—privileged women who lived in nice homes in wealthy neighborhoods and who came to the *poblaciones* to preach to their less-educated sisters about women's equality, even while many of them were exploiting poor women by using them as underpaid domestic servants. As Patricia Chuchryk has pointed out, "Roughly 25 percent of all women who work for wages in Chile are domestic servants" (1989, 153). In general, women, who make up over one-third of the labor force, are still concentrated in the low-wage sectors of the economy, primarily in service occupations.[15] Therefore, there is still some distrust of middle-class feminists by working-class and poor women, given the huge differences in lifestyle and inequities in distribution of the country's resources.[16]

In the early 1980s two grassroots women's federations emerged out of left-wing party traditions as a direct response to the political and economic crises—Comité de Defensa de los Derechos de la Mujer, or CODEM (Committee in Defense of Women's Rights) and Mujeres de Chile, or MUDECHI (Women of Chile)—which coordinated the activities of smaller neighborhood organizations (Chuchryk 1989, 164-65). In 1982 MOMUPO, Movimiento de Mujeres Pobladoras (Movement of Shanty-town Women) was formed to unite and coordinate the activities of some fifteen grassroots women's groups in Santiago. MOMUPO's aim was to develop activities that would help solve the immediate economic needs of the women and their families, and to involve them in a process of self-education that would increase their awareness of the social and political situation in Chile and encourage them to take a more active role. MOMUPO organized workshops on parenting skills, sexuality, women's legal rights, women's history, and other approaches to self-development and consciousness-raising. It also helped make these women, most of whom were housewives with no political or community experience, less vulnerable to the ideology being disseminated by the military-run Mothers' Centers (Centros de las Madres, or CEMAS), headed by Pinochet's wife, Lucía Hiriart de Pinochet.

The Mothers' Centers had originally been set up in the mid-1960s—during the government of Christian Democrat Eduardo Frei—as grassroots, community-based organizations whose objective was to empower women. But the military dictatorship used them as a means of strengthening its own conservative ideology regarding gender roles and the place of women in society. In October, immediately following the coup, Pinochet reorganized the CEMAS and established the National Secretariat of Women (SNM). To be sure, the Pinochet government put considerable effort into co-opting poor women by setting up skills-training workshops and free legal services in the *poblaciones*; it also built low-income housing

A meeting at La Morada Women's Center in Santiago (1993).

and provided maternal and pediatric health care in poor and working-class neighborhoods. But at the same time the Mothers' Centers taught women that their duty was to defend the family and the Catholic faith, to uphold and protect morality, to be the mothers of the nation and the protectors of the *patria* (fatherland). Thus, the ideology of motherhood was manipulated by the military government to serve its own purposes.

The Pinochet regime attempted to limit, if not eliminate, a public role for women. Many gains women had won in civil rights and labor were revoked. Employers were no longer required "to provide or to subsidize daycare for female employees and a new law made it possible for employers to sack pregnant employees" (Fisher 1993, 179). (Divorce and abortion are both still illegal in Chile, even now, and many women in the *poblaciones* still rely on unsafe, back-street abortions at enormous risk to their health.)

Grassroots political protests against the Pinochet dictatorship and the formation of human rights organizations whose participants were almost exclusively female must be understood within a broad cultural context of machismo and a long-standing patriarchal tradition. For women to come out of the shadows and take on a public role in organized resistance to authoritarian rule was a new phenomenon in Chilean society; it began to unsettle the very patriarchal structure upon which the society had been constructed and contributed to a period of transition within the home and in the community.

The devastating effects of the junta's neoliberal economic shock measures were especially felt in the *poblaciones* shortly after the 1973 coup. First of all, tens of thousands of men had been murdered, disappeared, imprisoned, or forced into exile, and many of those remaining had become unemployed. This absence of men from public life made it necessary for women to take on new roles in order for their families to survive the severe economic hardship the dictatorship inflicted upon them. Many women sought poorly paid work in the informal sector of the economy, working as domestic servants, or they became street vendors of crafts or food.

This was how the first communal kitchens, called *ollas comunes* (literally, "common saucepans,") came about—not as charitable activities like U.S. soup kitchens but as places where women collected, prepared, cooked, and served food to needy members of the community. Domestic life in some sectors of Chilean society thus began to undergo a process of collectivization to combat the widespread hunger experienced in poor neighborhoods, where unemployment, poverty, and misery had reached unprecedented levels. According to Fisher, "In 1983, an estimated thirty percent of all Chilean families were living in 'extreme' poverty" (1993, 10-11). In short, the responsibility for feeding the nation's poor fell largely on marginalized women themselves; some would go out into the streets to beg food from markets or donations to buy staples, while other women prepared the food. The Catholic Church did donate basic foodstuffs such as beans, flour, and oil and helped set up the kitchens, often in local parishes, where many destitute families and children would be provided their only hot meal of the day.

In addition to organizing communal kitchens, women began to collect and sell old clothing, start shopping collectives called *comprando juntas*, tend collective gardens, and form sewing and crafts workshops as survival strategies. These groups, usually headed and run by women, were called popular economic organizations (*organizaciones económicas populares*) or OEPs (Chuchryk 1989, 154-55). They also raised money by selling handicrafts, especially *arpilleras*, which are small tapestries; the Catholic Church, through the Vicariate of Solidarity,[17] would buy handcrafted articles directly from the makers and export them for sale abroad.

Margorie Agosín explains how the traditionally feminine crafts of sewing and embroidering became an effective means of denouncing the Pinochet dictatorship: "The tender and delicate needlework of years ago has now been turned into a powerful weapon against the enemy. This is the case of the Chilean *arpilleras*, small wall hangings with figures superimposed on the cloth to create scenes full of vitality and movement, whose principal effect is that of political denunciation. *Arpillera* means burlap in Spanish and since the backing cloth is often made of burlap, the finished work has come to be called *arpillera*" (1987, 11-12). Each *arpillera* tells a story about the life of the woman who made it, often depicting a personal tragedy such as the disappearance of a son or daughter, the discovery of a mass grave, a political arrest, or a graphic representation of communal suffering through housing and food shortages, unemployment, curfew, censorship, and so forth. The women who first made *arpilleras* in 1974 were also members of the Association of the Relatives of the Detained and Disappeared; they would gather in church basements to sew their stories of political protest. Then these women's artisan workshops spread throughout the country, especially in the *poblaciones*. The making and trafficking of these handicrafts had to be done clandestinely, however, since showing and selling *arpilleras* was illegal, considered by the military junta to be a subversive activity.

Through participation in arts and crafts workshops, some women were able to turn their personal suffering into collective action and group resistance. These regular gatherings with other women also helped raise their social and political consciousness. For many, it was their first group experience with other women; they began to gain self-confidence and pride in their contributions to the larger society outside the four walls of their homes; even women with little formal education achieved an increased political awareness and a growing understanding of the need for women to join together to resist the regime and to fight gender oppression both at home and in their communities, where alcoholism and domestic violence had been exacerbated by the economic crisis.

The rise of such grassroots women's organizations as communal kitchens, craft workshops, and human rights groups in the shantytowns, gave working-class women the opportunity for personal growth and development. The husbands of several women I interviewed were opposed to their wives' participation in these new social movements but eventually had to accept, or at least tolerate, the women's new sense of freedom and independence. If not, some of the women found the courage to leave abusive husbands and unhappy marriages and to begin a new life. For housewives and mothers who had become less socially isolated and felt valued because of their roles in their communities through participation in grassroots organizations, there was no turning back.

Immediately following the coup, a group called the Association of Democratic Women was formed to support political prisoners and their families. And then, in 1974, the Association of the Relatives of the Detained and Disappeared was established. Women whose husbands or sons and daughters or grandchildren had been murdered or imprisoned by the regime were the first to organize solidarity groups to support the political prisoners in Chile and to condemn publicly the violence and terror perpetrated on the civilian population. The Catholic Church, too, through the Vicariate of Solidarity, sponsored neighborhood humanitarian groups to look after the victims of military persecution and to help those in situations of extreme poverty.[18]

As Jo Fisher has observed, women's minor role in political organizations before the coup "gave them a public 'invisibility' which allowed them to organize without drawing attention to themselves. Women had also traditionally worked with the Church in welfare and humanitarian projects" (1993, 25). Progressive elements in the Catholic Church had been influenced by the new liberation theology, which emphasized social justice and working toward the creation of the "kingdom of heaven" here on earth, instead of preaching that this life is just "a vale of tears" in which one must endure suffering with the hope of a better life after death.[19] Some members of the ecclesiastic hierarchy condemned liberation theology, however, and remained closely associated with the military and the Chilean oligarchy, their former allies. As women's human rights groups took a more active role in political protests and in the organized resistance to Pinochet, the Church began to distance itself from these grassroots organizations.

In 1983 there was an upsurge of demonstrations against the regime. On the first day of national protest thousands of Chileans flooded the streets, banging pots and pans and calling for an immediate end to military rule. Additional spontaneous protests (and the subsequent repression) took place mostly in the *poblaciones* that had been linked historically to the Chilean Communist Party: "In traditional Communist *poblaciones*, such as La Victoria and Yungay, residents engaged in an avalanche of popular rebellion. They built burning barricades made from branches, tires, and garbage, and turned the streets into a battleground between military forces and stone-throwing *pobladores*. Strong grassroots networks, trust between neighbors, and a history of successful collective action imbued residents with the courage and confidence to confront the regime" (Schneider 1995, 157). This activity can be seen as an inversion of the original bourgeois propaganda marches organized by conservative forces against Allende's government.

According to Jean Franco, women's participation in new social movements in South America—in response to the authoritarian regimes of the

1970s and to the economic hardship caused by the debt crisis and neoliberal economic policies—has significantly influenced and galvanized Latin American feminist movements in general: "The power of such grassroots movements has had an impact on the feminist movement in which, more and more, their presence, their questioning, and their politics have become an issue" (1992, 69). Women's groups have also had a direct and indirect impact on culture, such as the emergence of a substantial corpus of writing by women.

From 1983 on the women's movement in Chile grew and began to take a more visible, public stand against the dictatorship. In addition to the co-ordinating council of women's organizations, MEMCH (the Movement for the Emancipation of Chilean Women), a group emerged called Women in the Defense of Life, representing a "broad political spectrum including partisan, independent and feminist groups." After 1983 "women, acting together in different instances, have earned a place as a recognized collective and social agent of opposition to the military government. They have achieved this through massive, disciplined, meaningful, symbolic and unified street demonstrations as well as by condemnations, campaigns, solidarity fasts, public statements and press conferences, despite the threat of government brutality" (Valdés 1988, 105-6). Through actions that redefined political spaces and broadened both the form and content of politics, women resisted authoritarian rule and promoted gender-specific demands. According to María Elena Valenzuela, women's new organizations and political activity "became the means for changing their condition of subordination and for re-democratizing all of society" (1991, 206).

Nevertheless, in the transition to democracy in Chile, women's demands have not been successfully met. The traditional political parties of the left and center have incorporated some gender-specific issues into their platforms but are not willing to share their power with women: "The Chilean political system has no legitimate form of participation outside the political parties and labor unions, and the parties are not prepared to incorporate women on equal terms" (Valenzuela 1991, 183). Therefore, the autonomous feminist movement and women's organizations, though still active, are excluded from the nation's power structure and from political and economic decision-making. Statistics provided by the *Women's International Network News* reveal the gross underrepresentation of Chilean women in positions of political power, despite their key role in opposing the military regime from 1973 to 1990: "When democratic government returned women found themselves out in the cold, with only seven members out of 120 in the House of Deputies and three of 47 senators. The new Congress installed in March of 1993 shows nine women elected to the House of Deputies and the number of senators falling from three to two" (*WINN* 1994, 74). Valenzuela proposes that the future of the women's movement in Chile depends upon "its capacity to work in conjunction with other power structures—the state apparatus, political parties, social organizations—without allowing those structures to subordinate or neutralize gender-specific demands" (1991, 184).

The stories of the women I interviewed, about their lives under military rule and what they did to fight back, are a tiny sampling, by no means representative of all Chilean women. Nonetheless, these voices of resistance point to the courage of thousands of "invisible" Chilean and other South American women who joined forces, at no small risk to their own lives, to oppose military rule and to protest the violation of human rights in their respective countries.

Elena Maureira

Speaker on Behalf of the Disappeared

Elena Maureira (1993), with her memorial to her husband and sons.

I interviewed Elena Maureira at her home in Isla del Maipo—not an island but a rural community of several hundred inhabitants approximately two hours by bus from Santiago, near the small town of Talagante. Most of the people in this community work on a minifundio, *a farm comprising many acres of vineyards. I visited Maureira on the hot summer afternoon of December 21, 1993. She lives in a small, three-room wooden house with a concrete floor. A large wedding picture of Elena and her husband Sergio hangs on the living room wall, faded photo in a simple wooden frame. The house is located behind the small grocery store owned and operated by Maureira's youngest son, Juan Luís, who is now thirty-seven years old. The Maureira family members have told their story to journalists and human rights workers from various countries: Elena's husband, Sergio Adrián Maureira Lillo, and four of their sons, José Manuel, Sergio, Segundo, and Rudolfo were detained on October 7, 1973, and there was no information as to their whereabouts until their corpses were discovered five years later in the Lonquén Mines, located in the hills not far from the capital city of Santiago.[1]*

Elena Maureira, now seventy-six years old, is a woman of modest means who did not have the opportunity to study beyond the sixth grade. She is only semiliterate and insists that she has never understood or been interested in political organizations. Yet despite the grief she felt while recalling and recounting her memories, occasionally wiping away tears, she impressed me as a poised, affectionate woman of deep faith who still has a twinkle shining in her dark brown eyes. She revealed a sense of urgency to tell her story so that not only her Chilean compatriots but also the entire world can bear witness to how she and her family personally suffered at the hands of the Pinochet dictatorship. Maureira's testimony also illustrates her eagerness to denounce the corrupt legal system that met all her inquiries, petitions, and attempts to find answers with lies and obstacles, and the military and police who, instead of helping her, served as accomplices in covering up the murders. Moreover, the Amnesty Law has granted pardon to the perpetrators of such crimes; that is to say, the individuals who terrorized and murdered members of the Maureira and other families from Isla del Maipo have not been punished.

Ironically, Sergio Maureira, a supervisor at the Nahuayán estate, risked—and lost—his own life in the struggle for better working conditions, increased salaries, and benefits for many of the same farmworkers who later, out of fear and terror, rejected his surviving family members. His "crime" had been his active participation in Salvador Allende's Popular Unity government and his leadership roles in a union organization and a left-of-center political party called MAPU.[2]

In a small room upstairs Elena Maureira has an altar where each day she lights candles and arranges flowers in front of protest signs bearing the names, pictures, and dates of the disappearance of her loved ones: these are the same signs that were carried by the Maureira family in demonstrations against human rights abuses; they are similar to those carried by thousands of relatives and friends of the disappeared at demonstrations not only in Chile but in Argentina, Brazil, and Uruguay, which also suffered under dictatorial regimes in the 1970s and 1980s.

My name is Elena Maureira. I am from a family of peasants from Buín, near the small town of Isla de Maipo. I was born in a rural area in the countryside, on a small *fundo* [farm] called Santa Victoria. But I was baptized and received my First Holy Communion in Maipo. I got married in Maipo.

I met my husband, Sergio, when I was living with my aunt in Santa Victoria. She had a small store there, and I was helping her out. Sergio used to come to buy flour at the store. He was still in school when we met; he was sixteen and I was seventeen when we got married. We had already been seeing each other for about a year when my aunt found out. She threw me out of her house and sent me back to my mother's place. But within the first week, Sergio came to talk to my parents and told them that he was in love with me, and asked permission to visit me every week. He came every week for about a month, and then his father came to the house to ask for my hand in marriage. Although Sergio was younger than me, he had a reputation for being a hard-working, responsible young man. So my parents agreed to let me get married. It was a very simple wedding at the church in Isla de Maipo; then we went to my in-laws' house, where the whole family was waiting for us with food, and two musicians sang for the small reception. That was my wedding day. My husband and I stayed there, living with my in-laws at their house, where our first two children were born. Then we moved to our own place and had ten more children. I had twelve children, eight boys and four girls. Just imagine! I always say, only God keeps me alive.

I remember the day the *carabineros*, the National Police, came and arrested and detained my husband Sergio. We were living on a large *fundo* in Nahuayán, where my husband worked as a foreman. Don José Celsi was the *patrón* (owner) of this *fundo*. Sergio was in charge of supervising all the farmworkers on this large estate, and two of my sons, Segundo and Rudolfo, worked there as laborers. On Sunday afternoon, October 7, 1973, Sergio went to play soccer with the kids. They got home tired and hungry about 8:00 P.M. Sergio asked me to bring him a basin of water so he could wash his feet. He cleaned up, ate something, and then told me he wanted to go to bed early because he was exhausted.

At about 10:00 P.M. the police came. All the children were watching TV when a police officer, Pablo Nancipil, who was a friend of the family, arrived at the house. He used to come over for cookouts and other social gatherings. Pablo asked me, "Do the Maureiras live here?" "Of course!" I answered. "You know we live here. You've been a guest in our home many times." But who could have ever imagined what they were going to do that night! "Is Don Sergio here?" he coldly inquired. And I told him that he was asleep, to go on back to his room. He entered the bedroom and said, "Don Sergio, please get up quietly and without resisting arrest. You must come with me to the police station. I have been ordered to detain you. Wear warm clothes because it's cold." I can't believe that jerk was so cynical. So Sergio got dressed and left with the police. Then they came back for his identification card, which he had forgotten to take with him. At this time they also went into the bedroom and began beating my son Segundo and asking him where all the weapons were hidden. Segundo replied that he didn't know what weapons they were talking about.

There were four other police who came with Pablo Nancipil that night: Mañuel Muñoz and Héctor Vargas came in the house, while Jacinto Torres and another guy we didn't know stayed in the truck. It was the *patrón*'s white pickup. He must have ordered them to come and lent them the truck. And then about half an hour passed and the police came to take away my two married sons, Rudolfo [age twenty] and Sergio Adrián [twenty-eight]. They arrested them at their own houses.

The following morning my daughter-in-law, Elisea Navarrete, Rudolfo's wife, came to the house, sobbing. Elisea was only nineteen years old at the time, and she was very much in love with Rudolfo. They had a six-month-old baby, and October 7 just happened to be their anniversary; Elisea had baked a cake for the special occasion. They were eating cake and celebrating when the police stormed into their home about ten-thirty that night. My son Rudolfo was brutally beaten; those scumbags kicked him in his stomach and slapped his face, right there in front of his wife, and almost killed him before throwing him into the truck and hauling him away. Elisea never saw her beloved husband again after that tragic moment.

Hilda, Elisea's cousin, is also my daughter-in-law. She was married to my oldest son, named Sergio like his father. Hilda and Sergio had spent that Sunday, October 7, celebrating their only son's first birthday. Sergio was already in bed and Hilda was watching TV when the same police officers came for Sergio. The baby started to cry when one of the police kept raising and lowering the volume on the TV. They turned everything upside down, going through papers and stealing things.

After that, these same police came back to my house for two more of my children, Segundo and José Manuel. Those criminals and murderers raped my daughter in the back room. Then they broke José Manuel's arm when they struck him with a club as he tried to reach for some money in his pockets so he could leave it with me (it was the farmworkers' salary for that week). They hit him so hard that the club broke with the force of the blow. They took all the money and stole many things from our house: two revolvers, my husband's gold watch, a necklace of mine, and an old rifle that hung on the wall—a family heirloom, something that had sentimental value and that I didn't want to part with. The police stole everything valuable that they found. They left the house in shambles. It was total chaos. They yelled all kinds of obscenities, like "You old bitch" and "Shut up, you mother fucker." And I told them that I was old enough to be their mother; how dared they speak like that? It was a nightmare. Can you understand what a horrible nightmare this was? I wanted someone to pinch me and wake me up from this terrifying nightmare.

My husband and my four sons never came back. I never saw them alive again. When my daughters went to the police station to take them some breakfast the following morning, they were told that everyone who had been detained had already been taken to the National Stadium in Santiago. That same day my daughters went directly to the stadium and searched everywhere but couldn't find any trace of them. How my oldest daughters and my daughters-in-law suffered looking for them! Every time someone said that some people had been detained at a certain place, they immediately went there in the hope of finding them. Over several years we spent the little bit of money that I had saved in trying to find my husband and four sons. It was horrible not knowing if they were dead or alive. I worried constantly, always asking myself if they were perhaps being tortured that very minute, if they were cold or hungry, if they were inside the country or if maybe they had been able to escape. I got no answers to any of these questions. My life had been converted into sheer agony. Not knowing was a form of torture for all of us. We never stopped hoping that they might be alive until, after enduring five years of anguish, we found out that their corpses had been discovered at the Lonquén Mines.

A police officer with a guilty conscience had confessed to a priest in Santiago, and that's how the mass grave site was found. His conscience wouldn't let him live in peace. So he went and confessed. And then the priest went to the Vicaría de la Solidaridad so that they could investigate and find out if it was true. One of the Vicaría's lawyers went with a group of people to Lonquén to look for evidence. And there they were! They found them. They went with large nylon bags, but it was difficult to get the bodies out of the mines because clothes and a spring mattress and a lot of rocks and dirt had been thrown on top of them and the hole covered up with cement. It appears that some of the victims may have been buried alive, because of the scratches and dried blood found all over their bodies. When I went there and saw the hair, the rocks, and the remains, I was in a state of shock! I almost fainted; I thought I would die from the horror! All of the relatives of the victims had to identify the corpses by the clothes they were wearing.

Our house was full of journalists, investigators, and doctors for the next several weeks. I couldn't even cook because there were people here all the time. My youngest son lost most of his hair from the shock. He'd been only eleven years old when his father and brothers disappeared, and the poor child had been forced to witness everything. He was traumatized from the impact of this tragedy. I finally took him to see a psychologist, because his hair started falling out and he was withdrawn and sad.

After I found my own family members, I continued working with the Vicaría de la Solidaridad. I felt it was important to offer support to other families who had lost their loved ones. I was invited to speak on several occasions. I tried to help families who had gone through similar experiences. Here in Isla de Maipo those assassins also murdered three members of the Astudillo family, four members of the Hernández family, one of the Floreses—to think that fifteen people were taken from this very small town the same night that they came for Sergio and my boys! Everyone knew that the Astudillos were Communists, but that was no reason to kill them. The Hernández family wasn't Communist or active in any leftist political parties. All they ever did was participate in the farmworkers' union on the Guayaba *fundo*. There have always been unions here in Chile on these estates, everywhere. My God! Those assassins had no right to kill them for that! Why didn't they just arrest them, or even send them somewhere far away, to an island or something? But not murder them!

Not too long ago I found out from an eyewitness who had been detained with Sergio that the *carabineros* beat him to death with a club the same night they took him away. And then they decided to kill everyone else held prisoner at the police station here so that no one would find out how Sergio died. They assumed that by killing all the witnesses they could hide this heinous crime. It wasn't until five years later that we found the corpses at the Lonquén Mine. Apparently, those prisoners who hadn't already been tortured to death were buried alive in the mine and then covered with cement.

We know the names of all the members of the National Police who were guilty of committing this crime. Their names have even appeared in books. And they are still working as police. Can you believe that? There has been no justice. Those assassins are still working for the government, receiving salaries and enjoying their lives as free men. They have not had to pay anything for these atrocities. The government of Patricio Aylwin didn't do enough to help the families of the victims of Pinochet's regime—

the military put a lot of pressure on him—and consequently, there was no justice for us and no real return to democracy. The Amnesty Law has allowed almost all the murderers of Pinochet's regime to go unpunished. Now that we have elected Frei [1993], we hope there will be some justice. The only thing that we are asking is that these guilty police officers be punished, that they pay for their crimes. Not that they be killed, just punished. We know that there is a cop working near Rapel, and a lieutenant working in Paine, and another one here at the Isla de Maipo. It's so damn frustrating.

Let me tell you what happened to my son Juan. He didn't know that this one assassin lived in Paine, where he raises pigs. Well, one day Juan was talking to his friend Claudio, who works as a manager at the dairy, and this cop arrived in a jeep (he had a rifle too) to get the leftover whey to feed to his pigs. Claudio wanted to introduce them, and Juan immediately recognized the cop. The cop, however, didn't recognize Juan and held out his hand. Of course, Juan refused to shake it. And when Claudio asked him why, Juan replied: "I'm never going to shake the hand of an assassin. How can I dirty my hands with the blood of my own brothers and with the blood of my father?" And he left, telling Claudio that he would explain later. That afternoon Claudio came to look for Juan at his job and asked him a lot of questions. Juan told his friend the truth: that just seeing the cop reminded him of the day when they came and took away his dad and his brothers. Juan was only eleven years old at the time; he remembers that day as vividly as though it were yesterday, but he had never before told anybody the story. After he finished, Claudio vowed never again to allow that killer to enter the dairy.

Later, Claudio told Juan that the next time this scumbag came to the dairy, he locked the doors. And when he kept honking the horn of the jeep, Claudio went outside and confronted the son-of-a-bitch: "I don't let assassins in here. Do you remember the Isla de Maipo?" And the guy just turned white and took off in his jeep. It's amazing how he didn't deny his guilt. And this asshole Muñoz was one of the worst. He's now retired but still living in Paine. And then there was Pablo, the one who confessed to a priest before he committed suicide. As I already told you, that is how we found the corpses at Lonquén. Let me tell you the names of the police who came to the house the night they took my husband and my four sons. They were Pablo Nancipil, Jacinto Torres, Mañuel Muñoz, Héctor Vargas, and another whose name I don't know.

Our life here in Isla de Maipo was very difficult after they killed Sergio. Everyone was afraid to talk to us. Some people tried hard to drive us out of town. Nobody wanted to get involved in the affairs of anybody else; everybody here was fearful and suspicious. Nobody wanted to have anything at all to do with us. We were harassed constantly. They even poisoned our dogs in an attempt to run us out. Another time, they slit open some pregnant cows we owned and killed them so that we couldn't earn money from selling their calves. The soldiers used to take me about three times a week in their jeep to the arsenal in Talagante, because José Celsi, the *patrón*, would order them to scare me. So they would take me there and harass me, point four or five rifles at my back, take my identification card away, and leave me there, all alone. Just imagine that. I almost went crazy. And you can't even imagine all of the terrible things these young soldiers said to me. When I was all alone they treated me so badly! But I give thanks to God and to the Virgin Mary for giving me the strength to endure. "If they killed my husband and children, then let them kill me too," I used to tell myself. I always answered back when they insulted me. One soldier was missing a hand, and when he would yell nasty obscenities at me, I would reply, "I am old enough to be your mother, and if you don't respect me, then I don't respect you either. At least I have two hands that both work, not like you, who only has one." I would shout back all kinds of mean things to defend myself against their abuse.

Another time I remember I was shopping in Santiago—I needed to buy my granddaughter some new shoes—and there was a policeman following me. First I saw him at the post office, and then I noticed he was walking next to me. When I stopped, he stopped, and then he continued to follow me. I was trembling with fear; my entire body was shaking and my legs almost gave out. Finally, he said, "I'm following you in order to protect you, lady." I was very frightened but also angry: "Why didn't you defend and protect my family when the National Police came to kill them? Where were you then, you son-of-a-bitch?" When he continued to follow me and then began to insult me, I walked faster and shouted and cursed at him. I called him every bad name you can imagine. I'm ashamed to think of all of the nasty things I said, but I was burning up with anger and needed to let off some steam. I carried all this rage inside me for so long that I had to vent my anger and get this off my chest. I told him that if he wanted to arrest me, to go ahead and do it. That I wasn't afraid of him. That he was a murderer. Finally, I got to the shoe store, where the owner knows me. He told the cop to stop harassing me and to get the hell out of his store. The cop left, and then I had a crying spell; I just sobbed and sobbed. I was shaking and crying, and the store owner brought me some water and some tranquilizers to help calm me down. I completely lost control of myself; I didn't even remember all the nasty things I had yelled at the policeman. The store owner gave me a discount on the shoes I bought and sent a young man with me to the bus stop to make sure that I got home safely. I have many memories of similar bad experiences with the *carabineros*.

I have told my story publicly on numerous occasions. People sometimes start crying when I tell them about the terrible, tragic things that have happened to me and my family. But there are many caring people who give me the strength to speak out, so that the whole country will know what happened to me. And God gives me so much strength to carry on. I have gone to speak at a number of places in Santiago. I always go whenever I'm invited. I just turned seventy last August. God has given me the courage to keep on living. Also, I still have two unmarried sons who need me. My boys are all alone and have only me, so I ask God every night to keep me alive for them.

I'm a member of the PPD [*Partido por la Democracia*, Party for Democracy].[3] But I must tell you the truth. I don't understand politics very much. I don't understand politics, but I like to be with people. I like to help others, and I want everyone to know the truth, to know what happened to me and my family. I'm often invited to speak at meetings and different types of events. But I'm just a peasant. I don't have any formal education. I need to be honest about that; everything I know I have learned from my own life experience and from other people. When my husband was alive, I always stayed at home caring for my twelve children. I never went anywhere without Sergio. I've always been a housewife. To tell you the truth, I am just a peasant, someone who doesn't know how to act or what to say in the presence of more educated people. But now, I do go many places, and people always treat me with such respect! They say that Mrs. Maureira, from the Isla de Maipo, ought to go speak to this or that group. Many people are aware of what happened to me and they know about Lonquén.

Let me tell you what happened when I was invited to speak in Melipilla. Everyone wanted to talk to me and ask me questions. And then when I went to Rancagua for several days, I was touched by how nice the people there treated me. They asked me all kinds of questions that I didn't feel prepared to answer. But God, my children, and my husband, whom I am always defending, gave me the strength and the courage to speak out. I'm telling you that I was able to respond to every question they asked me. It seemed as though I just had the answers ready on the tip of my tongue, and it turned out fine. Later, a young woman who was about eighteen years old and had just been released from prison came up to talk to me. We talked for a long time. She told me how she had been raped and tortured in prison, and how now she was very frightened to get involved again in the struggle against Pinocho.[4] She asked me, "Señora, what should I do? I'm terrified to get involved in anything." I told her not to be afraid, that she must continue the struggle and never give up fighting for what she believes in. "Look at me," I said. "You know that I had five of my loved ones killed the very same day, and I'm still fighting. I've been able to keep on going with the help of my friends. And with the solidarity of my *compañeros*, I've been able to continue the struggle and I'm not afraid of anybody. So, be strong, don't be afraid, keep working in the opposition." And then two little girls about eight or ten years old came up to me and gave me some flowers. They also recited a poem that was so beautiful I began to weep tears of joy and happiness. It also happened to be my birthday (August 18). They announced my birthday and everyone applauded; later, many people came up to me to hug me, to congratulate me, and to wish me well. I cried because I was so touched. I couldn't believe that this was happening to me. I felt as though my heart was going to come out of my mouth. I will never forget that happy day in Rancagua.

Mirta Crocco

SOCIAL WORKER AND COMMUNITY ACTIVIST

Mirta Crocco (right), with Monique, a French human rights organizer living in Chile (1993).

On December 18, 1993, Mirta Crocco invited me to join her family for after-noon tea and pastries at her home in Valparaíso. With two of her daughters and several grandchildren, we sat around a large round table in a garden full of colorful flowers, under large trees whose branches provided ample shade. Later, Mirta Crocco invited me to her book-lined study, where she allowed me to tape our interview.

A social worker and professor of social work by profession, Crocco has devoted most of her adult life to the cause of social justice in her native Chile. Immediately following the coup in 1973 she began working with the Committee of Cooperation for Peace in Chile (Comité de Cooperación para la Paz en Chile, or COPACHI) and then with the Vicaría de la Solidaridad.[1] For the human rights organization CODEP, founded in 1984, she served as executive secretary in Valparaíso, and then became its national president.[2]

Mirta Crocco is an elegant, sophisticated woman of about sixty, with dark, expressive eyes. She is slim, charming, and down-to-earth. She spoke frankly about the devastating impact of the dictatorship on her life, confessing that she has not been able to recover from the psychological trauma caused by the death of a daughter who was a victim of military rule.

Crocco's testimony emphasizes that her activism and her understanding of Chile's structural social inequities stem from knowledge acquired through direct experience working in the shantytowns, not from her formal education in the School of Social Work. It also suggests that as a feminist her commitment to the struggle for human rights is linked to issues of gender equality. One striking feature of her testimony is the way Crocco defines herself as both strong and vulnerable, as an independent woman who was reduced to feelings of impotence by the repression. Although a leader in the opposition to authoritarian rule, she was at the same time a victim of it and is still recovering from its devastating effects on her life.

Let me begin by telling you how I became involved in the struggle for human rights here in Chile. I am the oldest of four children. I was born and raised here in Valparaíso. I'm from a middle-class background; my family is politically conservative. In this regard, I am an anomaly, the only one in my family who was active in the opposition to Pinochet and involved in the human rights movement.

My parents couldn't afford to send me to the University in Santiago. That is why I entered the School of Social Work here in Valparaíso. I felt an inclination toward a profession in which I would be helping others; social work seemed a suitable vocation for me. After working for five or six years, I came to understand that most social problems are related to socioeconomic power structures and social hierarchies. For example, poverty, lack of opportunity, unemployment, underemployment, illiteracy, and prostitution are all linked to the unequal distribution of resources and wealth. They are not isolated problems independent from society's social structure. The way I had been trained to deal with these social problems as a social worker was not effective. My direct, practical experience in the field taught me to seek out other solutions to these problems. As I became more radical and politicized, I began to question the very premises upon which the whole field of social work was built.

When I entered the university, I converted to Catholicism. My mother was a non-practicing Anglican, and my father wasn't religious at all. I became active in a student organization on campus called Acción Católica Universitaria [University Catholic Action Group]. During a period of four years I devoted a lot of time and energy to volunteer work and to my own spiritual development. I had a passion and zeal for working with people. I mention this because there is a logical progression from my conversion to Catholicism to my vocation as a social worker, and eventually to my human rights work. I've always felt a strong desire to help others and to try to create a more just society.

When I was at the university, I started to identify with leftist political thinking and progressive student organizations, in spite of the fact that everyone else in my family was conservative. My father is really reactionary: he's a *momio* who supports Pinochet.[3] And I married a lawyer who was politically moderate, something like a Christian Democrat, although he never joined any political party. At the time we got married, our political differences weren't a major issue. But as I became more committed to leftist ideals and principles, these ideological differences became the source of serious marital problems and conflicts.

Because my work was so intense and brought me into direct daily contact with the subaltern, marginal sectors of Chilean society, it was easy for me to identify with the left. In fact, I was the first person here in Valparaíso to do community work in the *poblaciones*. We would go out into those shantytowns and poor rural communities up in the hills to work directly with people who lived in small shacks and had barely enough to eat. There was no medical care, and unemployment and illiteracy were high.

During this period, I began to distance myself from the formal training that I had received at the university. I questioned the methods and approaches I had been taught and started to think seriously about new approaches to the profession of social work. I was interested in a more scientific, structural analysis of society's problems, rather than the Band-aid approach. The story of my involvement in human rights is a long story that began as a consequence of my firsthand experience with the *pobladores* [slum dwellers].

This was a period of political transition and new political processes in Chile. The poorer *poblaciones* were beginning to organize and become politically active. Eduardo Frei, a Christian Democrat, was elected president in 1964, and I was offered an administrative position in the regional promotion of the popular sector.[4] But I didn't accept this job, because I had two small children and because I enjoyed my work with the *pobladores*. I thought a lot about community development. I recognized the need for community development projects but knew that they should be accompanied by educational programs for personal and social development. Development alone was not enough; access to education was essential for the lives of the *pobladores* to improve. When Allende was elected in 1970, he implemented many social reforms that really helped the marginal sectors. I was committed to the Popular Unity government and strongly supported radical social reforms in health care, education, land reform, job training, and the like. I always viewed Allende's program of social reforms from my own professional perspective; I could see the difference these policies were making in the lives of individuals who lived in the shantytowns.

I never participated in any political party. I must confess that I'm not suited, by temperament, for party politics. So many party members become dogmatic and narrow-minded, and I'm just not comfortable with the kind of discipline that is required of members of revolutionary parties such as the Communists. I support these parties and respect the people who join them, but it's just not for me.

When I went to a professional conference in Venezuela in 1972, I met many Venezuelans and Colombians who were committed to the revolutionary processes in their countries (the Cubans didn't attend this conference). As a result I established countless professional contacts with radical social workers throughout Latin America, and I became more and more politically aware and increasingly committed to leftist politics.

As I became more political, my husband and I began to have serious problems. The conflict between us was my first existential crisis. It was a period of intense suffering, confusion, and personal anguish. I had married thinking that our commitment was for life. We had six children, because both my husband and I love children; we wanted to have a large family. He was a successful lawyer, and I was also doing well in my career, a career that I loved. And since I'm well organized, I was able to integrate my professional life with my family life. We had a fairly happy marriage during the first few years. But after that, we grew apart. Our attitudes toward life and child rearing, as well as our values and ideologies, were very different.

I didn't care about accumulating wealth and material things, and he did. When I supported Allende, as a faculty member at the university, my name appeared on a list of Allende supporters. This was a very difficult moment for me, because I had to confront my husband. He's an intelligent man, but his political stance was much more conservative than mine. It was very hard for me, because all my family, my parents and my brothers, were so much more conservative. I was considered the black sheep of the family, just because my views were more radical than theirs.

It wasn't that I had read Marx or Lenin, or that I had been politically indoctrinated in some left-wing party. My ideas didn't come from reading books but from my professional experience as a social worker. My political convictions sprang from my direct contact with people living in the shantytowns. I found myself increasingly committed to those who were organizing at the grassroots level. I couldn't continue living with my husband and be true to myself. I realized that the rift between us was very, very deep and that I would not be able to spend the rest of my life with this man. Finally, we decided to separate because of these irreconcilable differences.

I began working full time. It was difficult for my children to come home from school and find neither their father nor their mother there to greet them. I felt bad about having to leave them alone, but I had to work full time in order to pay the bills. On the weekends I would always spend a lot of time with my kids. We would take excursions to the mountains, lakes, and countryside. I used to take several of them with me to the *poblaciones* up in the hills just outside Valparaíso. They would attend neighborhood meetings, workshops I held for the mothers, and all kinds of community events. But during the week my kids had to spend a lot of time alone.

It was interesting that during the Popular Unity government [1970-73], not just my children but many children who often heard their parents discussing politics formed strong opinions about Allende and Chile's changing political landscape. My own children, who attended the Italian school, were constantly discussing politics. Several of my kids supported Radomiro Tomic, and one of my daughters declared herself a conservative.[5] I considered this to be a very meaningful process. In the shantytowns the children were also receiving a political education. I remember that the day Allende was elected the streets here in Valparaíso were full of people dancing, all the way from the Avenida Argentina to Carampangue Street. All of us were dancing and celebrating! You could hear the music everywhere! It was tremendous, and I felt happy to be a part of this joyful celebration. It was a moment of victory for the Chilean people.

During the period of the Popular Unity government I worked very hard and firmly supported the revolutionary process taking place here in Chile. I was a professor of social work at the University of Chile, but as I told you, I had already begun to question many aspects of the profession. The entire social service system served as a buffer between the interests of the workers and the interests of the ruling elite. Thus, I viewed the profession as reinforcing the status quo, rather than doing something to transform these unjust class structures. Since many of my colleagues shared my views, we formed a committee and began working hard to bring about changes in the methods and approaches to the teaching of social work. During the Allende years I was the president of the National Association of the Schools of Social Work. There were eleven such schools at that time. I also helped to make some major changes in the social work curriculum at my own university here in Valparaíso. This new program was passed and implemented, although it still needed some fine-tuning and minor revisions.

Following the power grab in 1973 the military regime immediately shut down the School of Social Work. They claimed that it was not a school but a training ground for subversives. All of us lost our jobs; right after the coup we were fired from our positions at the university. It was a very difficult time for all of us. Everything that we had worked so hard to establish was eliminated overnight.

It is true that some of the most politically committed students studied in our program. They were interested in our innovative methodology, in the new courses we were offering, and in our broad, global approach to analyzing Chile's social problems. Our program was similar in its philosophy and methodology to the popular, democratic pedagogies developed by Brazilian social scientists such as Paulo Freire and Paulo Tarzo. We had a reputation for being the most avant-garde, progressive school of social work in the country, so it was logical that progressive students were interested in studying in this new program.

When my colleagues and I had attended Latin American social work conferences, we discovered that in Brazil, Argentina, Ecuador, and other countries, new approaches to social work were being discussed and sometimes implemented. It was very reassuring to discover that what we had been developing, based on our own experience, was not far-fetched nor completely off the wall. On the contrary, our work resembled what was being done on a grassroots level in other countries with similar social conditions and social problems. Naturally, our *compañeros* at work tended to be leftist; some were revolutionaries, and many of those who started out as centrist Christian Democrats ended up identifying themselves with Allende and the left. The Popular Unity government was the political channel that was serving the economic, educational, and cultural needs of the marginal populations. So when it came time to vote, almost all of us social workers voted for Popular Unity and other leftist political parties. These parties proposed policies that would help the marginal sectors, whereas the centrist and right-wing parties defended the interests of the rich at the expense of the poor. We voted for the candidates who supported our work with the *poblaciones* and who were committed to funding projects that would help the poor.

I discovered that there is a fine line between political science and social science. Thus, I really wasn't surprised when the military regime eliminated our school after the coup. It was logical that the fascist government would consider our work dangerous and subversive. Many of our best students in the School of Social Work during the Allende administration had come to us from other disciplines such as engineering, education, mathematics, and architecture. They switched to the School of Social Work because of their political convictions. Many were committed Communist Party members and had experience as militants and political activists. These students sought meaningful careers devoted to the service of the marginal sectors in Chile. This level of commitment on the part of students was very rewarding for us as professors and beneficial to the school as a whole. For the first time the male enrollment increased substantially in our program. Since social work had traditionally been considered a woman's profession in Chile, there were never many male students in our program until Allende was elected.

That was a very difficult period for me personally. For ten to twelve years I slept only about four hours a night, trying to juggle work, time with my children, and the domestic chores. My ex-husband paid for the children's education, but I didn't want to accept more financial help from him. In Latin America, as in many patriarchal societies, it is common for a man to maintain absolute control over the running of the home if his wife is financially dependent upon him. Given the life choices I had made, I wanted to be independent and to have control over the day-to-day running of my home. I insisted on taking most of the responsibility for the kids. Sure, my ex-husband would visit the children and take them out whenever he pleased, but it was very important for me to be financially independent and to manage my own household.

During this period, I was also responsible for supervising twenty-five student interns in Calera. They were working in the industrial sector, and this was a marvelous experience for me. I was learning and growing—and then suddenly everything came to an abrupt halt after the bloody coup. What I felt is indescribable! It was as though part of me died when the military took over. Since my association with Allende's campaign and with the marginal sectors had been so close, I felt the huge loss that these people suffered when everything that had been accomplished during the three years of the Popular Unity government was taken away from them. Our achievements seemed to evaporate into thin air overnight.

The popular sectors had put tremendous effort into the Allende campaign. They sold *empanadas* [meat pies] and did all kinds of things to raise funds so they could make posters and distribute propaganda for the elections. When the support for the Popular Unity government rose to 40 percent of the population, that was a crucial turning point. The conservatives became terrified and organized an aggressive opposition to Allende's government. Instead of losing support, the Popular Unity government was gaining, and had already won the parliamentary elections in March. Why? What was happening? The men and women in the slums and shantytowns began to say, "We never had shoes before Allende was elected; we never went to school before Allende was elected; we couldn't even afford to buy milk for our children before Allende was elected." I remember attending a community meeting in Cemento Melón, where a man stood up and began to speak, his voice trembling: "I have worked here at Cemento Melón for forty years, and this is the first time anybody ever asked me what I thought about my work. Now, with the change in government, I go to workers' meetings where what I have to say is taken seriously. For the first time ever, I'm treated with respect and dignity, as a man whose ideas are important." His voice broke and his eyes filled with tears. For the first time in forty years this man felt he had been treated like a human being on the job. We were all very moved by his comments. These were the kinds of things that took place every day during the Popular Unity government. I witnessed the homeless squatters take over buildings and occupy them. This was how they claimed their right to decent housing.

I will never forget the nightmare of September 11, 1973, the day of the bloody coup. I remember that tragic day so vividly. I sensed the darkness that would follow. I'm not a historian, but I knew there are thousands of examples in history of terrible repression following the attempts of people to liberate themselves by means of more democratic governments and liberal reforms. For example, the military coup in Guatemala in 1954, also financed and orchestrated by the CIA, followed the land reform of

Jacobo Arbenz's liberal government. Arbenz expropriated the land previously owned by the United Fruit Company. And there is the more recent case of Nicaragua in the 1980s. The U.S.-financed contra war was designed to crush the revolutionary Sandinista regime. And there was the invasion of Granada in 1984 to overthow another progressive regime. These are just a few examples in recent Latin American history of periods of economic and social transformation interrupted by military intervention and the extreme repression of the civilian population.

The day of the coup, we weren't allowed to leave the house, and for three days there was a state of siege here in Valparaíso. Varparaíso is located on the road to Santiago. The soldiers patrolled the area all day long with huge machine guns. I'm telling you, you just saw those weapons and sighed, "My God!" I spent those first days following the coup here in the garden, surrounded by my children, pacing back and forth like a dog in a cage. At this point I wasn't even angry yet; I still felt numb, just dead inside. And as my children and I were looking out the gate, we saw the police come and take away many of our neighbors. They were Communists, Socialists, other radical people, many who had been involved in social programs, and a lot of school teachers. I can't tell you exactly how many of our neighbors were detained and disappeared. But the repression was very systematic and calculated.

One day the National Police came and raided a particular neighbor's house. Since she and her husband were both Communists, the soldiers accused them of hiding weapons. I was so angry that I decided to go and try to help this family. As I jumped over the fence with my children, another neighbor warned me, "Mirta, be careful, your house has been marked with a cross. It is going to be raided, too." I thought of all my documents and papers that could be interpreted as subversive materials by the regime. I was extremely worried and frightened. I felt trapped. I decided I would try to explain that all these books and papers were science, history, and anthropology. But for the soldiers it's all the same—subversive and dangerous material that needs to be destroyed from the point of view of the barbaric military. Fortunately, they never did raid my home.

During those first two days following the coup, several of my students and others from the university came to my house seeking refuge. Some of the slum dwellers who were being persecuted also came to hide out at my home. It was very difficult; people didn't know where to hide, where they could find protection. And we had only a few hours to mobilize ourselves. We had to react immediately to save people from being killed by the regime. At this time, I began to feel rage at how my neighbors and people close to me were being abused and persecuted by the military. And of course, I had no idea of the full extent of the torture, the disappearances, the rapes, and the murder of tens of thousands in the days to follow! I didn't know that the National Stadium was full of people who had been taken away and held as prisoners.

One night a small child in our neighborhood who ran outside to see what was happening, and a young soldier, himself just a kid, got startled and shot at the little boy. The child was badly wounded and eventually died. Many young people, and even children, were persecuted by the National Police and the military. I left the back door open, thinking of the students and *compañeros* who might come here to hide. And many students did come here, to my house. When I think about it now, in retrospect, it was crazy. I had six of my own children to protect, and I was taking an enormous risk. I don't know if I would do today what I did back then. But in all honesty, I couldn't think twice about helping these people, because they were going to be killed if we didn't hide them and help them flee the country.

When they finally lifted the state of siege, I found out that two of my students had been detained. I went to look for them. The week before, one of my students from Norway came to tell me that her husband had been murdered. She was devastated. I began to see how people whom I knew, and who were close to me, were disappearing. It's a long, painful story!

Immediately following the coup I became active in the struggle for human rights because my students came to me seeking help. Some had been tortured and described to me in chilling detail what had been done to them. Many of my students came here to my home to tell me what had happened to them. All the female students had been raped! If the military suspected them of having been involved in any sort of revolutionary activity, they took them prisoner and raped and tortured them. It was so brutal and barbaric. I saw open sores on their breasts where many of the young women had been burned with cigarettes. I had to take care of their wounds and sores so that they wouldn't get infected. The soldiers would stick bottles in their anuses and do all sorts of horrible things to hurt and humiliate them. Many young people came here with bruises and cuts, and I would nurse their injuries and hide them. I remember that those first months after the coup—September, October, November, even December—were such difficult months! I felt intense rage toward the military that had hurt and abused so many innocent victims. So many of my students were young, idealistic people who only desired to create a more humane, just world. Their only crime was wanting to help others!

In October 1973 an organization called the Pro-Peace Committee was established in Santiago. Catholic bishops from all the dioceses in Santiago, as well as Lutheran, Anglican, and Methodist clergymen all came together and said: "We cannot allow this violation of human rights to take place here in Chile." Regardless of their diverse political views—many of them weren't even Allende supporters—they all united in denouncing the violence against the civilian population and agreed that they could not allow these atrocities to continue. So that is how the Pro-Peace Committee was formed to help victims of the regime and to offer support to the families of the disappeared and the detained.

I remember one day my ex-husband stopped by the house and saw some of the people I was hiding here. He was worried about the kids and decided to take them on a camping trip to the south of Chile for a few months. The courts had shut down, and he had some vacation time. So during the months of January and February 1974 I was able to go to Santiago and work directly with Pro-Peace Committee in the building on the corner of Quintero and Pascua. And finally, in March, we established a branch of the Committee of Cooperation for Peace [COPACHI] here in Valparaíso. I was very active in the creation of this branch.

Two of my *compañeras* who had also been fired from their jobs at the university were living here with me at the time. One of them was separated from her husband and had two children to support. They stayed here and helped out with the Pro-Peace Committee. We took turns cooking, cleaning, ironing, and taking the children to school. Since all three of us were unemployed, we started making pies to sell them at the Naval School and doing other odd jobs in order to survive. I still have the letter from the university saying that I had been dismissed because I had supported Allende's government, and my views and philosophy weren't compatible with those of the university.

After all those years of service the university didn't offer us a pension or even severance pay. How were we supposed to survive and support our families? Following the military takeover I had enough money to get by until September 30; after that, nothing. I had no other income. I had a large Toyota that could hold about ten people, so I began a "taxi" service to earn some money for food and the bare necessities.

I remember that one day a friend of mine named Miguel Bustos, a priest, stopped by to visit me. He had been working in Calera, where he participated in JAP[6] and had done some community organizing in Cerro Placeres. He told me that the police had been following him, but that he had nothing to hide. His friends and I told him to protect himself and not to show up at the police station for interrogation. But he went there anyway, and they killed him! They took him to Lebu and tortured him using electric shock. We found out much later when another priest also a friend of ours, came to visit us. He too had been detained at Lebu, where there was a ship used for torture. He told us that they had tortured Miguel Bustos to death! These were the kinds of horrible atrocities that we witnessed and experienced for many years.

For a long time, I worked in the statistics section of the Pro-Peace Committee; we gathered information about *compañeros* who had been assassinated. There were falsified accounts of confrontation with the military, but all of them had bullet wounds in their backs. I became very familiar with the Law of Escape, frequently used by the military to justify the murder of political prisoners. It was now 1975, and the government demanded that the Catholic Church shut down the Pro-Peace Committee. I don't know exactly what happened within the Church hierarchy, but the committee was closed down and a new organization, the Vicaría de la Solidaridad, was founded. The Vicaría provided legal defense to people who had been persecuted by the regime—but it defended only those members of the opposition to the dictatorship who were never engaged in armed struggle.

Among the people actively involved in the formation of the Committee in Defense of the Women's Rights [CODEM] were Rafael Maroco, a priest; Blanca Regina, a nun who worked at the Vicaría and had previously worked in the Pro-Peace Committee; and Fabiola Letelier, who had gained international recognition after her husband was assassinated in Washington.[7] All of them agreed that even in a dictatorship, *everyone* ought to have the right to defend him- or herself and to be protected. That is how CODEM was born.

At this time I went to England on a scholarship. When the Pro-Peace Committee shut down, I had once again found myself unemployed. I had a friend who organized trips to Argentina for people who were going into exile, and I had gone on three of these trips when they finally arrested me. The Secret Service interrogated me, asking me all kinds of questions and even threatening to come for my children. It was so frightening that they knew every detail about me: where I had been, what work I had done, and even everything about my private life. So I took advantage of the opportunity to go to England, with a scholarship. I was there for four and a half years and returned with my youngest son while my other five children stayed in England until they finished their college degrees.

While I was there, I worked to establish a Center for Latin American refugees in London. It was very important for us to maintain our cultural identity while living in exile, because we all experienced a profound sense of culture shock. Most of us had gone through similar experiences, and it was helpful and cathartic for us to get together for social and cultural events. There was a strong sense of solidarity with our Latin American *compañeros* from Argentina, Uruguay, Brazil, Peru, and Ecuador. Most of them had followed the events leading up to the coup d'état in Chile and had supported the political reforms of the Popular Unity government.

When I came back to Chile, my youngest son studied at Santa María University. He formed part of a group of rebellious student activists and was sent into internal exile in the south of Chile the same year that my daughter Laly died. She had graduated with a degree in sociology in England and then had come back to Chile in February 1984. The following December she died when the bicycle she was riding exploded. The circumstances surrounding her death remain a mystery. I still have not recovered from this. I'm still in anguish. I haven't been able to recover psychologically and emotionally from this terrible personal loss. I will always suffer from Laly's absence. This pain in my heart will never go away.

Even after my daughter's death, I continued to work as the executive secretary of CODEM here in Valparaíso. We became more active in the defense of students who had been persecuted by the dictatorship; we worked closely with a student organization called the National Union of Democratic Students [UNED], which was active throughout Chile. CODEM also defended the human rights of the slum dwellers. I employed the same approach and methodology that we had used in the School of Social Work. I went out into the shantytowns and gave short seminars and classes on the abuses of human rights under Pinochet. We started a local newsletter here in Valparaíso and also a national newsletter that was distributed throughout the country. It discussed issues and analyzed what was happening in the country. This bulletin was very educational, very general and accessible to everyone, and it contributed to the organization of the working class in the growing nationwide resistance to the dictatorship. This was in 1983 or 1984 here in Valparaíso; the bulletin began earlier in Santiago, in 1982.

I think it was very important that we began to organize the opposition, because we were all so repressed and suffering so much. It was important that we began to talk to one another about what was happening and to realize that we had a right to rebel against the injustices being perpetrated on the civilian population. We reread the United Nations Universal Declaration of Human Rights; Article 5 in the Preamble says that people, as a nation, have the right to use arms if they are mistreated or repressed by their government. This was how the people began a popular, armed opposition movement. There was less of a climate of terror by then; the political parties once again became stronger and more organized in resistance to the regime; and people gradually became a little less fearful to get involved in some form of grassroots opposition movement. This is, of course, just my own analysis, from my perspective as a CODEM leader.

Both men and women participated in CODEM, but it began primarily with the women, and women have the leadership role. I had never before been in a situation where women were the leaders. I had never been executive secretary or national president of any organization before this. I had been involved in social groups, not political groups. The women who began to organize in the shantytowns were also the first ones to get involved in the human rights movement, and then later the men joined in and supported them. That was more or less the process. Among the labor organizations the leadership was mostly male. Among the student organizations the leadership was mixed; there was a good balance of male and female student activists in leadership roles. The women's grassroots organizations coincided with the international feminist movement. Many different kinds of women's organizations were formed in different sectors of the society.

CODEM contributed significantly to the educational processes related to the best ways to organize and recruit people for the human rights struggle in Chile, and so forth. And then CODEM also participated in a group that was formed to diagnose and treat victims of torture, because at this time we began to see the psychological and emotional trauma that the survivors of torture were suffering. This service is still being provided by CODEM throughout the country. (What happened here in Chile is that after MIR broke up into splinter groups, CODEM also divided, and smaller groups were formed.[8] We went through some very difficult times trying to defend the political prisoners who were still in jail, because we were more isolated and weaker after the organization split into smaller groups.)

I had to resign from my position as national director of CODEM because I had a car accident and broke my back. I was bedridden and unable to move at all for more than seven months. I withdrew from the world for a long time. It was very difficult for me to recover from the accident, and suffering so much after Laly's death made it even harder. Once I was able to move around again, I did do some research here at the Casa de la Mujer, a women's community center that provides social services and does research on women's issues here in Chile. But it was virtually impossible for me, because I had to go out into the *poblaciones* in the hills, and with the changes in temperature I was in excruciating pain.

Now I'm doing much better, and I'm currently working with a program designed to help those political prisoners who were released and are suffering from physical or mental problems. This program was proposed by the Ministry of Health and financed by the Aylwin government with the reparation funds that were allotted to victims and families of the detained and disappeared. I was interested in working with this program so I sent my résumé. It was very important for me to show my *compañeros* and *compañeras* that they were not alone, and that even though there had been a change of government, we were still with them and cared about all they had gone through in prison. The program is designed to help them recuperate from the trauma they suffered so that they can begin to work again and to reintegrate into society. I'm not exactly sure what kind of work I want to do next. I know that it will be something committed to improving society and helping others, but I still need to give it much more thought before speaking about these plans.

All my children became socially and politically conscious. Blanca studied sociology from the perspective of the transformation of Latin American societies through the unification of different countries with similar social problems. I have two more daughters who were born after Laly— my daughter who was killed mysteriously when a bomb exploded near her bicycle. Pati, who is living in Germany, also studied sociology; she is interested in working with victims who were traumatized by torture during the dictatorship. And my youngest daughter is a historian. The official history of Latin America is in need of revision, and she understands the importance of studying history from the perspective of those who have been humiliated, massacred, and oppressed and yet rise up again and continue their struggle of more than five hundred years. My two youngest sons are very different. One is an industrial engineer who lives in Italy, and the other is a civil engineer. The latter was the rebellious student activist who was expelled from the university and sent into internal exile in the south of Chile. Well, he finally went back to school and finished his studies.

There hasn't been a real return to democracy in Chile since the plebiscite that said "NO" to Pinochet. The most pathetic thing, in my opinion, is that we denounced the Constitution of 1980 for such a long time, and we are still stuck with that same constitution; we denounced the Supreme Court, and the same court members are still in power. The same actors who staged the military coup are still running the country. And the army is still powerful, with the same protagonist, Pinochet, as commander in chief. Contreras is still in a position of power without having received any punishment for the heinous crimes for which he is responsible. The Secret Police, the *Central Nacional de Información* [National Center of Information, CNI] and the *Dirección Nacional de Inteligencia* [Directorate of National Intelligence, DINA] remain intact and untouched.[9] How can they speak of democracy? What a farce! We have the same economic model that was imposed during the dictatorship. We have the same poverty and health problems, so please don't try to come and tell me that this is a democratic solution. Honestly, it is a pity. And I can't tell you right now what the best solution would be. The moment you begin to criticize or denounce the policies of the present government, you are labeled a "nonconformist" or "intolerant" or "out of touch with reality" or "lacking a practical approach" to the transition toward full democracy.

In my opinion, this is pathetic! The State Department has been perfectly successful in Chile: Chile no longer has a dictator, yet it continues with the same economic policies that serve the national interests of the United States. There are laws in Chile to keep this economic model intact, and there is a parliament that has the appearance of having been democratically elected. And all this functions to serve the interests of the foreign economic model that has been imposed upon us. I'm telling you, this makes my blood boil! And to see how we Chileans accept this "transition to democracy" without questioning or analyzing the reality of the situation! There is a definite need for a new social movement denouncing this sham. Right now I'm in a support group with other *compañeros* who feel the same way I do. And there must be many people, both young and old, who are experiencing similar frustrations regarding the general decline of the Latin American left. There is a general feeling of apathy, and a profound sense of impotence and helplessness among many former activists in leftist organizations and political parties. We need to begin to rethink things at a grassroots level, to talk with people, both educated and uneducated, and to think seriously about new solutions to our current problems. The old paradigms no longer correspond to the present-day reality, and we need to develop new models in order to fight back!

ꜛꜛꜛꜛꜛꜛꜛꜛꜛꜛ *12* ꜛꜛꜛꜛꜛꜛꜛꜛꜛꜛꜛ
Elena Pinilla

DOMESTIC WORKER AND POLITICAL MILITANT

Elena Pinilla (1993).

I interviewed Elena Pinilla at the home of Alicia Oyarsún in Valparaíso. I had gone to Oyarsún's house to interview her about her involvement in human rights activities, and she introduced me to Pinilla, who works for her as a housekeeper. After a conversation of several hours with Pinilla, I asked her if she would allow me to record her life story for my book on women activists in Chile. She agreed and offered a powerful, moving testimony.

Elena Pinilla is a miner's daughter who left home as a young teenager, and by the time she was only seventeen years old, she was the mother of three small children. Despite her courage and militancy in the struggle for human rights in Chile, she is a modest, unassuming woman. Her testimony is compelling and poignant; although she risked everything by participating in the armed struggle against Pinochet, she expresses remorse for not having done more and for the years that she was politically unaware. She narrates a dramatic story about how she was transformed from an apolitical, lower-middle-class housewife into a Frente de Liberación Nacional (National Liberation Front, or FLN) militant who fought in the clandestine armed movement against the military regime.[1]

Elena Pinilla is separated from her husband; she works cleaning other people's houses and cares for her emotionally disturbed adult daughter, who still lives at home. But she has not abandoned her dream of a new Chilean society based on social justice and gender equality. As she points out, Chile's patriarchal judicial system still does not allow a Chilean woman to divorce legally or to travel outside the country without her husband's permission.[2]

My name is Elena Pinilla and I was born in 1952 in a mining town on the outskirts of Valparaíso. My father was a miner, just as my grandfather had been. Since my dad was a miner, I could have developed a social consciousness at a young age, but I didn't. I had a happy childhood. At the Melón cement mines in Polpaico, I do recall that sometimes there were miners' strikes there, and I remember a dramatic difference in the quality of housing between the miners and the managers: miners lived in overcrowded two-room apartments, and owners and managers lived in what we called *chalets*, spacious two-story houses with several bathrooms. These were the kinds of class differences that I did notice.

When I was still a child, my father became ill with black lung, the miners' disease, and was fired from his job! My dad was still a young man when he became ill; I don't think he was more than thirty-six. The pension they gave him wasn't enough for us to live on, but with this money he was able to buy a small plot of land in Santiago. We moved to San Felipe, because my grandfather had a house there, and went to live out in the countryside at Quebrada Herreranos, where my father planted and harvested, trying to eke out a meager living as a small farmer. When I was twelve years old, my parents sent me to Valparaíso to live with my great-aunt.

After I finished sixth grade, I was working during the day as a domestic servant and attending night school. But then I got pregnant, and my life changed drastically. I was so inexperienced; I didn't have anyone to teach me how not to get pregnant. I was only thirteen, was just a child myself. I couldn't imagine myself as a mother, with the responsibility of raising a child. When my daughter was born on November 27, 1966, I had just turned fourteen. This was very difficult for me to face. I felt all alone and didn't have anyone to turn to for help.

In fact, I was all alone during this pregnancy. My aunt threw me out of the house, and I didn't have anywhere to go. I couldn't let my parents find out because they would have been devastated. I was so frightened. I went on cleaning houses and then would sneak into a friend's house at night to sleep there. Before the baby was born I married the father. We went to live with his aunt, and our daughter was born there. Within a year a second child, our first son, was born, and after that we had another boy. I was only seventeen and already the mother of three children. When I think about it now, it was because I didn't have any guidance in my life. I was all alone. I just did what I thought was best for me. And my opportunities and options were very limited.

My husband worked at the post office here in Valparaíso. I stayed home taking care of our three children. I also raised my niece; when my sister got divorced she wasn't able to take care of her daughter, so she came to live with us. Then I began to work at a vegetable stand near the house and would run home to check on the kids. We couldn't afford to hire a babysitter, so I had to leave them alone. My daughter took care of the younger children. I lived a very sheltered life; I was unaware of social issues and uninterested in what was happening in the world. I was just concerned about myself and my family. And since we were comfortable and not lacking any of the basic necessities, I didn't have to worry about not having food to eat or money to buy clothes for the children.

When my older son was about fourteen or fifteen, he would some-times be gone for a long time without telling me where he had been. I began to worry about him. I realized that he had become involved in pol-itics and was participating in a leftist political party. I found out that he was a member of the Young Communist League, La Jota, and I was very scared.[3] But it was because of my son's involvement in politics that I started to realize what was going on all around me with the detained and the disappeared in Chile. My son began to talk to me and explain things to me. He told me not to worry about him because he was doing some-thing that was meaningful to him: "Mom, you know my *compañero* Roberto; his father is a political prisoner. My other friend Manuel's father was killed by the military." This was how I began to become aware of what was happening, and I really suffered to think that these horrendous atrocities had been committed against innocent civilians. That was how I began to come out of my shell.

It may seem hard for you to believe, but I really hadn't heard anything about the disappeared and the political prisoners in Chile before this, until 1980 or 1981, some seven or eight years after the coup. No, I honestly didn't know anything about the disappeared, the tortured, the political prisoners, the exiled.

These are the memories I have of September 11, 1973, the day of the coup. I remember getting up early to take the kids to the dentist, and the military wouldn't let me leave the house. I asked them why, and they told me that the Allende government had been overthrown. I turned the radio on to see what had happened, because I had always liked Allende. My father had voted for Allende, all of my family voted for Allende; I liked him because he was the president of the poor, as far as I was concerned. And I didn't think any more about it. I heard the bombing on the radio and the violence had a terrible impact on me, but then I just shut out everything and remained concerned only about my immediate family.

I did go to visit my father in Santiago on September 13. There was a curfew, and you had to be back home by five o'clock in the evening. I took the train to Santiago, and near the Mapocho station I saw many corpses in the Mapocho River. You can't tell me that there weren't any dead bodies there, because I saw them with my own eyes! I was very scared. I went to my parents' house and they were fine. Then I went to see my younger sister, who was an activist in the La Jota, very politically committed. I remember helping her burn papers and documents that could be used against her if the soldiers raided her apartment and found them. My sister's face was all black and blue and terribly swollen. She told me that she had had a fight with a girlfriend and I believed her. It wasn't until years later that she confided to me that she had been raped by the soldiers on September 12. They raped her in front of the student housing at the university. They ripped off her clothes, and they raped her repeatedly and beat her till she was all bruised and bleeding. She was only nineteen years old at the time, and too frightened and ashamed to say anything to anyone. This was especially traumatic for my sister, because we had been brought up peacefully in the countryside. We were very innocent and had never been exposed to violence like this before.

When my son became active in La Jota and talked to me about the detained and the disappeared and political prisoners. I began to understand many things that I hadn't really noticed or understood before, like the ways in which we were being repressed by the regime, and how many people didn't even have enough to eat. Slowly but surely, I began to develop a political awareness. My son told me that he was going to take me to the Human Rights Commission here in Valparaíso. I hadn't even known that this agency existed. I went, and he introduced me to some wonderful, caring people. I was eager to learn more about what had happened to them and to others. They began to tell me stories about how their children had been murdered by the regime, or had been disappeared, or were being held prisoner, and my heart went out to them. I met people who were militants in the Communist Party.

I felt an affinity for the Communist Party because my grandfather had been a militant in it, working with the peasants in Renca. I remember that they were often hiding up in the hills, and my grandmother would have to go up there to take them food and other provisions. But I was very young then and really didn't understand what was going on. Anyway, as I was telling you, my son introduced me to Communist Party members and I started to get a political education.

Actually, very soon I became active in the armed resistance to the dictatorship. I participated in what was called a combat unit. We received military training, learning how to load and unload a gun, how to make and use bombs, how to use dynamite, and so on. And then they would take us out into the countryside to practice using weapons. Later, we would bomb the electrical lines at the military headquarters.

I remember once we were in the middle of a "mission" and I was armed with a rifle when a *carabinero* walked by. I was hiding behind some bushes and was so quiet that you couldn't even hear me breathe. I knew that if the cop saw me I would have to kill him. I had never been so terrified in my life. Yet I knew that if it was necessary I would have to shoot, because it would be either him or me. One of us would have to die, and I was certain that it wasn't going to be me. I knew that I had to stay alive, because I was needed here to continue our struggle. We took a lot of risks and were exposed to many dangerous life-or-death situations. But at the moment I had to act, I was always able to become cold and detached in order to carry out my mission.

My husband didn't know anything about my political involvement in the clandestine movement or my participation in the armed struggle. Actually, he didn't even have a clue about any of it. I had to be very secretive. He never found out anything about our son's participation, either. From about 1980, though my husband and I still lived in the same house, we were already separated and had separate bedrooms. That made it easier for me to sneak out at night when I had to take part in some operation. I remember that one night, when it was already very dark outside and I left through the back door, I heard somebody. I was so scared. But then I heard my son's voice: "Mom, Mom, don't worry. It's me." And we both immediately understood that each of us had our duty to perform. And that understanding was stronger than any fear I may have felt for him as his mother or the fear he may have felt for me as my son. We just hugged each other, and we both laughed, because he thought that I was asleep and I thought that he was asleep, yet we were both sneaking out of the house at the same time to perform a mission. It was funny. We laughed, and then my son whispered to me: "Mom, you know what you have to do, and it's important, and I also know what I have to do." And we said goodnight and went our separate ways to carry out our tasks. And this pretty much sums up my participation in the military unit. After that, the Secret Police [CNI] began to follow me constantly, and I had to withdraw from these activities and from my participation in the Communist Party.

Then I began to work actively in the Human Rights Commission here in Valparaíso, [Agrupación de los Familiares de los Presos Políticos, Exiliados, y de Ejecutados]. At that time there were a number of political prisoners, and we were working for their release. There was so much work to be done; I was active in educating and informing people about the political prisoners. We planned protests and demonstrations. We made posters and banners with pictures of the prisoners and their names and the dates they had been detained. We participated in hunger strikes to show our solidarity with the political prisoners and their families. The families of the prisoners felt isolated and all alone. Nobody seemed to care about their suffering.

During the years I worked with the Commission, 1986–87 there were approximately fifty political prisoners here in Valparaíso. There was so much work to be done at that time. It was right before the plebiscite that would finally bring an end to the Pinochet dictatorship. I remember the first march we organized from Valparaíso to Santiago, in order to draw attention to the issue of the political prisoners. This march was so successful that we planned another. In the second one we walked the entire way, and so many people joined us along our route that by the time we got to Santiago, we had become a river of people! That is why it is so discouraging to compare the apathy and lack of participation now with the tremendous fervor and passionate involvement of many Chileans during the final years of the dictatorship. The opposition movement was so strong and widespread that we had great hope for real changes in the future! But it didn't work out that way. Now there is a general atmosphere of political apathy on the part of the younger generation; they don't want to have anything to do with politics. And many older people just want to forget about the past, to bury it and get on with their private lives.

Let me tell you about when we occupied the jail. I took part in organizing the occupation of the jail by the families and relatives of the political prisoners here in Valparaíso. Did you know that this was the first place ever in history, anywhere in the world, that family members occupied and took control of a jail or a prison? I was one of the people who spent the night there. It is very exciting to think that we made history with that event.

During visiting hours my godson, Lautaro González, who was one of the prisoners, asked me: "Elena, can you stay here all day and spend the night here?" And I told him, "Yes, sure I could." It was all planned so that when the prisoners signaled to us, we would all enter at the same time. They were able to disarm the guards in just a few minutes. And we all stayed in the jail from about 5:00 P.M. until the following day. The governor and other officials came, trying to convince the families to leave the jail, but we refused to budge. It was very emotional because for the first time in many years the families of the political prisoners were able to spend some time together. But we were also very frightened because the military threatened to remove us by force. It would have been possible for them to massacre us and then to say that it was in self-defense, since we were hiding arms. The *milicos* [soldiers] often justified their homicide with those kinds of lies. But we resisted, and I'm proud of that.

It's funny, but I don't think my ex-husband ever found out I was involved in taking over the jail. But I was seeing someone else at the time, and when *he* saw the morning paper and read the headlines about the jail in Valparaíso being occupied by the families of the political prisoners, he thought to himself, "I wouldn't be surprised if Elena is involved in this." And sure enough, when he turned to the next page, he saw my picture!

It was very sad to see how the political prisoners lived. The conditions were terrible. The small and overcrowded cells had tiny windows from which you could only see other prison cells. The bunkbeds barely fit; in a cell where there should have been only one bed, there were four beds cramped together. And then the stench was disgusting. They had communal bathrooms with showers, but there was only cold water, and winters are very cold here in Chile. At first the political prisoners had been put together with the regular inmates who were charged with criminal offenses, but finally the families of the detainees were able to get them moved to a separate part of the jail where they could lead somewhat more normal lives. They could read, exercise, and receive visitors. Their conditions were much better than those of the other inmates, but they were still definitely overcrowded, and that created a lot of tension and stress. Many of them belonged to different political factions and had different ideologies. Some had been imprisoned for merely distributing pamphlets; others had been accused of more severe acts such as killing police officers. So there was a diverse group of prisoners with different temperaments, and sometimes there were conflicts among them.

What saddens me most is that nothing has really changed in Chile. If you read the newspapers or listen to the news, you will discover that there is still repression in this country. Behind this so-called democratic government you find Pinochet, and Contreras, and a whole band of assassins. They still hold positions of power; as you know, Pinochet is still commander in chief of the armed forces.[4]

The recent elections [December 1993] here in Chile demonstrate that we are a country without a memory. What happened during the seventeen years of the fascist dictatorship was that the regime killed off most of the leadership of the left, and other progressive people were forced into exile. That is how we became a nation without a sense of political consciousness. I am grateful to my son for making me aware. I'm also ashamed, because I am his mother; it should have been me who taught him. But instead, he taught me and made me open my eyes to the reality that surrounded me but that I didn't see. Or, perhaps, that I didn't want to see. I'm telling you, honestly, I am so ashamed of all those years that I lived unaware and untouched by the state terror imposed by the regime. I often ask myself, "How could you have lived like that for so long? How was it possible for you to live in your own little world, Elena, and not care about what was happening to your brothers and sisters here in Chile?" To tell you the truth, it is very difficult for me to live with my guilty conscience. To think that so many thousands of my *compañeros* and *compañeras* died and were disappeared, and I just turned my head the other way, preferring not to know what was going on.

I don't remember exactly how many, but there are still some political prisoners in Santiago. If this were a democracy, do you think that we would still have political prisoners? It's already 1993 and Pinochet is no longer the dictator, so why are there still political prisoners? How can they say that Chile has changed?

The average Chilean worker still isn't able to support his or her family with the current low wages. The minimum wage is about $150.00 a month; but when you go to the grocery store you find that the prices for food are so high that a family of five cannot eat on this amount of money.

You can buy potatoes, bread, pasta, and tea, but you can't afford to buy fruit, milk, cheese, or meat—all the foods that are necessary for a balanced diet. Our reality today is one in which the poor are getting poorer and the rich are getting richer. If you take a bus up into the shantytowns in the hills, you will find people living in shacks and suffering extreme poverty. There are thousands of kids dying of curable diseases because they don't have access to proper medical care. I am poor, but you will find people who are much poorer, people who don't have anything to eat, people who live in shacks without running water, without indoor plumbing or a kitchen. The level of poverty has increased in Chile. I don't understand much about the economy, but I do know that the standard of living of the poor has gotten worse.

For example, my son is now married and has two beautiful daughters. But in order for his family to survive, he had to quit school and is now working at two different full-time jobs. It would be impossible for him to pay the bills if he were working only one job, because the wages are so low and the prices of food and everything else are so high. There is also a problem with day care: since they can't afford it, my daughter-in-law must stay home with the children. The baby is only one year old. And they are a typical working-class family that is barely getting by.

Chile is still a sexist society. Women are still treated as second-class citizens. I wish there could be some real changes with respect to women's liberation here in Chile. Please excuse my language, but in my opinion the government doesn't give a shit about women. For example, we don't have a law protecting married women who are unhappy, or physically or emotionally abused in their marriages. According to the law they are stuck in these terrible marriages, because divorce is still illegal. Abortion is also still illegal. If a young teenager makes a mistake and gets pregnant, she is forced to have an unwanted child. You have to be rich to afford an abortion in Chile, and even then, if you get caught you can be put in jail. If you aren't able to raise a child for economic or any other reasons, Chilean law still forces you to have the baby.[5] Even if it wasn't planned or if you don't have the means to offer the child a decent standard of living, you must still have the baby. Even in cases where the mother is at risk of dying or has other health complications, she must still have the baby. The men who made these laws are obviously insensitive and indifferent to the reality of women's lives. These laws are very backward. Before we can speak about women's liberation in Chile, these laws need to be changed, allowing women the freedom to get divorced and the freedom to choose whether they want to bring another human being into this world.

What are some of my own dreams and aspirations? Well, I am forty-two years old and at this stage in my life, I am already going downhill. For people my age, especially here in Latin America, there aren't many opportunities; there isn't much possibility to dream about a better future. What dreams? If you haven't fulfilled them by now, then it is probably already too late. The plans I have are to continue working as I do now, cleaning in several private homes. I hope to save a little money for my old age. I would like to be able to save enough to buy a sewing machine so that I could work at home as a seamstress. Another of my dreams is to work with an organization that is dedicated to women's rights. But this is very difficult for me to do, because my daughter, who is twenty-seven, is mentally ill and I have to take care of her at home. She is severely depressed and blames me for all her problems. She complains that because of my political involvement in the Commission for Human Rights, I used to leave her home alone and she felt abandoned. Even though I explain to her that when I became active in this work she was already an adolescent, she refuses to understand! I tell her that if she wants to blame anybody she ought to blame the dictatorship and not me. But she doesn't seem to want to understand. There are many young people who have emotional problems as a consequence of all the years of repression here in Chile.

My other son is now twenty-five. Although he had leftist views when he was an adolescent, now he is very apolitical. Like so many of the youth in this country today, he doesn't want to have anything to do with presidents, elections, or political parties. All he cares about is working and maybe going out partying now and then. But he is fed up with politics and doesn't want to have anything to do with it!

All the terrible things I witnessed here in Chile during so many years of the military dictatorship left me feeling vulnerable and full of pain. I get emotional and cry very easily. But all this terror has also made me very strong, because I know that I'm capable of confronting almost any situation and surviving. Everything that I suffered, and that my *compañeros* suffered, made me stronger inside. I was able to mature and grow as a person as a consequence of my experiences; I also learned from and was enriched by the lives of so many other *compañeros* and *compañeras* who suffered from the violence and repression here in Chile. Each of us contributed a small grain of sand, and they all add up.

I hope that my story about how I changed from an apolitical housewife to a political activist may help other women to take an honest look at their own lives. Perhaps my testimony may inspire some woman to open her eyes and see what is going on in the world around her, instead of being blind to the suffering of others. I really hope so.

Alicia Oyarsún

MILITARY WIFE AND
MOTHER OF POLITICAL PRISONER

Alicia Oyarsún (1993), with a painting of streets in Valparaiso done by her son while a political prisoner.

I interviewed Alicia Oyarsún on December 17, 1993, at her home in Valparaíso. She lives in a large, older house with many rooms. On the walls of the living room, where we spoke, hung several paintings done by Oyarsún's son while he was detained as a political prisonor in Valparaíso.

Alicia Oyarsún is a robust, strong-willed, middle-aged woman of Mapuche descent. She is the wife of a retired naval officer and the mother of six children.

Oyarsún became active in the Agrupación de los Familiares de los Presos Politico's (Association of the Relatives of Political Prisoners) after her son Marcelo was detained in 1988. As she told the gripping story of her experience as the mother of a political prisoner, tears sometimes rolled down her cheeks; at other times she raised her voice, barely containing the rage that still remains.

Oyarsún tells of her transformation from a sheltered middle-class housewife into an activist deeply engaged in the struggle for human rights in Chile and arrested numerous times because of her militancy. But she expresses a sense of having been abandoned by the international solidarity groups that were active in the struggle against the Pinochet dictatorship. Oyarsún longs to continue her community service with the poor in Chile, especially with the women, but is limited by a lack of financial resources and a prevailing feeling of apathy among Chilean youth.

My name is Alicia Oyarsún. I am fifty-one years old. I would like to speak to you about three different stages in my life: my childhood, my married life, and my life after my son was taken prisoner. I remember my childhood as being rather sad and unhappy. My mother died when I was only eleven years old, and my father was a sailor who used to drink too much. Actually, he was an alcoholic who got violent and abusive when he was drinking. After my mother died, my dad left my three brothers and me with my grandparents. My grandparents are of indigenous descent; my grandmother was a Mapuche. I am proud to say I have Mapuche blood; my other last name is Canicura, a Mapuche name. I've always said that my strong, fighting nature comes from my Mapuche heritage. As you know, the Spanish colonizers were never able to conquer the Mapuches. They were great warriors and always resisted domination.

My brothers and I were living with my grandparents in the southern tip of Chile, in Punta Arenas, for a while. Then we returned to Puerto Montt, another small town also in the south of Chile. My grandparents were very poor and couldn't afford to take care of us, so they put us in an orphanage. I hated the orphanage and felt very lonely there. I think that since I suffered so much as a child, I became socially conscious very young and also felt compassion for people in pain.

I stayed at this orphanage for only two years and then I ran away when I was fifteen. I ran away because the German nuns who ran the school treated us very badly. They used to hit us and verbally abuse us. I came by myself to Valparaíso when I was only fifteen, and I began to do housework for a well-to-do family. When I was only sixteen, I got pregnant and had to get married. Nobody had ever taught me about birth control and how to keep from getting pregnant. So I ended up in a terrible marriage. My husband was very macho and physically abusive; I decided to leave him shortly after we were married. He used to beat me up, leaving me all black and blue. I remember he even hit me in the stomach when I was pregnant. I refused to let anybody abuse me, so I left him.

I worked and took care of my daughter for two, almost three years, until I met the man to whom I've been married for almost thirty years. My husband was in the armed forces, and we were transferred to Punta Arenas on the southern tip of Chile. We were very isolated for five years while my husband was stationed at a naval base in Puerto Williams, an island only thirty-six hours by boat from Antarctica.

We were still living in Puerto Williams when Allende was elected. I remember that I was happy when I heard the news. When I was a child my grandmother, who was a Socialist, used to tell me that someday a Socialist would be elected president. My grandma was a strong independent woman; she participated in clandestine meetings during the dictatorship of Ibáñez.

My husband and I came to Valparaíso in 1972. Everything here was in a state of confusion and chaos. One could sense that a military coup was imminent. There were shortages and long lines for food. The economy was in a state of crisis. After the coup in 1973 I remember thinking, "This is just one more military insurrection," and I didn't worry too much about it. Nobody close to me had been imprisoned or disappeared, so I wasn't aware of what was happening in the country. Since we always lived on military bases, I wasn't exposed to civilian life. I was very sheltered and unaware of Chile's political and economic reality. Mainly, I was devoted to caring for my husband and small children.

I do recall that several days after the coup my father-in-law, who was seventy years old and had been a member of the Communist Party all his life, came to me and said, "Alicia, the military are looking for me; they are going to detain me if they find me." I remember telling him to come hide at our house, because we were living on the naval base in Viña del Mar at the time. They would never have thought to look for him there.

Several years later, I remember asking my husband whether it was true that people were detained and disappeared here in Chile. He told me, "No, Alicia. Those are just lies." He said that the people who were claimed to be missing were probably living comfortably in exile somewhere outside the country. And so I believed him and didn't question things too much until about 1980, when my son and daughter, who were sixteen and seventeen at the time, became involved in politics. By 1983 the student protest movement against Pinochet had become very strong. Once in 1984, after a large student protest here in Valparaíso in front of the cathedral, my daughter was wounded in the head by the police. She was taken to the hospital in an ambulance and had to have eight stitches. My husband was very angry and told both Niza, our daughter, and Marcelo, our son, not to participate in any demonstrations because he would be thrown out of the navy immediately if his superiors found out. He told them he would retire with thirty years of service in just three more years, and that they should withdraw from their political activity until then. They did decrease their participation until January 1987, when their father retired from the navy. Then they both became openly involved in the growing opposition movement.

Of course, I worried a great deal about my children's political activities; I was afraid they might be detained or even killed by the repressive regime. But I told them that if they felt that they were doing the right thing, then I would respect their decision and support them. I started to become politically aware myself when three university professors in Santiago were decapitated. That horrendous event was a turning point for me; it made me realize just how brutal and terrible the repression was here in Chile! I remember very distinctly an argument between Marcelo and his father when Marcelo asked his dad, "How can you be so closed-minded not to understand that this is the truth? The military murdered and beheaded those three professors!"

After this chilling event I began to support my children's participation in the resistance and to protect them from their father. If he asked where they were, and I knew they were at a protest march or a meeting, I would lie in order to protect them. As a military man himself, he wasn't capable of understanding his children's commitment to their ideals and to the protest movement. After retiring from the navy, my husband went to work in the United States to support the family. He had been gone for several months and was coming home for a visit on May 5, 1988. After picking him up at the airport, we heard on the radio that a CNI officer named Roberto Andaur had been killed in Gómez Carreño, near Valparaíso. The first thing that came to my mind was, "Thank God! Marcelo didn't do it, because he was with us; we were all at the airport at the time of the murder." I was relieved that it wasn't Marcelo, because I knew those assassins would get revenge against whoever had killed Andaur.

The day my husband came home from Florida was his birthday. We celebrated with drinks—*pisco* sours—a cake, and balloons. We were all so happy to be reunited as a family! He had brought back gifts and new clothes for the children. That evening our son was invited out to a bachelor party; he told us he wouldn't come home to sleep and not to worry about him. We were exhausted and went to bed about 1:00 A.M. We were awakened from a deep sleep at about 4:30 or 5:00 A.M. by a loud noise. Armed navy personnel had forced open our front door and broken all the windows in the house. My husband jumped out of bed with only his boxer shorts on, and asked them, "What is going on here?" Excuse my language, but they just yelled at him, "Shut up, you mother fucker!" And then they threw him down and kicked him in the face. I heard my husband telling my son to surrender to them. I didn't realize what had happened. I hadn't heard Marcelo enter the house upon returning from the party, so I thought that the soldiers had followed him home. Our daughter Niza was shouting obscenities at the soldiers. They tied her up and took her away. This scene was horrible for my husband. The house was full of soldiers, and even his own fellow marines were now beating him, abusing him, and taking two of his children prisoner. Four Secret Police also accompanied them.

I couldn't believe what was happening! I was truly in a state of shock! I got on my knees and prayed to God: "No, not my children. Don't let them take my children away from me." I could see that my son was bleeding, and when I tried to console him a soldier put a machine gun in my face and said, "Where do you think you're going, bitch?" And he pushed me aside. It was such a horrible night! It was worse than my worst nightmare! My four-year-old daughter was screaming and crying. We were all terrified! They even took my seventy-year-old mother-in-law to the bathroom, where they interrogated her. They also pointed a machine gun at my niece, who was only ten years old, and then they took her to the kitchen and asked her for the names of my son's friends. The house was surrounded with armed navy personnel who were ready to shoot Marcelo if he tried to escape. Next, they brought in some boxes and showed me some black plastic bags. They told me, "Listen, lady, your son had these bags and they contain bombs." I replied, "That is a lie. These don't belong to my son, you just brought them here. I saw you bring them. You are trying to frame Marcelo." That cynical scumbag said that my word didn't count against his word. Then they began to raid the house and to steal everything of value from the closets and drawers. I had a gun that was registered and a rifle that was made in 1879, and they took both of them. They stole our stereo and all the money my husband had saved during the months he worked in the United States. It seemed as if the soldiers were here forever; it was after 7:00 A.M. when they finally left. They hauled away both Marcelo and Niza. I was trembling with fear and rage!

I remember that I had a huge fight with my husband, because he blamed me for the kids' involvement in "this mess." He said that he didn't want to have anything to do with them. And I told him that I would do everything possible to find them; I would go look for them, and I would get them back. There wasn't anything he or anyone could do to stop me. Then I went to the bathroom and I discovered my twelve-year-old daughter sobbing. I tried to comfort her. She was traumatized by the violence that her young eyes had witnessed. My poor baby remained withdrawn and introverted for a long time after this. I had to take her to see a child psychologist.

The first thing I did was go talk to my landlord. I knew I needed to explain to him what had happened before the neighbors told him anything. So I left the house at 8:15 A.M. and by 8:35 I had arrived at the office where this gentleman works. When I told him the story of the previous night, he was very kind and supportive. I just sobbed and sobbed and sobbed; he put his arms around me and tried to console me. I remember that when I was crying on the bus, a man asked me what was wrong and I told him. He said that he was shocked that the military could be so savage and so brutal!

The next thing I did was to go look for my children. First, I went to the parish church. They sent me to the bishop's office, where I got the address of the Human Rights Commission. Their office was located at 264 Blanco Street. I went there immediately and reported that my kids had been detained. After that, I went to the university where Marcelo had been studying. They already knew that Marcelo and Niza had been taken prisoner; some students had already made posters with their names on them, to be carried in a demonstration they were planning. I asked to speak to the chancellor, who I knew was a fascist. He seemed concerned about my children and told me that the university was investigating the matter. In fact, he made a phone call to an officer at the naval base, and they told him where my children were being detained. Thanks to that phone call, I found out where Marcelo and Niza were being held.

Of course, I went there immediately and demanded to see them. What hurt me most was to discover that they had been tortured. I'd had no idea that people were being interrogated and tortured like that. It was a shocking revelation. They interrogated my daughter all day Friday, Saturday, and Sunday; not until Monday was I finally able to see her at the naval base detention center. She was still blindfolded and had her hands tied behind her back. My poor daughter had been held in solitary confinement and not allowed to talk to anyone, not even to me, her mother. I don't know how she survived such abuse! The Red Cross would go visit the prisoners, but they didn't help at all. They would just say that the prisoners were fine and then leave. But from what I saw, this wasn't the case. I was their mother, I could see the open sores, the bruises, the visible traces of torture. How could the Red Cross say they were fine? I was ready to explode with rage!

They finally released my daughter on Tuesday, but Marcelo was kept there as a political prisoner. When I was allowed to see him, it was so terrible that I will never forget that day. The sight of my son was horrifying! I was heartbroken to see Marcelo like that. He was covered with blood from the wounds and beatings they had inflicted upon him. It was awful to see him like that! There are no words to describe the pain I felt! But I tried hard not to show how upset I was. I knew I had to be brave and strong for Marcelo, so he would have the strength to keep resisting.

The military had arrested about two hundred young people during that period, and they kept twenty political prisoners. Since my husband was a retired naval officer, they mounted a show. They called my husband in for a hearing, just to humiliate him. Marcelo told these military officers, "I have a mind of my own, and I think for myself. I don't think what my father tells me to think." And my husband just lowered his head in shame. It was very painful for him to see what his colleagues were doing to his own son. After thirty years of service to these people, and to see how cruelly they were treating his own son! Marcelo was then sent into solitary confinement for another twenty days. On May 21 they moved him to another cell, but he remained alone, isolated, and incommunicado.

Both my husband and I would go to the detention center every day to ask how Marcelo was doing and to take him some food—though we found out later that they never gave him any of it. By this time my husband was fully supportive of Marcelo and my efforts to get him released. I began to get involved in a human rights organization called Agrupación de los Familiares de los Presos Polítics [Association of the Relatives of the Political Prisoners]. Marcelo was detained as a political prisoner for three years! It was very difficult for us as a family, especially during the holidays like Christmas, New Year's, and Easter.

Marcelo was badly tortured while held as a prisoner. It was horrible what they did to him. When they used the electric shock in his mouth, he lost seven of his fillings. This was a very difficult period for me, because my husband went back to the United States to work, and I was left with all of the responsibility for raising our six children and managing the house. Also, my daughter Niza was being followed by the Secret Police constantly, so we sent her to Canada, where she remained in exile for three years. I don't know how God gave me the strength to carry on, with my son in prison and my daughter in exile in Canada. In addition, my youngest daughter broke her arm and was in the hospital for nineteen days.

As I was starting to tell you, Marcelo smiled one day and I could see that his gums were all swollen and red. I was so ignorant about methods of torture that I innocently asked him why his gums were bleeding. And then he told me about the electric currents they had used. I wanted to die, right then and there, from the pain I felt listening to him describe in chilling detail how he had been tortured! But I was strong and didn't cry in front of him. I knew that even if it killed me, I had to be strong for him. I would come every day and bring him chocolates. On his birthday, I brought him a big cake to share with the other prisoners.

Marcelo was still covered on my husband's insurance, so I decided to make an appointment to take him to see the naval dentist. The day of his appointment, I went to pick him up and eight soldiers with machine guns escorted him from prison to the clinic. He was handcuffed and also had his legs chained together. It was so sad for me to see him being treated like a criminal. Marcelo looked up at me and said, "Mom, hold your head up high. And don't be ashamed, because I'm not a delinquent. I haven't done anything wrong."

A few days later those bastards were beating Marcelo until they broke his kneecap and he needed to be hospitalized. He was in terrible pain for over a week, but none of the hospitals would treat him. When I went to talk to a chief administrator at one of the hospitals, he was extremely rude to me and threw me out of his office, shouting that he refused to treat "subversives" in his hospital. "Get out of here," he yelled at me, treating me worse than a dog. I raised my voice at him: "Tell me, whom did my son kill? Perhaps you, as a doctor, have killed people, because right now you are proving to me that you have violated the oath you took, promising to heal people. Perhaps you even work for the Secret Police and are one of the doctors who supervised the torture and interrogation of detainees." I left the hospital crying and went directly to the office of the Commission of Human Rights, and they were able to help me get Marcelo registered in another hospital. They operated on his knee. Just imagine, even though he had a cast that went from his ankle to his thigh, the soldiers had him fastened to the bed with two chains and four padlocks. It made me want to throw up! I was so angry, but felt helpless. There was nothing I could do to stop them from treating my son so badly. I wanted to die from rage and frustration.

At the time, I didn't have any extra money at all. We had a lot of financial problems and were barely getting by. I would try to save a little money by walking the thirty blocks each day, instead of taking the bus, when I went to visit Marcelo. If I had some spare change I would buy him a few cigarettes or chocolates—or a newspaper; since the soldiers would open and read all his mail, I would hide the letters that his father had sent him from the United States between the pages of the newspaper. I would write him letters too, telling him how much I loved him and supported and respected him for not abandoning his ideals and the struggle for justice.

I became more and more involved in the Agrupación de los Familiares without ever belonging to any political party nor espousing any particular political ideology. At first, it was difficult for me to leave the meetings and go out into the streets to confront the police at demonstrations. I was beaten up and taken prisoner many times. They would release us from jail after a few hours and then lock us up again. But we continued to attend demonstrations calling attention to the tens of thousands of detained and disappeared in Chile. We would go to each demonstration knowing beforehand that we would end up in jail! This was our way of resisting the dictatorship and informing others about the violation of human rights in our country.

I remember we went to Santiago to protest the presence of Patricio Guzmán, a fascist who was going to speak before the parliament that day. Ten of us were mothers of political prisoners from Valparaíso, and ten were mothers from other places. We put black hoods over our heads and joined hands as a form of protest. The police beat us with clubs and cursed at us, telling us that we were old bags and crazy women. Those murderers shouted insults at us that I would be embarrassed to repeat here.

Another time, we decided to occupy the detention center on Christmas Eve and Christmas Day. We took our entire families and stayed at the prison overnight. The soldiers couldn't do anything to us to make us leave! This event was very successful; there was some newspaper and television coverage. Even outside of Chile, people heard that the families of political prisoners in Valparaíso had successfully occupied the prison!

Each time a political prisoner was released, all of us from the Agrupación would go there to celebrate with a bottle of champagne. I would think to myself, "When will Marcelo get his freedom?" That happy day finally came on April 26, 1990, after the plebiscite, when Chileans voted against Pinocho. The morning Marcelo was supposed to be released, many of his friends from the university and from the neighborhood went to visit him. His case was to be decided in court at one o'clock that afternoon. All the family was there waiting for the decision. When it came, I was so happy that I cried tears of joy! That night we had a huge party at the house. More than a hundred people came over to celebrate Marcelo's freedom from prison!

But I also felt deep pain for the families of people who were still detained; I empathized with their anguish and frustration, and even after my son's release, I continued to work for the political prisoners and their families. When the president of the Agrupación was invited to Europe for three months to do international solidarity work, I substituted for her as president. Gradually, we were able to take over more and more space within the prison. At first, we were allowed to visit the political prisoners only in a small waiting room. Eventually, we entered the patio and took over that space. The first day, the guards fired three shots into the air and tried to push and shove us out of the patio. But we just stayed there! After that, during all our subsequent visits we would insist on staying in the patio.

In time, many of the thirty-six political prisoners here in Valparaíso were released. After the plebiscite, only four remained in detention; the last one was finally released on August 17, 1993. But even though all the political prisoners here in Valparaíso have been released, I feel that our work is unfinished. Many of my *compañeras* and I have looked into the possibility of starting a human rights commission in Valparaíso, but we don't have the funds to finance this project. It is a shame, because there is so much work that needs to be done! In Chile there is still so much poverty, prostitution, abandoned children roaming the streets, a lot of homeless people—you just have to go to the Plaza Echaurrén, for example, to see the horrible conditions in which these street people live. And we need to find a way to help teenage girls who get pregnant and don't have anywhere to go. These are the kinds of issues related to social justice and human rights that need to be addressed here in Chile.

Rosa Alfaro

SECRETARY AND WIDOW OF
SLAIN YOUTH LEADER

Rosa Alfaro (1993), beside a mural painted by a young artist from Valparaiso. It includes fragments of poems and lyrics from a song dedicated to this port city. The final fragment of a poem written by an eleven-year-old boy speaks of the women and children of the disappeared.

I interviewed Rosa Alfaro on December 18, 1993, in her working-class neighborhood of Valparaíso. Alfaro, now thirty-eight years old, and currently employed as a secretary, had been a militant in the Communist Party's youth organization and participated actively in the opposition movement during the dictatorship of Pinochet. Her husband, Julio Guerra Olivares, a construction worker and a leader in the Frente Patriótico Manuel Rodríguez (Manuel Rodríguez Patriotic Front), or FPMR,[1] was one of the victims of "Operation Albania," in which twelve young activists were gunned down by the military on the night of June 15–16, 1987.[2]

Alfaro explicitly addresses the topic of her development of a working-class consciousness. Her memories of Allende, the Popular Unity government, and her own involvement with Communist youth organizations form a central part of her narration. Also visible in her testimony are the devastating psychological consequences of the repression in Chile.

Rosa Alfaro perceives the younger generation of Chileans as, for the most part, apolitical and heavily influenced by the consumer-oriented, capitalist model that is pervasive in the mass media. Nevertheless, she continues to believe in the principles of class struggle and has not lost her idealism.

My name is Rosa Alfaro, and I'm thirty-two years old. I'm from a working-class family. I was born and raised here in Valparaíso. My mother worked as a maid, and my father was a carpenter. I am one of six children.

One of my most important childhood memories was the election of Salvador Allende. I was nine years old at the time. My mom was very active in the campaign, and my older sisters also helped out. It wasn't just my own family; everybody here in the neighborhood supported Allende. Everyone around me was active in his electoral campaign. It was the beginning of something new in Chile; it was the beginning of what would come later with the Popular Unity government. My father is a Communist, and my older brothers and sisters participated in La Jota [JCC]. I was still too young to join at the time, but I do remember making posters and doing little things like that. The day of the elections everyone was listening to the election results on the radio, and when they declared Allende the winner, everyone went out into the streets and danced and had parties to celebrate the victory. This was a victory for all of us as working-class Chileans. Finally, we had a president who was going to respond to our needs!

When the Popular Unity government was in power, I remember having to wait in long lines to buy bread and other food. There were shortages of many things. When you needed toothpaste, for example, it was very difficult to find it. My mother participated in the JAP [the neighborhood-based rationing organization]. You would have to line up early in the morning in the park to get meat and milk. We were given ration cards to buy basic food staples. At school they would give us milk and notebooks. We had plenty of meat and chicken to eat because of the rationing system. But as you waited in line for food, you would see people fighting, some defending Allende's policies and others very angry about them, especially about the lines and the shortages.

And then there was the military coup. I remember that day, September 11, 1973, very well. You could hear the machine guns firing and see the soldiers patrolling the streets. I saw them raiding different houses and burning books. We had to dig holes in order to bury our books so they couldn't burn them. My family lived in a neighborhood up in the hills, and the planes would fly very low over us. They were trying to intimidate and terrorize us. We were all very frightened. We listened to a shortwave radio in order to follow the news about what was happening here inside Chile. But one could see the atrocities taking place all around us. We saw that people were being rounded up in trucks and being detained. And many others disappeared, but we didn't know if they were in hiding somewhere, had escaped from the country, or had been taken political prisoners. And everyone was too afraid to ask what had happened. Of course, none of this was announced on the radio. There was complete censorship and a state of siege.

My family lived in a working-class neighborhood that wasn't that poor or marginal. Some of the women in the neighborhood supported the fall of the Allende government. These conservative women were the ones who had been banging pots and pans to protest Allende. They knew that my mother was a Communist, and they harassed us by asking us if the military had come yet to detain her. But Mom was a very strong, dignified woman with firm convictions. She never, not even for one minute, denied that she had been an Allende supporter—unlike so many others who, out of fear, denied that they had ever supported the Popular Unity government. Many people, even some of the conservative right-wing people, respected my mother because of her unwavering commitment to her beliefs and because of her extraordinary courage.

The time right after the coup was very difficult for us. We feared for our safety, and we felt all alone and very isolated. There was martial law and a curfew. We weren't allowed to gather for meetings, and the soldiers were coming and taking away many of our *compañeros*. Hundreds of people, people we knew—Communists, Socialists, teachers, labor-union leaders, and other people who didn't even have anything to do with politics—were being detained and disappeared. It was a nightmare!

And then finally we began to organize again. I was about fourteen years old when I joined La Jota. Most of us were young people from working-class families and from the marginal sectors of Chilean society. More and more of us joined together. We would have meetings up in the hills. We were taking great risks and facing the possibility of being killed. I remember once, when a group of us had gotten together for a meeting after the curfew, a truck with armed soldiers drove by, and we didn't know what to do. If we had stayed where we were, they would have found us and shot us; if we had started running away, they would also have shot at us; so we just had to hide and hope that they hadn't seen nor heard us. We were so scared we couldn't even breathe! This accumulation of fear and terror took a toll on us.

I remember when La Jota became directly involved in the formation of the *comedores infantiles* [youth lunch program]. There were so many hungry kids on the streets that we began to go to all the houses throughout the neighborhood, asking them to contribute whatever they could so that we could provide hot meals for these kids. In doing this, we were rebelling against the military government, which didn't allow us to organize collectively. But the problem of hunger was so widespread that eventually the program provided food for everyone who needed it, not just the children. And finally, because so many people were literally starving to death, the municipal government took over the program and started a few other social service programs. The youth organization at that time, in the middle of the dictatorship, became very strong. I remember that we would have big festivals, in spite of the risk of being detained.

It wasn't until 1975 or 1976 that we began to find out just how many people had been detained and disappeared during the early years of the dictatorship. We learned about the people who died in concentration camps and in the torture chambers that had been established on ships; we found out about Lebu, Esmeralda, and other places. We began to distribute this information clandestinely and to denounce these atrocities. We wanted everybody to know what the Pinochet regime had done to so many innocent civilians.

We, the young people, were primarily the ones openly confronting this terrible repression, a repression unlike any other in the history of our peaceful nation. The old people had never lived through any dictatorship like the one that was inflicted upon us. Many young people—I would say about 70 percent—joined the opposition in our effort to overthrow the dictatorship. Many young people surrendered themselves totally to this struggle; they were willing to die for it.

It was at this time that many of us opted for armed insurrection. I remember our discussions: some of us argued that if we took up arms, then we would become assassins like the military; others argued that we had the right to defend ourselves with arms, since our human rights were being violated with violence by the military regime. It was a difficult decision for us. We had never even seen guns and rifles before and didn't know how to use them. In an armed confrontation with the military, either you died or a soldier died, and often that soldier was a young man from your neighborhood. Often the soldiers were there because they had to do their obligatory military service, and it just happened to be during the dictatorship. But the military had opened fire on us first. How many thousands of children and young people were murdered from September 1973 until about October 1974? Entire families had been massacred by the soldiers, including small children. This taught us that we couldn't just cross our arms and respond merely with propaganda; instead, we had to respond to violence with violence. This controversy over the use of violent means of confronting the military brought about a split in the Communist Party. Many long-time members, especially of the older generation, couldn't support the path of armed resistance.

I remember one time when my brother and I were detained for a few days and then released. We had been taken together with a large group of young people. The *carabineros* threw all of us into a filthy, overcrowded cell. We were mistreated, but not tortured to death, like some of the political prisoners. In this particular incident my *compañero* Julio was also captured.

Julio and I got married shortly after that. And then, after our daughter was born, we had to make a decision as to how deeply involved in the resistance movement we would become. I finally decided to remain in the Communist Party but not to participate in the leadership or directly in any clandestine operations. But Julio was deeply committed: he was at the center of the clandestine movement and an important leader. As a result, he was followed by the Secret Police. The military and the CNI were highly organized structures with sophisticated surveillance methods. They had scientific devices for detecting conversations and for gathering information about all of us. It was very difficult to escape from this system of absolute control.

My husband Julio was killed by the military in what has come to be known as Operation Albania, which started the night of June 15, 1987, and ended the following morning. Ignacio Valenzuela, one of the principal leaders of the FPMR was the first of the twelve leaders to be murdered. He was shot in the back on Alhue Street. Patricio Costa and his wife, Patricia Quiroz, who was four months pregnant at the time, were both badly tortured before being killed. These were clearly assassinations and not a confrontation, as the military later claimed.

My *compañero* Julio was killed at about midnight on the night of June 15 in the apartment he was renting in Santiago. (Although we were married, Julio and I weren't living together at the time. He was sent to Santiago by the Party, and I remained here in Valparaíso.) About sixty members of the CNI carrying machine guns raided his apartment and murdered him there in cold blood. When they arrived, they cut off the electricity, threw tear gas into his apartment, and had him completely surrounded. It was obvious that they had come with the intention not of detaining him but of killing him. The military officer in charge of this operation was Corvalán. Pinochet had given him the order to carry out this assassination of the top leadership of the Frente. A total of about five hundred soldiers participated in Operation Albania.

I heard on the radio early the following morning that Julio had been killed. Even before they mentioned his name I knew it was Julio, because they reported the address of the apartment where he was murdered and then gave a physical description of him. I was in a state of shock! It seemed as though this awful tragedy was happening to someone else, not to me. I remember that they announced Julio's death Wednesday morning, and they made us wait until Friday to bring his corpse home from Santiago to Viña del Mar. Because it was a holiday, we needed to get a special permit to remove his body from the morgue. I had to identify Julio. It was horrible—you can't imagine how horrible—to see Julio's body full of bullet holes! My *compañero* had beautiful blue eyes, and those assassins shot right through each one. He had seven or eight wounds: several in the head and several in the chest. Any single shot would have killed him immediately. What they did to him was so brutal! It's hard even to imagine that anyone could be so cruel and barbaric! I never dreamed anything so terrible could happen to Julio. He was such a good man.

Needless to say, the families of all the victims of Operation Albania were shattered by the news. Some of them became emotionally and mentally ill as a consequence of this tragedy. Several of the parents of these young activists even died from a broken heart.

Like many other legal cases related to the violation of human rights here in Chile, these cases weren't tried in a civil court; they were tried here in the military court. It is such a sham! The military always protects itself and claims that such assassinations were committed in self-defense. However, Operation Albania, along with the highly publicized Tucapél Jiménez and Orlando Letelier cases, was condemned by the United Nations.[3] It was during this period when Pinocho said that no one in Chile could even lift a finger without his knowing it. The dictator felt he was all-powerful and invincible, that he could crush all the opposition movement by killing off the leaders!

After Operation Albania, the Frente Patriótico was badly damaged. The military regime had successfully killed off all of the most important, intelligent, and committed leaders, leaving the movement weak and without direction and leadership. Also, everyone was very frightened in the wake of this horrendous repression. Following Operation Albania, there was a general climate of terror. Each day there were signs of increasing repression. Many of us were being followed by the Secret Police; I remember being followed constantly for many months. I was terrified, not so much for me as for my daughter, Irene. I remember that my friend Laura Soto offered to help me leave the country; she was going to get me a ticket and a safe place to live outside of Chile. Many people did opt to go into exile at this time, but I decided to stay here because it was important for me to let people know that Operation Albania was not a confrontation between armed youth and the military but, rather, a slaying of defenseless victims. I didn't want to flee! I wanted to stay and resist! I couldn't give in to the military and let them win this battle!

I felt strongly that it was my responsibility to make the truth known about what happened to my *compañero* and the others who were murdered in Operation Albania. I knew that if we, the surviving family members, didn't do this, nobody else would do it. Julio had given himself completely to this struggle for the people of Chile, and I felt that I owed it to his memory to stay here and keep fighting. Julio never really belonged to me, because from the very beginning, even before I met him, he was a youth leader in the Party. He belonged to everyone, to all Chilean people who were struggling to overthrow the dictatorship. He had sacrificed his own personal life for the greater good of the larger community. I had tremendous respect for him and strongly supported his commitment to this battle.

At the site where Julio was murdered, there is now a plaza named after him. The people from this neighborhood in Santiago got together and decided to pay homage to Julio by renaming this plaza. It was a gesture of solidarity and a tangible act of resistance against the unjustifiable violence and the gross violation of human rights. Many of these neighbors had wanted to help Julio the night of the slaying, but the military stopped them with tear gas. Every year, on June 15, there is a commemorative service in honor of Julio. Throughout the country there have been memorial services to remember these youth leaders who were brutally slaughtered in 1987. The students have a big annual event; smaller events in Santiago, in Lota, and also here in Valparaíso are organized by the family members of the victims of Operation Albania.

We, as the surviving family members of the victims of Operation Albania, have gone repeatedly to speak to members of parliament and to many other political representatives. The only one who listens to us is Don Andrés Aylwin. We are demanding justice. We want Corvalán, the military officer responsible for this operation, and the others who participated to be tried in the civilian courts and punished for their crimes. We need to get the case out of the military courts and into the civilian courts. We are also demanding that the truth about the victims be told publicly and that all the lies that came out in the papers, saying that they were a bunch of terrorists, assassins, and thiefs, be retracted. We are demanding that their reputations be restored! We want to reconstruct the truth about Julio and the other victims. We also want to reconstruct the history of the FPMR so that people can appreciate the commitment and the courage of these young martyrs. Julio was a photographer; others were writers—they were very sensitive, talented young people. Many political prisoners wrote poems and essays about them, paying tribute to their dead *compañeros*. They were also known and loved in their respective neighborhoods. We are now in the process of gathering testimonies about them by family, friends, and *compañeros*. We are planning a big event honoring these victims next June 15 and 16, on the anniversary of their deaths. It is very important for us to keep their memory alive!

I'm no longer active in my political party (PCC) because of some political differences and problems, but I still believe in the ideals of social justice. As I mentioned earlier, I am from the marginal, working-class sector of Chilean society. I think we need to work at the grassroots level in order to raise young people's class consciousness, so they can understand the social structures that are oppressing us. We need to combat the growing consumerism that is being promoted on TV, in advertisements, and everywhere here in Chile. The working class needs to be aware that some of these new economic policies that the government is implementing are working against us as working-class people. We are still very poor; even though there is a new class of millionaires who are benefiting from all of this, the people are suffering a lot of poverty and lack of opportunity. We must demand educational opportunities, health care, day care, and a decent standard of living. I think that by working with young people and trying to teach them about their rights, we might be able to forge a new left, from the grassroots. In my opinion, this is the only way we can renovate the traditional leftist parties here in Chile.

Another matter of concern to me is that Chile is still a very sexist country. We still have a long way to go in order to eliminate machismo. We have very few women in top-ranking positions of national leadership. How many women are senators or representatives? Unfortunately, very few. This space—that is, the political arena—is still closed to us. We, as women, have always been denied positions of power. We need to work hard toward the goal of conquering these male territories, because we are certainly capable of being excellent leaders. But the men aren't just going to step aside and hand over their power; we must fight for our right to share power and decision-making together with the men who now control everything!

Belinda Zubecueta

POLITICAL PRISONER

At the time of this interview in December 1993, thirty-five-year-old Belinda Zubecueta was one of nineteen remaining political prisoners in Chile. She had not been released, despite the country's return to civilian rule. Zubecueta was detained in 1986 and endured more than seven years of imprisonment, torture, and isolation. Her resilience and unbroken spirit point to her inner strength. Here is her personal story about life as a political prisoner in Chile during the Pinochet dictatorship.

I did not personally interview Belinda Zubecueta. Her prison testimony as presented here is based on my transcription of a tape-recorded interview conducted in a prison in Santiago by Monique, a human rights activist from the French Communist Party who has been living and working in Valparaiso since 1970 as a full-time community organizer and journalist. Since I didn't have the opportunity to meet Belinda myself, there are visible gaps in the following testimony: information about her childhood, family background, and the like. Therefore, the format of this testimony is somewhat different from that of the previous narratives.

I had just turned fourteen when Salvador Allende was elected. I remember that the Popular Unity government really tried to bring about social justice. Allende was concerned about the marginal sectors of society and committed to giving the children of working-class parents enough to eat, a good education, employment opportunities, and access to culture. This was a giant leap forward for us as a nation. It was also the first time that a Socialist had ever been elected president anywhere in Latin America. Allende's election offered hope to the popular sectors of Chilean society!

But of course, it became clear very soon that the capitalist system [especially in the United States] wasn't going to allow us to go on just like that, developing the kind of egalitarian society that we wanted to build. So there was a boycott of Chilean merchandise, and an economic blockade was imposed on us. These forms of economic sabotage brought about the shortages and the infamous long lines in Chile. The wealthy capitalists bought up large amounts of food and other supplies. They hoarded everything. They refused to sell any of these products; in fact, they preferred to throw food into the rivers rather than to sell it. Enormous amounts of food were dumped into the Mapocho River. It's amazing to see how effective the capitalists were in sabotaging the Popular Unity government. They successfully undermined Allende's attempted transition toward socialism.

After the military coup, Chile suffered the darkest period of repression in her history. There had been repression during the dictatorship of González Videla, but Pinochet's military junta was by far the most atrocious and brutal. Nobody was respected, neither men nor women nor children. Not too long ago some clandestine cemeteries were discovered, and the remains of young children were found there. So you see, the military regime didn't persecute just members of political parties but the entire civilian population. Throughout the years of the dictatorship there was severe repression of everyone who tried to organize, not just of the leftist political parties. Even social groups whose aim was to help the poor were persecuted by Pinochet's regime. This was a period of not just political violence but also economic violence. And the marginal sectors of Chile were the hardest hit. The only thing that mattered to the regime was maintaining power through widespread state-sponsored terrorism.

I was a typical, unaware housewife who was fulfilling her domestic responsibilities at home, enclosed within the domestic space of four walls. I was worried about the day-to-day survival of my family. My main concern was whether we had enough to eat. Slowly but surely, I started to realize what was going on all around me, and I began waking up to the violence in the country, particularly in my neighborhood. I began to see that people who were close to me had been tortured or assassinated. We were suffering from a lack of decent housing, from unemployment; there wasn't any day care for our children. Our young people didn't have access to cultural activities; the only culture they knew was a culture of violence and death. Inside of me I began to feel a rebellious spirit growing against the injustices of this oppressive system.

So I became involved in many social activities. I worked with a committee for the homeless and joined the squatters who took over land and occupied buildings. Even though they were brutally repressed, many of these very poor people felt that they had nothing more to lose. They had already lost everything that they had achieved and that had been given to them during Allende's government. So what else was there for them to lose? The only solution seemed to be to organize and to fight back. And from there, I felt that what we were doing wasn't enough, so I made the decision to join the armed resistance, the Manuel Rodríguez Patriotic

Front. I worked actively with the FPMR until I was detained in 1986, and I've been a political prisoner since then. My *compañero* also participated in the FPMR. He was killed in a confrontation with the military. I felt that I had nothing else to lose, so I just kept on struggling and fighting back.

I've been locked up for seven years. Seven years of my life here in jail! This experience has caused me so much anxiety and anguish. I've tried to learn how to turn this experience into another form of the struggle, into resistance on a different front: to be able to survive the physical and psychological torture, as well as the isolation. This has been my goal from the moment I was taken prisoner by the CNI until now.

Here in jail, I've learned to take everything that is negative and to crush it, and to try to draw from this experience anything that is positive in order to continue growing as a woman. I have had this constant desire to learn and to grow as a person, so that when I'm released from jail I can better serve my people. Because in my own social sector, the working class, we desperately need women who are intellectuals and can be leaders within the community. Nothing—not the experience of seven years in jail, not even the horrible torture that I have been subjected to—nothing has made me lose my convictions as a revolutionary committed to the cause of creating a more just, socialist society. This is my objective in life: to gain my liberty so that I can continue working for my ideals.

Sometimes I'm filled with rage because the only way that it was possible for us to end the dictatorship was through a coalition government led by a conservative centrist political party, like the Christian Democrats, who defend the interests of the capitalists. We knew that it would be very difficult and that we would confront a series of obstacles, but we never dreamed that these past three years of Patricio Aylwin would be so humiliating for us, especially regarding the violation of human rights. Fundamentally, this government has served not the interests of the Chilean people but rather the interests of the military and the elite. Beginning with us, the political prisoners, this government hasn't been able to help us, and we haven't seen any justice yet. The judicial system is dealing with us as though we were delinquents or common criminals, not political prisoners. When we are released, we are viewed and treated as second-class citizens. When we go to look for a job, nobody wants to hire us; we are considered to be terrorists. People don't understand that we, as a people, have a right to defend ourselves against the state-sponsored terrorism inflicted upon us by the dictatorship.

Who is going to pay the price for the torture and the isolation we have endured, for the disintegration of our families, for the suffering of our children? Just wait and see; nobody is going to pay for the crimes committed against us. The same people are still controlling the mass media. They even had the audacity to allow Contreras to appear on television, with a diabolical and threatening expression on his face, denying all the charges against him, and all the atrocities committed by the regime. The same thing happened with Corvalán not too long ago. What's happening? Despite the fact that there are military officials who are guilty and we know who they are—they have been recognized as the principal protagonists of the terror—there still hasn't been any justice. When a case is supposed to be tried in the civilian courts, the military puts pressure on the judges to transfer the case to the military courts. And these officers are usually found innocent and are released from custody after only a few months.

There were approximately five hundred political prisoners when Patricio Aylwin took over as president, and now there are only nineteen political prisoners who haven't been released yet. The nineteen of us have been kept in jail as part of a deal that the government cut with the military. Right now, there are eight *compañeros* who have been freed of all charges and granted pardon. Nevertheless, their files are still sitting on the president's desk. He refuses to sign for their release because of pressure from the armed forces.

I am grateful for all the support that the international solidarity groups with Chile offered throughout the years of the dictatorship. Now, however, by articulating their support for the present government, they have helped to legitimize the false notion that there has been a return to democracy in Chile, that there are no longer political prisoners or violations of human rights. But that is not the case. The government says that there are no longer Chilean political exiles. But that isn't true. Many prisoners who have been released were offered the alternatives of either staying in jail or leaving the country. It's important for the international solidarity movement to continue denouncing this violation of human rights, to demand the release of all remaining political prisoners, and to demand justice for the victims of the repression and their families.

Chiloé Sasso

STUDENT LIVING IN EXILE

*This final testimony was not based on a taped interview. Rather, it is my transla-
tion of a Spanish text written by Patricia "Chiloé" Sasso, who tells her own story,
based on her memories as a young child growing up in Chile during the Pinochet
dictatorship.[1] I met Chiloé, who is now thirty-two years old, in 1992 when she was
an undergraduate in a Spanish composition class I was teaching at Ohio State
University. She recently completed her master's degree in the Department of
Spanish and Portuguese at Ohio State. Chiloé is slim and attractive, with wavy
black hair, piercing brown eyes, olive complexion. As a student, she is articulate,
insightful, passionate, and eager to express her point of view in class discussions.
She is also a gifted writer. In my classes she fulfilled several assignments by relat-
ing her childhood memories of the coup and subsequent repression in Chile, the
repercussions of the political climate of violence on her own psyche and personal development, and her experiences of culture shock and interracial tension as a young
Latina living in the United States.*

*When I visited Chile in December 1993, I was invited to spend several days
with the Sasso family at their home in Santiago. Chiloé's mother is a retired elementary school teacher, and her father is a copper miner. Her older sister, Angela,
invited me to spend an afternoon at the biology lab where she works as a techni-
cian. All the family members spoke with nostalgia about Chiloé, whose presence
they have missed since her voluntary exile to the United States. Although the
Sasso family can be classified as middle class according to Chilean standards, it is
interesting to note that Chiloé has a perception of herself as "poor." (This self-
construct is one of the elements of self-fashioning through narration in these
Chilean testimonies.)*

*In Chiloé Sasso's personal narrative, what is omitted is as important as what
is written; this text speaks through its silences, its ruptures, and its gaps. Interestingly, Sasso chooses to speak little about the circumstances leading to her exile in
the United States, or about her marriage to an Anglo-American and their divorce, although this was a major part of more than seven years of her life. Sasso is
currently struggling as a single mother to raise three children. When I asked her
why she had omitted so much information about her life in the United States, es-*

pecially about her ex-husband and her relationship with his family, she responded that after writing that part of her essay, she deleted it on purpose: "It was as though I was trying to erase the cause of a major disaster of my life; my marriage was a mistake that contributed to a depression that I'm still trying to recover from." I respect Sasso's desire to remain silent about these and other events (and their consequences) in her private life. I will not try to fill in the blank spaces and ellipses in her personal testimony. She also chose not to submit a photo of herself to be included in this book.

When trying to describe the past, we find ourselves faced with a series of personal elements that turn out to be that which enables us to put the past in a comprehensible context. I say "comprehensible" because a child does not understand the true meaning of life's events at the time. A recounting of our past carries with it our present—who we are. This is because we are what time and circumstances have made us.

My past and my memories of the coup in Chile go back to when I was ten. A few years before that, without understanding anything about politics, I learned from the talk around me that Allende's victory was also a victory for the Chilean people. But what did it mean to be a part of that group? At my age I didn't understand the concept of "nation," and in my innocence I couldn't understand the division that existed among Chileans, either. Until 1973 I thought that this division was just a disagreement between young and old—a generation gap. What caused this disagreement? I saw the contradictions everywhere in the adults I knew—parents and relatives of friends from school, people in the stores and businesses we frequented, neighbors, relatives, and friends of my family.

I considered the words "the Chilean people" to be something beautiful, perfect words for a song by Violeta Parra or Víctor Jara, without realizing that they referred to the poor, to workers, and to anyone underprivileged. Nevertheless, they were beautiful because they were what was moving the country. They seemed even more beautiful when I discovered that I, as a miner's daughter, also belonged to those people. By listening to my father I came to regard Allende as representing social progress and a better standard of living for the Chilean people. He was the hope that made the difficult daily routine and the sadness of the poor bearable.

Nevertheless, these simplified political notions that I received from my father were constantly being challenged, even before the coup, by disturbances in downtown Santiago and the daily reports on radio and television. Gradually, the violence engraved itself in my memory—the violence of a country that slowly bled, but not to death, with the coup and the assassination of Allende on September 11, 1973. The weapons and the brute force of those who would rule ended the capacity of the Chilean people to reason, silenced their voices, and doused their fervent desire to create a socialist nation—one based solidly on well-being as the prime re-course of a country. They bled Chile for almost seventeen years, annihilat-ing human beings like animals, as well as lowering the ability of those who lived (if you can call it that) under repression and fear to exist and to think.

The years leading up to the coup were recorded in my mind via the black- and- white television set of a great-aunt of mine, and there the images of horror remained, images of a slow war in which women and children ran in desperation to escape death. On that TV screen I saw suf-fering I had never before imagined, yet it was real and palpable in my own land. The contradiction between the words of my father (in support of Allende) and the social upheaval raised a great question in my mind, and it was only after the coup that I was able to answer it. Even then it was only a sketchy answer. Many years later I was able to understand it on a deeper level, in the context of global economic and political realities. My father, like so many others, had placed his confidence in and devoted his energy to the labor unions. For him, membership in the union meant active par-ticipation in the fight for labor rights and also an expression of a common vision for change.

Perhaps even more than my brothers and sisters, I saw the violence up close, since I studied ballet in the municipal theater located in downtown Santiago. The distant violence of that faraway war came closer to us every day, touching us. Unable to understand, I asked myself why, who were the bad people? My mother took me to the theater every afternoon, and what we really feared was going home afterward. She made me walk fast and stay by her side, although it wasn't necessary for her to say so, since I was already so afraid. Dozens of people would be waiting for the bus; the people always seemed calm but expectant, their eyes fixed in the same di-rection. I couldn't be sure, but the people in those places always seemed shadowed with fear; in their faces you could see the exhaustion after a day's work and fear and insecurity. For them life seemed to be an endless rou-tine of waiting for the bus every evening, and then continuing the tedium on foot, walking down lonely streets or perhaps among the crowds, every-one wanting to escape from the humdrum, burned out from the routine, seeing before their eyes the crumbling of their world.

After the coup, on many occasions while we waited for the bus, stand-ing on the sidewalk with many others, the violence was right in front of us, with no television screen or the safety of distance to protect us. Tear gas would be sprayed routinely to disperse crowds, and the feared fire hydrant would soak everything and everyone within its radius.

The progression of attempted killings and acts of savage violence perpetrated against anyone who tried to rise up against Pinochet was sad—the weapons used were beatings of those who resorted to disobedience, starvation to manipulate the thoughts and actions of those who remained neutral, silent death for those who wanted to organize, and a common grave in an unknown or unestablished cemetery for those who still believed Allende's socialism possible and dared to identify with it.

Violence was put down with more violence. Sometimes my mother and I would have to run into a store to keep from getting soaked; other times we were able to catch the bus and get away. I also remember a burning sensation in my eyes and throat, something like a light and slow torture. I would hear people say, "Those are the students walking around revolting again." Were they just students? I knew they weren't; I had seen all sorts of people in those demonstrations. After seeing these things my mind would keep going round and round: "What happened to those who were left behind?" "Why did those people expose themselves to beatings?" "Why do innocent people suffer from the violence as well?" On one occasion I saw a *carabinero* following a man; I realized it only when I heard the man rush by. What impressed and frightened me was to be close to the *carabinero* and see his face filled with rage, a purple vein popping out from his temple—a look that stayed with me, his eyes almost leaping out and staring at the man as if the obsession of catching him strengthened the *carabinero's* vision so he wouldn't lose sight of him. The man ran without even looking behind him; the crowd opened to swallow him as if wishing to help. I remember thinking that he was the winner at the same time that I heard the *carabinero* shouting insults. The man ran and ran until he lost himself in the crowd; his race had saved his freedom and even his life, at least this time.

After this, my mother and I went home. She looked worried and fearful, and I asked her if she was afraid of these revolts. She replied, "Yes." It seemed more and more dangerous to go downtown, so my parents decided that I shouldn't go to ballet class anymore. I remember that I was saddened by this decision. Even though I had been in the midst of these revolts many times and perceived the atmosphere of hatred and suffering, I could never imagine the atrocities. I knew that in Germany the Nazis developed all sorts of cruelties in order to destroy other human beings; nevertheless, perhaps because of my age, this kind of cruelty was completely inconceivable to me.

I also recall that people seemed tired of living, of standing in line for hours just to get food. From my bus I could see them standing there, feeling the fatigue in their feet, with fear and exhaustion hidden behind their faces. Later on, these faces would cease to show any feeling at all; neither could words express the suffering and terror from the abuses of the military regime. Anger was evident all around me; regrettably, I didn't understand it as a social problem or relate it to hunger or poverty. I didn't comprehend the infinite repercussions of repression in those suffering from it. So many people saw the possibility of a better life rapidly dwindle away. I grew up watching these people and myself wait, wait without hope and with frayed nerves, while clutching the tickets that rationed the sale of meat, cooking oil, sugar, rice. The rations never satisfied the need but denigrated the soul. In waiting, one lost one's dignity but not one's anger.

I remember how before the military seizure of power the *carabineros* were creating as much violence as the students on campuses around Santiago or the civilian groups protesting the sabotage of Allende's government by the Chilean elite. Thus, before I could even articulate the increasingly violent world around me, another image of violence was forming. Perhaps I was too young to understand the reasons for it; supposedly the bad people were those trying to destroy order, but the enemy hid itself and attacked from behind. I never knew who the enemy was. I just knew words that I had heard which to my mind described invincible individuals: Marxists, Socialists, Communists. I imagined them planning together, conglomerates brainstorming some revolt downtown, or stealing food from the supermarket through the back door. The most revolutionary idea that I had was of the black market, as a business hidden in the basement of an abandoned building. The poor people (including my family) didn't have access to this black market, I thought, just the rich.[2] In addition to being very difficult to get into, I imagined this abandoned building as being very far away, reached only by car. This conditioned my thoughts regarding the class division that existed among Chileans. I thought I was starting to understand it all: the good Chileans were the rich people who were allowed in the country club, the same people who passed by in their cars sticking up their noses at the poor people waiting for the bus under the pouring rain or scorching sun.

On radio and television they showed and described acts of violence in detail: students were wounded, imprisoned ferociously, and beaten by the *carabineros* or by the butt of a rank-and-file soldier's submachine gun. As I remember it, depending on who did the reporting, sometimes you could identify the face or the name of the enemy. Santiago was a time bomb. I would hear an endless stream of words that I would memorize, not knowing what they meant. I was part of an incoherent world. What was happening to the Chilean people? Where was Allende? Why didn't he come to save the people? Who were these Marxists that everyone hated? Who was hiding all the food? What for?

Before the coup, my questions were almost never answered. The anguish was killing my father, who would say, "Here they are going to punish the just as sinners." The fear of becoming a victim of the violence downtown was my mother's constant worry; she had to go to the other side of town to get to her job as a teacher at a little school in Barrancas, one of the poorest neighborhoods in Santiago. I honestly did not realize the magnitude of my parents' fear until that tragic day, September 11, 1973, when without knowing what was taking place downtown I tried to go to school. My father arrived just as I was leaving and told us that they were bombing La Moneda and that no one could go out on the streets.[3] The feeling of being a prisoner in my own home made me look at the street demonstrations differently. We turned on the radio, and the announcer's voice filled the space of our house day and night, constantly reporting on the current crisis. This news penetrated the ears of those who didn't want to listen, and of those of us who didn't understand and asked why. The announcer's voice invaded my mind while I wished I were deaf so that I wouldn't have to hear anything, anything at all.

That day schools were closed until an undetermined date. For those of us who thought that having no school for one day was great, not knowing when our school would reopen again was awful. We kids thought it was great only in the beginning of what turned out to be a long time. As the days passed, we were bored stiff and going stir-crazy. Being forced to stay inside all day wasn't fun for anybody. This feeling of confinement only added to the already high level of tension in Chilean homes.

One day, while we were all at home listening to the news and waiting, the new military regime declared a state of siege and a curfew. For me, as a ten-year-old girl, these words meant that we were already prisoners of something, of someone. My mother was at work—what would happen to her if she was out after curfew? Would she be all right? Where was she? The hours passed by much too slowly for each and every person who didn't know the whereabouts of someone in their family. Finally my mom got home, three hours late and her face white with anguish. While we ate dinner, she told my father what things were like downtown: traffic jams and detours, *carabineros* and soldiers carrying submachine guns and protective shields grouped together on many streets. Downtown was an unimaginable battlefield to me. My mother was saying that where she had passed by on the bus, they had thrown smoke bombs, and that they smelled terrible. Now everyone knew that the Moneda had been bombed. Had anybody died? How? It was years before we were able to answer these questions, but from then on, most Chileans had someone to mourn. What would happen now?

For me that day marked a new stage in my childhood. I sensed that all of us were affected by the coup, even though I didn't understand the socioeconomic implications, or the extent to which this tragic event would change the Chilean people and the course of our history. Meanwhile, the afternoon hours passed by slowly; the radio announced the time along with the news, and as the curfew approached, the hours seemed unending.

Six o'clock would come, or perhaps eight—I was intrigued because I didn't think the people could be so obedient to an order that in my mind simply seemed impossible to carry out, since there was no way to monitor millions of inhabitants. What I didn't know was that disobedience through political affiliation with Popular Unity was met with torture and death. I wanted to go out to watch; regrettably, I had to settle for looking out my window. I didn't want to see the violence; I wanted to prove for myself that all I had heard and seen about the soldiers wasn't true, not in my country. Everyone was confined in their houses; my father said that it was dangerous even to go out on the patio. I didn't believe him; I couldn't believe that human beings would invade the homes of others. I naively thought that we were safe in our own home. Being young was like wearing a blindfold, and to find out that we weren't safe even in our own homes, that even our own fathers could be defenseless creatures, unable to face the military that "was only following orders"—this was the birth of my consciousness about, and terror of, human cruelty. This was also when my mistrust of everyone was born.

The silence of the night of the coup has stayed with me ever since. I envisioned that silence as something round, yet indescribably penetrating. It was and it wasn't. In the silence you might hear a dog barking. I could never before have imagined our neighborhood streets without a single taxi or bus. Now there were no voices, no noises. I remember trying to compare it to death, to a cemetery—that must be what it is like to be dead, not seeing or hearing anything. Yet fortunately or unfortunately, we were still alive, yes, alive, and we could hear, see, and perhaps feel in our bones the violence of this war. It might have been bedtime, but to be able to go to sleep one must be tired and at peace. We were tired but not at peace; peace had vanished from our lives. The restlessness of a bloody night ran through our veins, exchanging sleep for additional hours of wakefulness in which to hear gunshots, to visualize beatings, and to feel the fear day after day. As the night advanced, the silence in our house was accentuated. The dearth of conversation wasn't for lack of words or a topic; in those moments words or human noises were swallowed up by our fear. And that desire to live or to survive and to save oneself without knowing exactly from what demanded silence, obliged us to stay silent.

My older sister and I talked about what might be happening. She as much as I felt the impotence of our youth. In the darkness both of us would concentrate on what could be heard in the distance, but I really didn't know if she was imagining the same things as I. We opened our bedroom window a bit; through it I could prove to myself that that fat silence didn't actually exist: in the distance we could hear the sounds of vehicles passing by at great speed, made invincible in the darkness; we could also hear gunshots blasting in all directions, and a uniform murmur spread out into the vastness of the night—a murmur with no identifiable start or finish. These sounds entered my imagination and mixed with my reality. What is that sound? Do you think they are killing someone nearby? Whom? How many people? Years later I learned that the National Stadium, just a few blocks from my house, had been used as a concentration camp. I later discovered that the murmur I had heard night after night had been groans, shouts, cries, beatings, torture, and death.

Midnight wasn't the middle of the night for those people who didn't sleep and awaited their destiny in that stadium. Nor was it the middle of the night for those who formed part of the military and carried out orders to torture and kill Allende supporters. Grecia Avenue is the closest main street to my parents' house; this street leads to several other *poblaciones* of Santiago, including Hermida and Peñalolén. Along this avenue, in the darkness of the night and the nearly round silence of the curfew, the military transported its war arsenal—dark and silent tanks advanced, mixing with the shadow of the night. To see a tank just a few feet away always scared me, but to imagine the destruction left in its wake chilled me, erasing the innocence and the ignorance of my ten years.

The day following the coup the bustling of the city had been reduced to the mechanical sounds of the motors of a few public buses. It was as if the night continued; nevertheless, it was daytime. The lack of sunshine and the drab dankness and overcast sky foreshadowed the gloom of disaster, reflected the anguish. What had happened? The silence was fearsome; voices weren't heard; children weren't seen playing or laughing; everyone stayed inside their homes. That first day after the coup was like death in life. For me it was such a strange experience to be a prisoner in my own house. This wasn't a prison like the one I had seen near the train station, dark and ugly. My house, like other houses in Chile, had a fence that separated it from the sidewalk along the street; that fence now delineated our territory and our security. Nevertheless, our jail wasn't just the small, physical space in which we were confined; it was also being unable to talk about the fear we felt. And most of all, our jail was the uncertainty of the situation. This jail was fearing that you might be killed for no reason; it was not being able to ask about a relative or a disappeared friend; it was having to trade exile and silence for life.

Soon after the coup, television broadcasts were reduced to channel 7, the National Channel. The censored reports it aired told "the truth" exclusively from the military's point of view: "The armed forces have intervened so that Chile may return to democracy; but first, the Communists must be eliminated." That was what I heard, and what I really didn't understand was that those words convinced me and the ignorant people that there was an enemy in Chile: Allende and his followers who had pursued economic and sociopolitical change. The other television channels and radio stations were to remain silent or to comply with the censorship of the regime. Radio Cooperativa stands out in my memory as never having stopped its broadcasts, but I remember a somber-toned voice talking about what had happened in La Moneda—an official communiqué saying that Salvador Allende had committed suicide with the weapon that his friend Fidel Castro had given him as a gift. We all knew this wasn't true; the military violence showed this clearly. I couldn't understand how a president could lose power in such a way that the armed forces would betray him. In my limited knowledge I listened to words that at the time meant nothing to me: CIA, ITT, DINA, United States, Nixon—names associated with the control of Chile in ways I didn't understand.[4]

Living with this sense of uncertainty caused a feeling of impotence and frustration, of not knowing what to do and not being able to do anything. It was a mutilating, belittling sensation. I was just ten years old, miserably poor, and insignificantly small; I couldn't do anything for anybody. My father spent morning, noon, and night with a cigarette in his mouth, out of work, frequently in a bad mood. Perhaps he was desperate? Perhaps he was silently chewing on his rage, his shame, his disillusion, or perhaps he was counting his days in fear of dying? I didn't know. I didn't find out that we might have been one of the many families whose houses the military was beginning to raid until very late one night: while other houses in our neighborhood had their lights out, my parents were destroying papers and documents. In our bathroom they burned informative pamphlets of the miners' union and the magazines my father had collected—some of them were written in Chinese and showed people dressed almost identically. I didn't know what significance these things had, but thanks to the magic of that controlled fire, the traces of my parents' connection to the "enemy" were gone. I don't know, it seemed so unreal to me that traces of evidence could be found anywhere. Merely to be a member of a labor union meant to be a "subversive"; my father's name appeared on more than one list. I began to understand his fear and his silence. It was something that I felt, without being able to articulate or explain why.

I grew up thinking that the most normal thing in the world was to have a mother and a father. Just thinking about not having one of my parents made me sad, made me bitter, and clouded the happiness of growing up in my idea of a normal home. Even though poverty was a reason for constant worry, I preferred being poor to not having a father. That year my desire (or my mother's desire for me) to be a ballerina in the Municipal Theater was permanently frustrated. To have had such an opportunity was a privilege for a poor person, because there were so many obstacles: the schedule, transportation, lack of money, just to name a few. I didn't feel privileged at the time, but over the years my desire to continue my ballet or academic studies were often reduced to the same limitation: I couldn't, because there wasn't enough money.

Life continued, but it was strange. When school reopened and activities resumed in general, I realized that people wanted to pretend that nothing had happened. In spite of what little I knew, I was certain that something atrocious had happened. Teachers, neighbors, and even relatives repeated the same dampening phrases: "One can't talk about that," or "One never knows who could be an informer." Even worse was to be told, "They are political things and you don't know anything about that; they aren't things for little kids," or "Women don't know anything about politics." All these words belittled and angered me. I wanted to ask questions, but everyone hushed me up. The catechism teacher was a nice woman who seemed understanding, but it was just the topic of religion that had made her seem that way. In reality she didn't possess as much tolerance as she had taught in her classes. When I asked her what party she belonged to, her eyes popped out as if she had just seen Satan. She told me that wasn't a topic for a little girl, least of all in a class preparing students for first Holy Communion. I felt ashamed again, and doubted my questions, and even my right to know and to ask questions. I didn't consider it an impertinence; I just wanted someone to fill in the gaps in my understanding. I wanted to talk because I knew that the military was killing a lot of people—anyone who was suspected of having supported Allende's government. On another occasion when I asked my teacher something, she smiled and asked me if I had studied math during our vacation. I had to accept this as a nice way of telling me that she didn't want to discuss it, and I had to learn not to ask anyone anything. To learn about the situation from other children only caused other problems, because if an adult overheard, I would be punished.

During these times, when thousands of things passed through my mind, I slowly realized that I was growing up and that life was going on around me, but as if I were looking at it from the outside. Who was I? At the age of ten I realized that as a human being living on this earth I didn't have the necessary attributes to shine in any area in this world. The world of television and film was made up of blonds, of people with last names reflecting cultural and economic influence. I felt small and insignificant because I couldn't see a better future for myself; perhaps I couldn't see myself in the future. I had memories of the coup and, in my daily life, news of economic problems. I decided when I was very young that I would never be a teacher, because teachers were exploited; and I didn't aspire to be a miner, because I had never heard of any women working in a mine.

My perspective on life was sad and without much hope for the future. I saw my mother running around taking care of the household and then going to work; her salary never lasted to the end of the month, and this saddened me. I was afraid to ask for anything because I already knew the answer; moreover, I began to realize the frustration my parents felt. My father, who was at home only when he was laid off, always seemed unhappy and bitter, and I was afraid of his fits of temper. If one asked him for something, the answer was always "No," unless it was something of dire urgency, in which case he would buy it. I confess that I was never without a coat or shoes, but neither did I ever have a penny that I could call my own to spend on something frivolous. Sometimes I viewed our poverty with shame, other times with anger. I remember always saying that we were broke, which would sometimes make my mother smile at my realistic perspective. To have to ration your food and to not be able to buy something delicious in the outdoor market or at the supermarket because it was too expensive melted away the illusion of happiness, of feeling the satisfaction of enjoying something that you wanted but didn't need. Such a thing wasn't possible if you were poor. I've always wondered about the relativity of poverty. Even though I didn't want to be labeled as "poor," it seemed there was no way to escape it.

Because I was bad at math, and because I began to hate my teachers, I changed high schools many times. I thought I was free. These changes allowed me to see myself in many different lights. I compared my poverty to that of my schoolmates. Fortunately, I never became a vicious social climber. I watched the people who rode the bus; no doubt others saw me the same way. I was like all the other people who rode public transportation day after day. I thought a lot about these kinds of class issues and often wondered why the people who surrounded me didn't do anything to change their lives. Many of the people I talked with had lives filled with obstacles, and the impotence of not being able to do something had often destroyed them and erased their hopes; their lives were limited to a struggle for survival, to the drudgery and boredom of routine that fate had meted out to them. In my observations the people who made my heart shudder the most were the mothers juggling small children in their arms while trying to grab the bus rail and pay the fare, and the frail old people with poor eyesight who risked falling down, whether from the trampling of other passengers or from the aggressive impatience of the driver. At school you would see everything—the poor and the extremely poor—but thanks to the fact that we all wore uniforms, the tears in our clothes were less noticeable, and the holes in our shoes less visible.

Going to different schools taught me about other people, but perhaps the most important thing I learned was to begin to get to know myself as a human being. I didn't see myself as different from anyone else; therefore, I treated everyone as though we were all on the same level. It wasn't until years later that I saw that I was intruding in places I didn't belong. Maybe it was an innocent attraction to the "beautiful people" for whom everything was permissible, people who had everything I didn't. I know that it was also a question of personality, because I'm a friendly person; nevertheless, I often felt like a traitor to my family for hanging out with rich kids. For those with a better economic position, the difficult times had started with Allende's government. They didn't understand the reasons for poverty or hunger, and they categorized those whom they considered their inferiors as simply "lazy": "Otherwise they wouldn't be in the position they were in," these rich kids would callously remark, echoing what they had heard their parents say. These words made me think less of myself—I also felt hungry sometimes. I only had one pair of shoes, sometimes two. I had to wash out my socks and underwear so that I could use them again the next day. I walked to school, and my family mourned Allende's death.

These rich children lived in another world, one in which they didn't lack food or clothing, one which was almost hermetically sealed from the news of death and disappearances. For them, the military was simply restoring order to the country; the military junta was in charge of putting the rebels in their place and restoring the ideals of democracy. Their parents had taught them to make enemies and to hate the persons and ideas that were different from those of their own social class. When faced with these attitudes, I would remain silent and reminisce: I had been one of those many lucky children carrying two bags of milk given to them by the Allende government. My father and mother were what I was afraid of losing; they were not to blame for being poor, for salaries that barely covered expenses. It was the rich who kept recycling their fortunes and the elite their privileges. At first, I was surprised; I was disconcerted to hear and be with these types of people, but I couldn't open my mouth, I hardly felt anything. I couldn't say or deny their words while I felt that heat that burns the stomach with hunger and which is also felt when one is faced with belittlement and humiliation. I didn't have any way to defend myself, and I had convinced myself of my inability to do so; I lacked the economic resources that seemed to be necessary to have value as a human being.

I think that having attended such a school was also to my advantage because I saw with my own eyes the reality of other lives—how the rich people lived and thought—something that I wouldn't have been able to see or understand in depth if I had gone to the same school the whole time. During those times, I could see that even the girls who wore a different blouse every day and those who were picked up after school by car had problems at home. Many years later, some of these same girls didn't score high enough to get into the university. Yet they became secretaries as if by magic—thanks to a fabulous course offered by Manpower which their parents could easily afford to pay for. Some of them got good-paying jobs because of family ties. That wasn't going to be my future; I was just one more Chilean woman from the Chilean lower-middle class, if you want to classify me somehow (even though I didn't feel like a part of any class or group). Nevertheless, I did have the possibility of going on to study at the university.

When I started high school in 1977, four years of death and repression had already passed. I wanted to believe that things were all right, and my adolescent illusions let me, first because of my ignorance and second because of my fear of seeing obstacles in the road ahead of me. In the first year of secondary school, they announced that we had to go to the National Stadium for a student convocation. It was disguised as a folkloric act to seduce young people into believing that it was a social event meant to boost the spirit of this tormented generation. Because of my rebellious personality, I decided that it was better not to go to school; that way no one could make me go to a meeting that I wasn't interested in. The director announced to us that since it was such an important event, buses would provide round-trip transportation. And at the end of the announcement, the director, who was a plainclothes *carabinero*, said in a loud, intimidating voice that unless one was hospitalized, one could not be absent. They would take attendance and suspend anyone who missed without a medical excuse. ATTENDANCE IS REQUIRED . . . the echo of that powerful and authoritative voice left no murmur unhushed. In an instant the students became ecstatic; the director continued standing, staring at an undefined point as if his voice echoed even in his own ears. He was another of those thousands who just followed orders. I remembered my father's words, that he would never again enter the National Stadium, which had been a torture chamber and a death camp. That day when I got home, my mother arrived with news that all the teachers had to go to a march downtown. Any absentees would have their pay docked, and the attendance list would be sent to the Ministry of Education.

I started to look at anyone in a uniform with so much suspicion that at times I imagined just my look could give me away. Things I knew were true but couldn't believe nonetheless resonated in my mind; it hurt and terrorized me to think about them: when the policemen take university women as prisoners, they rape them and run electric currents through their nipples; at Calama they brought dogs trained to rape the women of the miners that they killed. That day in the stadium they made us watch a parade of low-ranking soldiers. I watched them with hatred; I was thinking that these young soldiers were only three or four years older than me, and they probably believed that human destruction was the solution to our problems; they probably felt that their valor and macho pride resided in the submachine guns they held ready to fire. My friends made jokes and laughed. Now I think that perhaps they weren't aware of the gravity of the matter. We had been herded to the stadium whether we wanted to be there or not, and now we were breathing the air of warfare and control. The soldiers in uniform seemed to me to be made of stone. They didn't move. I remember that as well as hatred, I felt the impotence of not being able to escape, of not having the leisure to walk all the way home, because the only alternative to staying was to feel a few bullets, should I start walking off, and not even live; or perhaps they would take me to the police station and nothing would ever be heard of me again.

For years I fantasized about facing up to the oppression, but my cowardly voice remained silent, and I justified my fear with such thoughts as "They only do such things to people who go to demonstrations." I tried not to see what was happening, not to wonder about what they did to the people they took away in the paddy wagons. I soothed my cowardice by thinking that the most important thing was to live peacefully, or that it was better not to get involved. Perhaps my unconscious shame kept me beating pots and pans once a week, although only in my mind, silently, thinking of justice for the disappeared, for the women who had been raped. I dreamed of a justice that perhaps doesn't exist in such a corrupt world.

Now that I don't feel hatred, my reason causes me to picture Pinochet in his world of economic glory and power. He made himself untouchable with the horror that he sowed. In my dreams I would like to have the power and the boldness to face him and ask him . . . tell him . . . and then I wake up, listening to the echo of his loud voice, and the mocking words with which he once sarcastically and coldly replied to a reporter's comment that they had found two dead people buried in unmarked coffins in a Santiago cemetery: "What can I tell you? What a great economy!"

In my third year of high school I participated in a student exchange program and traveled to the United States, the country that I both idealized and hated. I wanted to study English, and although they were poor, my parents nevertheless made the necessary sacrifices so that I could go. Ironically, it was during this trip that I learned about the role that the United States and Nixon had played in Chile. I found out that Pinochet wasn't a general acting out of pride and duty to save the nation. He was just one more puppet serving the political and economic interests of the United States. It became clear to me that nothing could justify the plot to overthrow Allende's government. Right there, seated in the library of my new high school in North America, my soul shattered into a thousand pieces. I realized that I was in the enemy's nation—a nation that could annihilate people in another country like cattle carrying some virus and beat them to a pulp, break them and drive them insane with torture, simply because it's part of their foreign policy and military strategy, because it's in their economic interests. My fury grew; it was treacherous to assassinate thousands of innocent people. Yet this is what this powerful country, which preached peace, liberty, and the pursuit of happiness, had done to my country and to my people.

I was only sixteen years old and very confused; I didn't know why I had really come here. I began asking myself many questions. Was English more important than Spanish? Was this culture better than mine? Was this mechanical life, detached from the expression of any affection for others whatsoever, better than life in my country where people kissed each other hello and goodbye? Was this country better? Were its citizens conscious about what their government was doing in other countries in the name of liberty? Did they know that in the name of fighting Communism, the CIA and State Department trained generals and financed coups d'états in other countries? Were they aware that in Chile the Secret Police electrocuted the testicles of the men, trained dogs to rape women, saved up excrement to torture prisoners, took hundreds of men out of some town or factory and riddled them with bullets and then threw their corpses into the sea?

What a way to grow up, surrounded by an atmosphere of fear. At the beginning of the 1980s the tension in Chile was made visible. The campus near my parents' house organized demonstrations on the eleventh of every month. As if preparing for war, the heavily armed military gathered for these demonstrations. The enraged students, protected behind building walls and railings, protested that they couldn't find work because there were no jobs. They were demanding justice in a world ruled by the irrationalism of the military. The demonstrators' street barricades, made from tires and branches and a few fires, seemed weak compared to the tear gas used by the police. But these demonstrations became a ritual at the old Pedagógico, as the school was called; organized protests served as an escape valve for the rage and anguish of the people. When I would come home after participating in a demonstration, I would try to forget about it—not that my own life and feelings of personal frustration and desperation were any better to think about.

So many times I thought there was no end to this unhappiness, that we were destined to live in an atmosphere of educational, moral, and economic decay. The poor continued to go to church on Sundays, without knowing that the priests and God himself were required to follow Pinochet's orders. I don't remember when or how I realized that a solution was in the making. I wanted to declare my protest, to change something, but I didn't want to die. I wanted to live in better conditions and to have a peace that I know now doesn't exist. I wanted this without knowing what I was looking for or even where to find it. After finishing high school, I decided to prepare to take the university entrance exam and find a job. For the exam one needed money, and for a job one needed contacts. I didn't have either. Perhaps I could stay and learn bit by bit, but what was I going to do in the meantime? Some of my girlfriends resigned themselves to study to become secretaries; many others went to the university. I wasn't doing anything, and I couldn't imagine living resigned to my fate.

Now fifteen years have passed since I finished high school, and I'm still tormented by resignation; I've progressed slowly and painfully. I'm still not happy—I don't feel the peace I've looked for for so long. I was married for seven years and everything turned gray. I remembered my childhood and my dreams, and I saw myself imprisoned again in my own home. I discovered that the strength of women is in never letting ourselves be convinced by men or others that what we want and are searching for isn't what's best for us. I discovered that my strength is in never giving in to the temptation to cry with my arms crossed for hours, as I used to do in the past. But the discoveries I have made aren't as important as the difficulties I've faced as a single mother; carrying three children through life is like trying to sidestep a claw without getting scratched up. Writing this, I have asked myself, "Who am I?" In my response are mixed the tears of five years of divorce, six torturous years of studies, eleven years of being wife and mother and having to guess my way along a path no one helped me travel. I left my country because there I had neither support nor opportunities. I have struggled and remained alone because I decided to change my life when I filed for divorce. I have faced things I never imagined, and I have carried on with determination, but my soul is tired from the suffering and fighting. In this country I will always be a foreigner. In the family that I had during my seven years of marriage I discovered the scorn felt in this land by anyone who doesn't belong to the Caucasian race. As a Latin American woman I was left with the bitter sensation of being unable to be accepted by them as an equal—something that doesn't hurt me anymore, but I remember it well.

I would like to have the certainty of having won my own war, but I still have much to resolve. It makes me sad not to have enough money to visit my parents and to watch them grow old. It causes me anguish that I can't give my children the chance to experience Chile, that other world that I miss so much. I remember the past, and I find my parents on an unending road of struggle as well. I don't want to suffer the same problems. I feel the impotence of not being able to change anything, of not being intelligent enough to achieve my desires, of not having enough time to see and enjoy being with my children. There is no definitive answer to the question of who I am. Material poverty doesn't mean anything anymore. The important thing is the impact of that poverty and lack of privilege on my spirit—that's what defines me. My desire to overcome it all and my search for human quality and warmth make me without doubt a rebel with a cause.

Political Awareness in Chilean Testimonies

From the standpoint of their present social and political roles, several of the formerly apolitical women I interviewed in Chile recounted their awakening of class and gender consciousness. For example, Mirta Crocco, a social worker by profession, explicitly addressed the nature of her political education as she became more and more committed to her work with the *pobladoras*. Her increased awareness of class inequities was followed by political action; she eventually became the president of CODEM, one of the most important Chilean human rights organizations. Likewise, Alicia Oyarsún and Elena Pinilla both told how they were radically transformed through their direct involvement with the human rights organization Agrupación de los Familiares de los Presos Políticos (Families of Political Prisoners).

The borders of social class are problematized and sometimes transcended in the Chilean narratives. Crocco is a border-crosser who increasingly identifies with the poor women of the shantytowns with whom she works, and consequently distances herself from her former bourgeois lifestyle in a traditional marriage to a political moderate. Her testimony highlights the process by which she became more and more leftist in her political views and less interested in middle-class consumer values. She speaks openly about how this personal transformation culminated in the breakup of her marriage. Her newly formulated class (and later gender) analysis of Chilean society, based on her firsthand experiences working with the *pobladoras*, also influenced her professional contribution to the revision of the core curriculum of the Social Work School at the university where she was employed.

When the university was militarized after the coup, Crocco lost her job. She was not alone: several thousand Chilean university professors were fired and subsequently forced into exile in 1973; others were detained and murdered. According to one source, following the military take-over, roughly 2,000 faculty were dismissed and more than 20,000 students expelled (Chuchryk 1989, 161). Military officers were installed in key university administrative posts; they rewrote and controlled the curriculum. Crocco not only lost her career; she also had her middle-class standard of living ripped away from her by the new regime and was forced into the informal sector, where she started her own taxi service as a survival strategy.

Chloé Sasso crossed a different class barrier when she, as a lower-middle-class Chilean, was sent to a private school with more affluent children and, later, came to the United States as a foreign exchange student. Although Sasso repeatedly defines herself in terms of her childhood memories of poverty, it is important to keep in mind that a family such as Sasso's—a family that owns a television set, whose house is in a middle-class neighborhood, and whose daughter travels to the U.S. as a high school student—cannot be considered as belonging to a destitute group. To own only one uniform and two pairs of shoes in such a society does not constitute poverty. Sasso tended to feel poor only in relation to an increasingly consumer-oriented world. During her teenage years she constantly compared her own life-style with that of her classmates, who were members of the upper and upper-middle sectors of Chilean society. One should not forget that Chile during the 1970s was not a rich, developed country; the typical middle-class lifestyle was much more frugal than that of the middle-class families that Sasso came to know during her stay in the United States. Her testimony reveals that much of her alienation and confusion as a child came about as the result of ideological differences between her own leftist-leaning parents and her school friends' parents, who tended to belong to the elite ruling class that supported the military regime.

Chloé Sasso's written (not spoken) story stands out as a different sort of text from those that precede it. It is far more eloquent than most of the others, reflecting narrative skill and, especially, Sasso's extraordinary eye for telling detail. The ability to reproduce childhood memories and to capture the sensations that went along with them is one of the most powerful features of this text. The critical distance that Sasso achieves in order to interpret and analyze her own life experiences is another salient attribute.

In contrast to Sasso's questionable representation of her social class, Elena Pinilla explicitly articulates a more accurate understanding of the relativity of poverty. By Chilean standards Pinilla is less affluent than Sasso: the former works as a domestic servant; the latter is a graduate student at a U.S. university. Nevertheless, Pinilla compares her own life (recall that she dreams of being able to purchase a sewing machine) with the lives of the less fortunate slum dwellers, whose inadequate housing lacks running water and electricity, and whose children are often deprived of shoes, adequate clothing, and three meals a day. Pinilla's class consciousness, like that of Crocco, seems to have evolved as a direct consequence of her political militancy and firsthand experience working with the *pobladoras* in the shantytowns. Like Crocco, she experienced a decline in her standard of living after she decided to leave her husband, who was a postal worker. But the loss of her middle-class, more comfortable lifestyle was a price she was willing to pay for her independence from a husband whom she no longer loved.

Pinilla says that she regrets not having become politically or socially conscious much earlier in life; she expresses remorse about her former indifference toward the outside world. Nevertheless, once she "saw the light," through the intervention of her son, she became unequivocally committed to the organized resistance to authoritarian rule. A detail of her testimony that impressed me was her articulation of the feeling that at forty-two she was already old and tired. Clearly, many years of economic struggle combined with political repression and fear have taken their toll on Pinilla, making her feel older than her actual age. Also, her options as a poor, uneducated woman with the responsibility of caring for a mentally disturbed adult daughter are quite limited.

The sometimes fragmented discourse of these testimonies corresponds, in part, to the women's fractured identities. Those women who were direct victims of military repression speak from a personal space of pain and anguish. For example, Elena Maureira, Alicia Oyarsún, and Rosa Alfaro articulate the suffering caused by the loss or imprisonment of their loved ones through a sometimes disjointed uttering of words that express rage, grief, and a desire for justice. The Chilean political prisoner, Belinda Zubecueta, speaks of her vulnerability and tactical silence when facing interrogation by members of the male military regime. Although she confronted torture, rape, and solitary confinement with courage and inner strength, she is never boastful or self-righteous when narrating her story. Though still imprisoned when she was interviewed, she does not allow herself to indulge in self-pity.

Like the other women (Maureira, Crocco, Pinilla, Alfaro, and Sasso), Zubicueta associates military rule with the masculine domination of the feminine. Her testimony suggests that the female body, during the dictatorhip, was often mapped as a site of torture and violation as well as a site of resistance. State torturers, according to Ximena Bunster, use violent sexual attacks upon the body and psyche of female prisoners in order to violate their sense of self, their female dignity: "The combination of culturally defined moral debasement and physical battery is the demented scenario whereby the prisoner is to undergo a rapid metamorphosis from madonna—'a respectable woman and/or mother'—to whore" (1986, 298). Yet despite her torturers' attempts to break her spirit and force a confession, Zubecueta did not give in, and the tone of her oral narrative is remarkably upbeat for someone who survived such humiliation and torture and was still imprisoned; she emphasizes that her sense of self remains intact. What is silenced in her story, are the psychological and emotional scars left by years of torture—the untold story of many victims of the repression.

Regarding Zubecueta's frustration with Patricio Aylwin's human rights policies and, in particular, his continuing to hold some political prisoners, one must bear in mind that any civilian goverment elected after almost seventeen years of military rule will be unable to redress all of the grievances of the electorate. This was especially true in Chile, where Pinochet continued (and still continues) to function as commander in chief of the armed forces. The former dictator—outraged by the findings of the Aylwin-appointed Commission for Truth and Reconciliation on politically motivated killings, torture, and other violence during his regime—was prone to saber-rattling; thus, the threat of another coup still hung over the nation, severely constricting the measures that the Aylwin government could take without fear of reprisals from the military.

Alicia Oyarsún's self-portrait as a resisting woman highlights her Mapuche ethnic background and evokes the "bloodline" of her ancestors who fought the Spanish colonizers. Oyarsún also emphasizes the fact that she was an orphan; unhappy childhood memories are central in the structuring of her life story, and she displays more self-pity than any of the other women I interviewed. Still, Oyarsún takes pride in her ability to withstand adversity and defines herself in terms of her participation in the organized, collective female opposition to military rule. Ironically, she is herself the wife of a military officer, who was uncritical of the military government until their own children became its direct victims. Thus, Oyarsún's development of political consciousness also involved a confrontation with the patriarchal value system upheld by her spouse, creating an inner conflict; the personal and the political came together in a complex fashion. As Oyarsún stepped into the public sphere of demonstrations, political protests, and organized resistance, she simultaneously learned to challenge her husband and to form her own opinions and political convictions, rather than blindly submitting to his authority.

Several of the Chilean accounts affirm Kirkwood's view (1983; 1986) that many Chilean women became more aware of gender oppression and subordination at home as a consequence of authoritarian rule. The national crisis contributed to a rupture and crisis in the lives of tens of thousands of ordinary, often apolitical housewives who, like Maureira, experienced the disappearance of family members. This collective crisis led to a fracturing of individual identities. As a direct consequence of the repression, many women began a process of reexamination of their past personal and collective lives and a reconstruction of traumatic events. This introspection and self-reflection usually took place in a wider social context of active engagement in women's and human rights organizations within the larger community. In this way many women gained access to the space of the body politic once foreign to them; in this way they created a bridge between the quotidian and the political, offering a new, nontraditional, nonmasculinist model for engaging in political practice.

Conclusion

SELF-FASHIONING THROUGH NARRATION

> Looking for evidence of women's resistance only in articulated
> protests . . . I ignored the possibility that their resistance was to be
> found precisely in their self-constructions.
> —Lynne Phillips, "Rural Women in Latin America"

In the foregoing narratives, memories are the cornerstone upon which
each woman structures her story. The intersection of individual recollections with historical memory is rendered visible in these self-
constructions. Further, each woman's personal testimony contributes to
the nation's collective memory and documents historical events from a
nonofficial, nonpatriarchal, feminine perspective. It might be argued that
in so doing, the testimonies record the intersection of the struggle for personal and for collective survival. The cultural critic Stuart Hall (1989) has
suggested that identities are stories we tell about history, a retelling of the
past; these stories also constitute a site of memory. As Kamala Visweswaran
has observed, "The autobiographical is not a mere reflection of self, but
another entry point into history, of community refracted through self"
(1994, 137). The narratives in this book provide windows into Chilean and
Cuban history in the making. They fill in some of the gaps in "official" ver-
sions and render more fully the stories of the historical events and reconstruction in both Chile and Cuba.

It is not within the scope of my project to question the historical relia-
bility of these women's stories; rather, it has been my intent to collaborate
in a dialogical process of the narration of each woman's oral history, with
as little editorial intrusion as possible on my part. It is important to bear
in mind, however, that ethnographic writing (as discussed in my introduction) can be caught up in what James Clifford calls the "invention of
cultures." Clifford reminds us that ethnographic texts and, in this case, testimonies can reveal as much about the author-editor herself as about her
informant or the culture of an "other" she wishes to translate. Ethnographic writing in general and testimonies in particular are linguistic con-

structs and, as such, inherently partial truths. As Clifford argues, "It has become clear that every version of an 'other,' wherever found, is also the construction of a 'self,' and the making of ethnographic texts . . . has always involved a process of 'self-fashioning'" (1986, 23-24). This book, then, is both about self-fashioned women who participated in Chilean and Cuban resistance movements and about the nations they helped to build. To the degree that the narratives are about real, not fictional, characters and events, the histories are also real to the best of each narrator's recollection. The tone and details may be embellished or skewed as a result of fading memory or strong emotion, but the facts they are based on cannot be challenged: lives were lost; innocent citizens were tortured and disappeared; ordinary women became political overnight without realizing it; governments rose and fell and changed hands. In short, lives were altered irreversibly for anyone living in Cuba from 1959 and in Chile from 1973 to the present.

These women testify to their evolving political, social, and gender consciousness as they engaged in grassroots and human rights organizations. They are all subjects-in-progress whose identities are multiple, open, and fluid as mirrored in their stories of personal growth and collective transformation. These women are involved in what Michael Foucault has described as a "politics of becoming" (1980, 109-33). (I am using Foucault's notion in the broad, non-traditional sense of politics characterized by a struggle for subjectivity and a transforming of identity).

Jane Jaquette asserts that the feminist movements in South America in the middle to late 1970s "were shaped from the beginning by their role in opposition to the military dictatorships. Ironically, military authoritarian rule, which intentionally depoliticized men and restricted the rights of 'citizens,' had the unintended consequence of mobilizing marginal and normally apolitical women" (1989, 5). This is apparent in the Chilean testimonies, most notably those of Maureira, Pinilla, Oyarsún, and Zubecueta.

Each of the Cuban and Chilean women in this study structured her personal narrative around the temporal axis from *before* to *after* a major historical event that shook her country. For the Cuban women, this event was the 1959 triumph of the Revolution, which completely transformed the island's political and social structures. For the Chilean women, it was the 1973 military coup against Salvador Allende, which ushered in a brutal dictatorship and brought a long period of parliamentary democracy to an abrupt halt. Most of the Chilean women—such as Elena Maureira, whose husband and four children were murdered by the regime, and Rosa Alfaro, whose partner was assassinated in Operation Albania—focused on how their lives were shattered by the military takeover and subsequent repression. Nevertheless, these women did not passively accept their victimization; they fought back and formed part of the organized resistance to authoritarian rule.

One of the theoretical underpinnings of this study of women's self-representation is found in the practice of conjuncturalism emerging within ethnographic criticism and some feminist theories. The conjuncturalist approach to identity emphasizes the contingent and the conditional and, as defined by James Clifford (1988) marks the process of moving between cultures. The constitution of self revealed in these testimonies demonstrates that each woman occupies multiple subject positions and forms shifting alliances. She must negotiate her sometimes conflicting and multi-layered identities as wife, mother, activist, and spokesperson for different groups (groups within the women's movement, grassroots organizations, human rights organziations, and so on).

Many contemporary poststructuralist theorists, such as Michel Foucault and Jacques Derrida, underscore the notion that identities are shifting and multiple and are constituted by relations of power.[1] In his lucid discussion of the status of the "subject," Paul Smith makes the claim that theories in the human sciences which privilege the *subjected* state or status of the subject, or construe an abstract or essentialist notion of subjectivity, "tend to foreclose upon the possibility of resistance." He argues that "a theory of resistance becomes possible only when we take into account the specific history of the 'subject' and its implication into systems of knowledge, power, and ideology" (1988, xxxi). This theory of social resistance, which has been significantly influenced by feminism, calls for an understanding of the role of the subject as an active historical agent. At the same time, this theory of social agency sheds new light on the old slogan espoused by feminists that "the personal is the political." It is in this sense that I regard these Cuban and Chilean women as active social agents. Their voices of resistance constitute a political act and contribute in some small way to the transformation of their respective communities.

A slogan coined by Chilean feminists, "Democracy in the Nation and in the Home," calls for the transformation of the authoritarian patterns that structure both political and personal day-to-day relations (Valenzuela 1991, 174). The testimonies in this book attest to the power and relevance of such slogans in the lives of women who formed part of a new era of mobilization and politicization in Latin America. Verónica Schild, who has studied the role of women in recent neighborhood-based organizations in

Chile, argues that "linking the activities of economic-type organizations to a gender-specific process of political learning requires a notion of politics that goes beyond conventionally narrow conceptions" (1994, 64). These organizations have served as a means for women (especially *pobladoras*) to become political agents. Nevertheless, most middle-level or regional representative bodies of neighborhood organizations still tend to be dominated by party-affiliated men. Women activists of grassroots organizations (such as Crocco, Pinilla, and Alfaro) are often critical of the authoritarian style and structure of male-dominated groups that tend to follow a union or party organizational model. Yet all these women agree that there is a need for women to participate *with* men in the existing social and political structures of power. In the words of Rosa Alfaro, "We, as women, have always been denied positions of power. . . . We must fight for our right to share power and decision-making together with the men who now control everything!"

Although Cuban women were somewhat successful in the transformation of a social order that had previously marginalized women, the legacy of patriarchy remains firmly rooted in the authoritarian style of government in Cuba. The Cuban women interviewed in this book all worked actively for social reforms promoting gender equality. They were engaged in the translation of the political into everyday life as they participated in literacy campaigns organized by the Federation of Cuban Women (Pelayo, Carrillo), filmmaking (Vega), cultural production (Morejón, Revuelta), and organized labor (Alfonso González). Nevertheless, Cuban women are still excluded from the highest levels of power. The ideal of equality for women in politics, as Aído Pelayo put it, is yet to be achieved: "We did, of course, and still do consider ourselves feminists, but our struggle was also a revolutionary, political struggle for the full participation of women . . . in all levels of society, including politics."

As Third World feminists reiterate, middle-class feminists from the United States must not arrogantly presume to "speak for all women" but must keep in mind the enormous cultural differences that separate women whose worlds are far apart and unalike. Generally speaking, Anglo-American feminist theories tend to privilege gender over class struggle and are sometimes insensitive to (or simply ignore) the socio-economic realities of working-class and other marginalized women of color, both within the United States and in developing countries. I have tried to be sensitive to class as well as to gender, attempting to point out the complex ways in which both categories come into play in the formation of the subject.

Like feminist women of color in the United States—Gloria Anzaldúa, Cherríe Moraga, Barbara Smith, Joy Harjo, Trinh T. Minh-ha, and others—the women whose testimonies appear here reveal a struggle by women to rewrite their shifting identity in order to survive personally and collectively. U.S. feminists of color have theorized about the multilayered identities and shifting subject positions of Latina, African American, Asian American, and Native American women who are often oppressed because of their gender, their ethnicity, and their social class.[2] Through their writings, these women of diverse ethnic backgrounds examine and denounce both racism within the mostly white, middle-class women's movement and sexism within their own communities. As Gloria Anzaldúa explains in the introduction to *Making Face, Making Soul,* "'Making Faces' is my metaphor for constructing one's identity. . . . In our self-reflectivity and in our active participation with the issues that confront us, whether it be through writing, front-line activism, or individual self-development, we are also uncovering the inter-faces, the very spaces and places where our multiple-surfaced, colored, racially gendered bodies intersect and inter-connect" (1990, xvi). Likewise, the oral accounts presented in this book reveal shifting identities and an attempt to negotiate changing roles during a period of personal and collective transition.

A sense of urgency is revealed in the Chilean testimonies that is not present in those of the older generation of Cuban revolutionary women (especially Pelayo, Carrillo, and Alfonso González)—testimonies that are, for the most part, triumphalist and may be classified within the genre of heroic narrative. They are also utopian in that they evoke feelings of nostalgia for the Cuban Revolution. The past is appropriated and idealized by these narrators, who refuse to acknowledge that the final collapse of socialism may be imminent in Cuba. By contrast, the majority of the Chilean women do not consider the end of Pinochet's dictatorship anything near a real victory; they are very much aware that he is still head of the army and that the economic policies he set in motion still affect the daily lives of many poor women.

The Chilean women make use of the interview situation very differently from the Cuban women. Their narratives still contain the stamp of denunciation and an urgency to let the world know what happened to them and their families under Pinochet. The Chilean women also speak of their need to form tactical alliances (with other political parties, grassroots groups, women's organizations, institutions such as the Catholic Church, and so on) as means of combatting authoritarian rule. Despite the transition to civilian government, these women argue, there is still an urgent need to democratize the country, in order to meet their gender-specific demands and finally achieve justice for the families of the tens of thousands of victims of repression.

As is generally common in Chilean feminism, these women link the fight for gender equality with class struggle. According to Mirta Crocco, the debate over women's issues formed part of a broader, more general discussion within the democratic opposition. In the words of Jane Jaquette, "The search for human rights was tied to women's rights, and the analysis of military authoritarianism became a critique of authoritarianism in the family" (1989, 5). This echoes the feminist analysis presented by Chilean sociologists Julieta Kirkwood and María Elena Valenzuela (see Chapter 9).

In Cuba, by contrast, the task of establishing gender and racial equality was part of the official revolutionary platform for a new society. The Federation of Cuban Women and the literacy campaigns of the early 1960s were established to work toward this challenging goal. Yet as Nancy Morejón, Belkis Vega, and Naty Revuelta point out, despite enormous progress in integrating women into the work force and into professions such as medicine, education, and engineering, there is still an urgent need in Cuba for women to achieve more prominent positions of power and influence in policy-making. Also, with respect to combatting machismo, there is still a huge gap between Cuba's progressive Family Code—stating that all domestic chores and family responsibilities be shared equally between men and women—and the implementation of this legislation in everyday practice. And a common denominator in all the Cuban testimonies is an urgent call for an end to the U.S. embargo, which is strangling the Cuban economy and inflicting suffering on average people—*not* on Castro and high-level government officials. These women all agree that in the post–Cold War era this policy is obsolete and inhumane.

I consider this book to be an example of the advocacy scholarship that I briefly discussed in the introduction. I do not pretend to be a neutral observer or merely a detached academic researcher. On the contrary, this book embodies my desire to express solidarity with the women whose stories I recorded through letting their voices be heard by a general North American reading public. These women wanted to speak out so that other women could learn from their experiences. As Elena Pinilla eloquently affirmed, "I hope that my story about how I changed from an apolitical housewife to a political activist may help other women to take an honest look at their own lives. Perhaps my testimony may inspire some woman to open her eyes and see what is going on in the world around her, instead of being blind to the suffering of others."

Judy Maloof (1993) stands in front of the same mural in Valparaiso as Rosa Alfaro in the photo on page 181.

The oral testimonies in this book represent an act of memory, of not forgetting the atrocities committed in recent Latin American history. Reflecting George Santayana's famous observation that "those who do not remember the past are condemned to repeat it" is the statement of Elena Maureira, the Chilean woman whose husband and four sons were murdered by the military: "I feel compelled to tell my story to North American citizens so that perhaps these kinds of heinous crimes will not be repeated in the future." These "invisible" women have participated in the making of History; they are *active agents* involved in renegotiating their subjectivities and transforming their collective identities. Their voices contribute to the creation of new political identities and can be a source of inspiration for present and future generations of resisting women in Latin America and elsewhere.

Notes

Introduction: *Women's Testimonies of Revolution and Repression*

1. Mapuche is the name of indigenous peoples of central and southern Chile, direct descendants of the Araucanian Indians, who resisted Spanish colonial domination and were never conquered by the Spaniards or the colonizers.

2. For further reading on Latin American women's history, see Miller 1990 and 1991, Hahner 1976, Bose and Acosta-Belén 1995, and Jaquette 1989. On the feminist movement in Chile, see Kirkwood 1983 and 1986.

3. The collapse of the Soviet Union in 1989, followed by Cuba's subsequent loss of subsidies and trading partners from the former USSR and Eastern Europe, compounded the already devastating economic effects of the thirty-nine-year U.S. blockade.

4. Milton Friedman and his Chicago School are responsible for designing this neoliberal model of "economic success" in the Southern Cone. Conservative economists praise the Chilean economy and advocate implementing this model throughout Latin America, in order to create new "free trade" zones similar to those created by NAFTA.

5. According to Blum, "Bombing and strafing attacks of Cuba by planes based in the United States began in October 1959, if not before. In early 1960, there were several fire-bomb air raids on Cuban cane fields and sugar mills, in which American pilots also took part—at least three died in crashes and two others were captured." In the invasion of the Bay of Pigs, "over 100 exiles died in the attack as well as four Americans flying for the CIA. Close to 1,200 other exiles were taken prisoner by the Cubans" (1986, 209).

6. See Patai 1988, 1-35. My methodology in editing these testimonies has been informed by Patai's feminist ethnographic practice, which she outlines in her introduction.

7. I have retained in Spanish certain words whose translations into English do not adequately convey the exact meaning. For example, *compañero*, "companion" or "partner," is sometimes used to convey a deep sense of political solidarity, a bond not only personal but collective.

8. Esperanza insists that her authority as a storyteller is based on her personal experiences of suffering. Behar writes that from Esperanza's point of view, "the rage brought on by suffering and redemption through suffering give a woman the right and the need to author a text. Rage and redemption form the poles of her life as text" (1993, 12). Likewise, many of the women I interviewed were driven to tell their stories as a means of expressing their rage toward the regime.

9. The moral implications of the practice of feminist oral history are discussed at length in the introduction to Patai 1988.

10. For theories about interpretive anthropology and discussions of the ethics and politics of ethnographic research, see Geertz 1993; Clifford and Marcus 1986; Rabinow and Haan, 1983.

11. An excellent example of intersubjective fieldwork in anthropology is Behar's book about her relationship with Esperanza (1993). Also useful is Lancaster's brilliant ethnographic research in a working-class barrio of Managua (1992). In *Fictions of Feminist Ethnography* (1994), Kamala Visweswaran elaborates upon her understanding of feminist ethnography as a practice that questions ethnographic authority. In questioning the canon of works by women anthropologists, she examines the ways in which "female ethnographers confront their biases as Western women, and the processes of identification (or lack thereof) that inform description" (1995, 17).

12. See esp. the work of Randall (1981a; 1981b; 1992; 1995), Patai (1988), Alegría and Flakoll (1987), Sommer (1991), Marín (1991), Kaminsky (1993), and Harlow (1987). Two special issues of *Latin American Perspectives* (Summer and Fall 1991) titled "Voices of the Voiceless in Testimonial Literature" provide essays on testimonials of women, the role of the editor, and female practice in journalism.

13. John Beverley indicates that "the roots of the testimonio go back to a tradition of nonfictional Latin American texts such as: the colonial *crónicas*, the *costumbrista* essay (*Facundo*, *Os sertões*), the *diarios de campaña* of, for example, Bolívar or Martí, or the romantic biography—an important genre of Latin American liberalism. This tradition combined with the popularity in the early 1960s of two different kinds of participant narrative texts: the anthropological or sociological life history composed from tape-recorded oral accounts developed by academic social scientists like Oscar Lewis or Ricardo Pozas; and Che Guevara's *Reminiscences of the Cuban Revolutionary War,* whose reception, along with its corresponding manual, *Guerrilla Warfare*, was related to the general impact of the Cuban Revolution in the Americas" (Beverley and Zimmerman 1990, 173).

14. *Testi-novela* is a term invented by the Guatemalan author to denote a novel that transforms testimonies into a literary text with the intention of

preserving the collective memory of a particular oppressed community. Another example is Morales' own 1994 novel about the chilling massacre of more than 100,000 Mayan Indians in Guatemala by the military regimes throughout the 1980s.

15. Translating the stories of the Palestinian writer Ghassan Kanafani sparked Harlow's interest in the history of the Palestinian resistance movement and then an expanded interest in other resistance organizations throughout the Third World. She has studied the changing role of Third World women, especially Palestinian women in the occupied territories and southern Lebanon. She writes that following the departure of the PLO fighters from Beirut after the invasion of Lebanon in 1982, "Palestinian women, mothers, wives, daughters, and sisters, took over, as they had done before, the supervision and maintenance of many of the social services provided by the resistance organization" (1987, 133).

16. An assertion made by Patai in the introduction to *Brazilian Women Speak* is applicable to my own work: "Problematic though they are as texts gathered, edited, and translated by a foreigner, I still hold the conviction that these life stories should be seen as the identifiable and unique constructions of the individual women and not creations of mine. . . . I have tried to interfere as little as possible with the stories' own rhythms" (1988, 9-10).

17. An extensive and well-annotated source of Cuban oral histories is Lewis, Lewis, and Rigdon (1977). Oscar Lewis states in the introduction, "I am primarily interested in how the poor react to this kind of revolution. Basically, that is what this book is about. It contains the life stories of four Cuban men raised in poverty, three of them from Las Yaguas, a well-known Havana shantytown. The fourth man lived in a poor barrio in a small town in Oriente Province until he was eleven and then spent the next ten years in Havana, moving from one poor barrio to another" (xxxiii).

18. For a brilliant analysis of Partnoy (1986) and of the role of the writer as a "revolutionary presence who asserts herself and survives," see Kaminsky 1993, 47-59.

19. Omar Cabezas was a Sandinista guerrilla who fought in the Nicaraguan Revolution and wrote a testimony entitled *La Montaña es algo más que una inmensa estapa verde* (Havana: Casa de Las Américas, 1982), translated as *Fire from the Mountain: The Making of a Sandinista*. In contrast to the "collective" subject represented in most females' testimonies, his first-person narrator is individualistic and male-centered. Women are only viewed as offering the male guerrilla fighters repose and pleasure. This has been noted by Ileana Rodríguez.

20. For further discussion of the constitution of the revolutionary subject in Central American testimonial literature, see Rodríguez 1996, and Marín 1991.

21. John Beverley acknowledges the contradictions inherent in testimonial narratives, which he says "have to do with the testimonio's location at the center of the dialectic of oppressor and oppressed in the postcolonial word." He reads the relation between narrator (Menchú) and compiler (Burgos-Debray), however, as an example of interclass and interethnic solidarity that points to the possibility of important political alliances between privileged and subaltern groups: the relation between these two women can serve "as a powerful ideological figure or symbol of the union of a radicalized intelligentsia with the poor and working masses of a country, which has been so decisive in the development of movements for social change in the Third World" (Beverley and Zimmerman 1990, 176).

22. Doris Sommer analyzes the collective subject of the testimonial and Menchú's deliberate use of secrets as a rhetorical strategy in order to oppose "modernizing" Western codes to indigenous ones. Sommer suggests that "the audible protests of silence may well be responses to anthropologist Elizabeth Burgos-Debray's line of questioning" (1991, 32).

Chapter 1. Women and the Cuban Revolution

1. It is ironic that Radio Martí, financed by the CIA and the counterrevolutionary Cuban-American exile community in Florida, appropriated the name of this national hero in efforts to subvert and undermine the Revolution by destabilizing the island with a strong disinformation campaign and a constant barrage of anti-Castro propaganda.

2. The most complete anthologies of Martí's writings in English are three volumes (1975, 1977, 1982), edited and with an introduction and notes by Philip S. Foner.

3. On May 4, 1886, immigrant workers and activists gathered at Haymarket Square in Chicago to protest the death of six workers at the hands of the police in an attack on strikers at the McCormick Harvester Machine company the day before. When police attempted to disperse the crowd, a bomb exploded, leaving many injured and some dead police officers among them. Eight foreign-born anarchists were put on trial for murder and—although there was no sound evidence linking them to the bomb-throwing—sentenced to imprisonment or death by hanging. For Martí's essay "A Terrible Drama: The Funeral of the Haymarket Martyrs," see Martí 1975. See also David 1936, and Foner, 1970.

4. Especially useful on the history of U.S.-Cuban relations are: MacEwan 1981, and Foner 1973.

5. Margaret Randall observes that "Cubans and others writing about Cuba are fond of mentioning women such as Celia Sánchez (early rebel sol-

dier adjacent to the Revolutionary General Staff, and then member of the Central Committee of the Cuban Communist Party and Council of Ministers), Vilma Espín (once head of the underground for the entire province of Oriente, now member of the Central Committee of the Party, member of the Council of State, and president of the Federation of Cuban Women), Haydée Santamaría and Melba Hernández. Santamaría was a member of the Central Committee of the Party, member of the Council of State, and director of the Casa de las Américas cultural institution (until she committed suicide in 1980), while Hernández was Cuba's Ambassador to Vietnam" (1981b, 22).

6. This speech, given in Granma Province on Jan. 20, 1981, was published in the *Granma Weekly Review* on April 21, 1981.

7. On the role of women in the revolutionary struggle, see esp. Stone 1981, and Randall 1981b.

8. The Generation of 1930 were women who had lived through the Machado dictatorship prior to that of Batista. In fact, both Aída Pelayo and Carmen Castro Porta began their political activity during the resistance to the Machado dictatorship in the early 1930s. Castro Porta suffered imprisonment at the Nueva Gerona jail on the Isla de Pinos before becoming one of the founders of the FCMM, a women's group that played an important role in the struggle against Batista. Her 1990 book documents that struggle by means of testimonies from women who participated in this organization plus photos, letters, speeches, and more.

9. Reliable sources documenting the major activities and the important role of the FMC throughout the thirty years following the Cuban Revolution are Espín Guillois 1990a and 1990b.

10. For a personal account of life inside a women's prison as told by a female prisoner in Cuba during the Castro regime, see Rodríguez and Garvin 1995.

11. For accounts and documentation of the CIA's covert war against Cuba, see esp. Tarasov and Zubenko 1984, Ayer 1976, Kirkpatrick 1968, Blum 1986, and Franklin 1997. Tarasov and Zubenko have noted that "the Miami office became the largest CIA branch in the world, with a staff of up to 700 . . . aside from the U.S. army officers under contract to it. The annual budget exceeded 50 million dollars" (1984, 216). In addition, fifty-four other front organizations were involved in the secret war against the small island nation of Cuba.

12. According to Tarasov and Zubenko, "in 1971 the CIA had elaborated and implemented a plan of introducing swine pest in Cuba which developed into an epizootic. The container with the germs was delivered to Fort Gulick in the Canal Zone and then smuggled into Cuba near Guantánamo on board a fishing trawler. In early May 1971, an epizootic broke out in Cuba, killing hundreds of thousands of swine despite the measures taken by the government" (1984, 234).

13. Tarasov and Zubenko report that "over 450 modern fighter-bombers have been stationed close to Cuba's shores. Three U.S. aircraft carriers are patrolling the Caribbean. The U.S. is constantly building up its military and naval presence in the region. Aerial surveillance of Cuba by SR-71 planes has reached unprecedented proportions. Intensive naval exercises are conducted close to the island" (1984, 236).

14. Huberman and Sweezy (1969) tell us that in no other Latin American country is the infant mortality rate lower than 42 per 1,000 live births. In the highly developed United States, it was 17 per 1,000, according to World Health Organization statistics in 1977. One of the health goals set by Cuba in 1974 was the reduction of the infant mortality rate to 20 per 1,000 live births by the end of the decade. In 1979, the rate had been lowered to 22.3, with continuous improvement expected to proceed on schedule (Randall 1981b, 70). In 1996, according to *Population and Vital Statistics Report*, a United Nations publication, the infant mortality rate in Cuba was 9.4.

15. Padula and Smith note that "before the Revolution, 80 percent of all children were delivered at home. By the 1980s more than 90 percent of all births occurred in hospitals" (1985, 83).

16. See Randall 1981b, 152-62 (app. 3, "The Working Woman Maternity Law").

17. "Double blockade" refers to the loss of trade with former Eastern European and Soviet bloc nations as well as the continued U.S. embargo. There was also a loss of subsidies from the USSR, which had supplied Cuba with oil in exchange for sugar. Since 1991, Cuba has been forced to purchase oil at the prices established by the world market.

18. Hardest hit by Hurricane Gordon were the eastern province of Guantánamo, where, Carlos Lage-Dávila reports, "the coffee crop was devastated, 3,000 homes were completely flooded and fourteen bridges as well as long stretches of railway, the sewer system, roads and aqueducts were affected" (1995, 19).

19. Smith and Padula suggest that "the very notion of an effeminate man offended the heroic sensibilities of the revolutionary leadership. . . . The worst homophobic excesses occurred during the first two decades of the revolution, yet in the mid-1980s the FMC still reportedly barred known lesbians from its ranks and provided a forum for neighbors to denounce others" (1996, 173). Not until 1992 did both Fidel Castro and Vilma Espín publicly denounce homophobia and claim not to support discriminatory practices against gays and lesbians.

20. *Fresa y chocolate* was named Best Film and garnered most of the awards at the Latin American Film Festival held in Havana in December 1993, received more awards at the prestigious Berlin Festival, and was nominated for an Oscar in the Best Foreign Film category. It was a huge success in

Cuba, with people waiting in long lines to see it when it first opened com-
mercially.

21. In a speech at the opening ceremony of the twelfth Havana International Fair on Oct. 30, 1994, Carlos Lage-Dávila, vice-president of the Council of State, reported that "tourism grossed $850 million for Cuba in 1994,
surpassing the $720 million from sugar exports. The figure represents a 13%
increase in earnings over 1993; and a 14% increase in visitors, totaling
630,000" (1995, 19).

22. One Cuban prostitute I interviewed was in her early thirties and had
a law degree from the University of Havana but found working as a prostitute
and dealing on the black market much more profitable than her former job.
Darling (1995) discusses the lives of some Cuban *jineteras*.

23. See Ruth Behar, ed. *Bridges to Cuba/Puentes a Cuba*. In this valuable
anthology of poetry, essays, and other creative and critical writings by Cuban
Americans and by Cuban nationals living on the island, Behar has offered us a
sampling of pieces that themselves serve to bridge the gap between the perspectives of Cubans on the island and those in exile. Most of these writers and
intellectuals propose a new politics that emphasizes shared cultural identity
rather than divisive "national" politics that stress ideological differences.

24. Sandra Levinson reports that "the 14 poll-takers asked 46 questions
of 1,002 adults. Although the survey design called for 1,200 respondents, the
survey team assigned to the eastern third of Cuba was barred by officials from
carrying out its work, according to the *Miami Herald*, which commissioned
the poll. . . . In an ironic twist, if anything, the final results were probably
skewed 'against' the revolution, in that the eastern third of Cuba, where poll-
sters were barred, includes Cuba's second largest city, Santiago de Cuba,
known as 'the cradle of the revolution,' and the former Oriente Province,
known for its revolutionary fervor" (1995, 9).

25. On the policies and situation regarding women in Cuba, the
progress made toward gender equality, and the constraints that remain press-
ing, see Harris 1995, 91-113.

Chapter 2. Naty Revuelta

1. Before the Revolution, it was a common practice for well-off
Cubans to study in the United States—though less common for girls than for
boys.

Chapter 4. María Antonia Carrillo

1. Carrillo talked to me about how the saints from this African religion
were blended with the Catholic saints, and about healers and clairvoyants with

the power to see beyond what meets the eye. Clearly, the imposition of Marxist ideology, which teaches that religion is "the opium of the masses," has not eradicated religious belief in Cuba. Many Cubans continue to worship the gods of their African ancestors and to believe that our universe is not merely material but also an animated, magical world inhabited by the spirits of these gods.

Chapter 5. Zoila Elisa Alfonso González

1. Despite efforts to integrate the races in Cuba, segregation still exists: some neighborhoods remain primarily black; others—the wealthier neighborhoods, populated mostly by the revolutionary bureaucracy—are still primarily white. Nevertheless, in the public parks and the streets one sees many interracial couples and mulattos. In fact, despite its pockets of segregated neighborhoods and vestiges of racism, Cuba is more racially integrated than any other Latin American or Caribbean nation—or the United States.

2. This quarrel between Alfonso González and Juan is representative of the rift in Cuba between those who despise Fidel Castro and those who adore him.

3. Che Guevara, the famous guerrilla leader, was an Argentine doctor who came to Cuba late in 1956 to make a house call and did not leave until some ten years later; he fought in the Sierra Maestra and after the triumph of the Revolution became Cuba's minister of industry. In 1967 he was killed by Bolivian soldiers in the mountains of Bolivia, where he was trying to lead another guerrilla revolt. For many Cubans and other South Americans sympathetic to the ideals of the Cuban Revolution, Che Guevara became its symbol and a hero to a generation of young revolutionaries throughout the continent.

Chapter 6. Nancy Morejón

1. Casa de las Américas is a publishing house but also an institution that organizes cultural activities and supports research in the areas of literature and culture.

2. Ruth Behar has pointed out, "The poetry in this text explores the lyrical beauty and complexity of Cuba as a geography of identity and remembering" (1995, 129). Morejón's other collections are *Mutismo* [Silences] (1962); *Amor, ciudad atribuida* [Love, attributed city] (1964); *Richard trajo su flauta y otros argumentos* [Richard brought his flute, and other stories] (1967); *Parajes de una época* [Parameters of an epoch] (1976); *Elogios de la danza* [In praise of dance] (1982); *Cuadernos de Granada* [Grenada notebooks] (1984); *Octubre imprescindible* [Indispensable October] (1983); and *Piedra pulida* [On polished stone] (1986). For English translations of her work, see *Ours the*

Earth (Jamaica: University of the West Indies, 1990) and *Where the Island Sleeps like a Wing* (Oakland: Black Scholar Press, 1985).

3. According to this definition of transculturation, Cuban women's readings of the Revolution also constitute a transculturation: that is, a combination of the quotidian and the political. In this way, women can gain access to a space once foreign to them.

4. Morejón expands on this in the essay "En torno a Nicolás Guillén," in her *Fundación de la imagen.*

Chapter 7. Belkis Vega

1. Camilo Torres was one of the principal leaders of the Cuban Revolution.

2. Vega's approach to filmmaking represents an example of the transculturation discussed in Morejón's interview.

3. Major Saad Haddad was a renegade Lebanese army officer who established an autonomous "Free Lebanon" along the border with Israel in 1979. According to Peretz, "'Free Lebanon' became, in effect, a state within a state, an Israeli protectorate whose security forces were uniformed, fed, and trained by the Israeli military" (1986, 392). Israeli Prime Minister Menachem Begin sought to establish an alliance with anti-PLO forces within Lebanon to share responsibility in fighting the Palestinians.

4. Sabra and Shatila were Palestinian refugee camps in southern Lebanon. During the 1982 invasion of Lebanon, many Palestinians were massacred at these camps by Israeli soldiers.

5. In Cuba, there is a program that requires all school-age children to spend forty-five days in the country, working in the fields. The purpose is to teach children the importance of collective effort in the agricultural work that everyone depends upon, as well as to provide a source of unpaid labor for the planting and harvesting of crops.

Chapter 9. Chilean Women and Human Rights

1. Julieta Kirkwood (1986, 96-107) discusses the significance of this organization in the mobilization of women from mining communities in Iquique and Antofagasta, and the participation of women in labor strikes, protests, and demonstrations. The organization was named for Belén de Zárraga, a famous Spanish anarchist and defender of women's rights who traveled throughout Latin America early in the twentieth century.

2. With Socialist Salvador Allende Gossens as its presidential candidate, Popular Unity (UP)—a coalition of Socialists, Communists, and other leftist parties—won with 37 percent of the vote in 1970. The democratic elec-

tion of a Marxist president in Chile sent a shock wave all over the globe. As Drake and Jaksic have pointed out, "Since the 1930s, Chile had been a Latin American leader in state capitalist development, stressing simultaneous import substituting industrialization and welfare programs for organized workers" (1991, 3). To create state socialism, Allende's government expropriated the major means of production and instituted a program of redistribution of resources to the rural and urban working class. This accelerated class conflict, and the centrist Christian Democrats (PDC) and right-wing National Party (PN), backed by the United States, joined forces in their opposition to Allende: Drake and Jaksic observe that "in the showdown midterm congressional elections of March 1973 the nation was divided between 44 percent for the government and 54 percent for the opposition" (1991, 3). Among the best sources in English about the Popular Unity and Chile's political economy during the Allende years are Boorstein 1977, Debray 1971, De Vylder 1974, Steenland 1977, and Sweezy and Magdoff, 1974.

3. For an analysis of how bourgeois women were organized as an important part of the overall opposition movement against the Popular Unity government, see esp. Mattelart 1977, 172-207. The third chapter of her book, "Cuando las mujeres de la burguesía salen a la calle" ("When bourgeois women take to the streets"), documents this phenomenon of the mobilization of women by right-wing elements for the purpose of destabilizing the Allende government.

4. There was the 1891 "revolution" in Chile, also due to foreign (British) influence and a burgeoning military, followed by social movements at the beginning of the twentieth century and uprisings during the 1920s and 1930s; in 1938, a popular-front candidate from the Radical Party, Pedro Aguirre Cerda, was elected president, and Salvador Allende served as a member of his cabinet. For a general history in English of class struggle and social movements in Chile, see Loveman (1979), who argues that a unique variant of Hispanic capitalism remains a dominant force in Chilean society and interprets Chile's development from this new perspective; especially useful are the chapters titled "Politics, Labor, and the Social Question," and "Chilean Democracy." Another useful source on Chile during the 1960s and early 1970s is Valenzuela and Valenzuela 1976, an edited collection that assesses the constraints upon the Allende government and includes articles dealing with public opinion, electoral politics, the labor movement, agrarian reform, foreign capital in the Chilean economy, and the "invisible blockade" by the U.S. government.

5. For further reading in English on the military coup in Chile and the role of the CIA, see esp. Alexander 1978, Blanco 1973, Petras and Morley 1974, Rojas Sanford 1975, and the Church Committee report documenting CIA covert involvement in the overthrow of Allende.

6. "This is surely the last time I will address you. My words are not spoken in bitterness, but in disappointment. There will be a moral judgment against those who betrayed the oath they took as soldiers of Chile. . . . Long live Chile! Long live the people! Long live the workers! These are my last words. And I am convinced my sacrifice will not be in vain. I am certain that this sacrifice will be a moral lesson that will punish cowardice, treachery, and treason" (fragment of Salvador Allende's final broadcast, quoted in Spooner 1994, 17).

7. A *población* is a working-class residential district: some *poblaciones* are fairly new; others, very old and run down; some are housing projects for employees of private companies. *Población* can also refer to any village or settlement; in Chile it is often a shantytown on the outskirts of a city, which may have been established overnight by homeless squatters who improvise tents and shacks from plywood and cardboard.

8. Schneider 1995, 75, chronicles popular resistance in the *poblaciones* during the 1980s. The book is based on more than one hundred interviews in the shantytowns and offers an analytical perspective as well as a focus on the human drama of the rise of popular social movements in Chile.

9. See Houser 1978, *The Execution of Charles Horman;* a later edition of this book was titled *Missing.*

10. The Chilean New Song Movement, which emerged in the late 1960s and 1970s, produced political protest songs that were first sung at *peñas,* or small gatherings of poets, musicians, and young people. Later, this new folk music with a political message of hope and resistance became known throughout Latin America and, with the growing international movement of solidarity with Chile after the 1973 coup, throughout the world. See Joan Jara's life of Victor Jara (1984).

11. On military rule in Chile under the Pinochet regime, see Valenzuela 1978, Valenzuela and Valenzuela 1986, Angell 1980, and Petras 1973.

12. Roman Polansky's riveting film *Death and the Maiden* (1995), based on the Chilean writer Ariel Dorfman's play, deals with the case of a doctor who supervised the torture of political prisoners and was never tried or punished—until he is held and interrogated by one of his victims, whom he had repeatedly raped and sadistically tortured as he listened to Schubert's quartet "Death and the Maiden."

13. On the women's movement in Chile, see Kirkwood 1986; also useful is Klimpel 1962. For more on women's movements in Argentina and the Southern Cone in general, see Feijóo 1978, Little 1978, and Masiello 1990.

14. In Santiago in 1993 I attended several meetings and a Christmas party at La Morada. This center provides a meeting place for a variety of

women's groups whose members come from a wide range of class backgrounds.

15. For statistical data on the inequality of men's and women's labor, see Leiva 1987, which indicates that women's wages continue to be significantly lower than men's, even if education is taken into account: "Women with a university education in Chile made 49 percent of the average male wage in 1985" (189). There is still a wage differential between men and women in most industrialized and developing countries, including the United States.

16. The better-off women were often perceived as being "anti-men," though I recall one middle-class feminist telling me in Santiago, "I'm a feminist, but not the type of feminist that hates men." Many self-defined Chilean feminists that I met in Chile expressed this same sentiment. They were interested in knowing more about the women's movement in the United States, especially the situation of women of color within U.S. feminist organizations.

17. The Vicariate of Solidarity was an office established by the Catholic Church following the coup in Chile. Its primary purpose was to investigate human rights abuses and to provide material assistance and support to the victims of military repression.

18. On the role of the Catholic Church in contemporary Chilean society and in the struggle for human rights, see Mutchler 1971 and Smith 1982.

19. Gutiérrez 1973 provides a detailed history and description of the doctrine and practice of liberation theology in Latin America.

Chapter 10. Elena Maureira

1. After the interview, Maureira showed me a video documenting the mass burial at Lonquén. The case is recounted by Isabel Allende in her novel *De amor y de sombra*.

2. MAPU, Movimiento de Acción Popular Unificado (Movement of Unified Popular Action), founded in 1969 by the former Christian Democrats, was one of the parties that formed the Popular Unity coalition.

3. The Party for Democracy is a moderate Socialist party that was formed in 1987 to confront the regime in any election. Garretón notes that the PPD is composed of "one Socialist party that joined with other leftist groups and a segment of the nonpartisan right" (1991, 227).

4. Pinocho is a derogatory nickname used for Pinochet.

Chapter 11. Mirta Crocco

1. The COPACHI, an ecumenical human rights organization that functioned in the early days of the military regime, was replaced by the Vicaría

de la Solidaridad, which was dependent on the archdiocese of Santiago. See Schneider 1995, 116-18.

2. CODEM, a human rights organization that defined its principal objectives in terms of the antidictatorial struggle, at first refused to identify itself as a feminist organization; later, however, "the silence of the opposition with respect to gender demands led twelve women's organizations—including MOMUPO and CODEM—to formulate the 'Women's Demands for Democracy' three months before the 1988 plebiscite, which asked for the full incorporation of women's concerns in a democracy" (Valenzuela 1991, 174).

3. The Spanish word *momio*, which means "mummy," is a popular pejorative term in Chile for someone who is right-wing and reactionary. During the dictatorship, it denoted those who supported Pinochet.

4. On the 1964 elections in Chile, see Loveman 1988, 313-14. During this campaign the moderate Christian Democrats received the support of Chile's Catholic Church and a rising Catholic rural labor movement that represented a major alternative to the Marxist-dominated FRAP coalition of Communist, Socialist, and smaller reformist parties. Loveman observes that "if anticommunism was the rationale for massive U.S., West German, and Church support for Chile's Christian Democrats, there existed within the Christian Democratic party many sincere reformers and even a small number of committed revolutionaries. President Frei's call for 'Revolution in Liberty' was not empty rhetoric. The Christian Democrats intended to alter dramatically the very foundations of Chilean society, to redistribute income and wealth, to improve the living standards of, and to broaden opportunities for, the nation's workers and peasants, and to democratize the country's political and social life" (1988, 314).

5. Radomiro Tomic was the presidential candidate of the *terceristas*, a political party that was formed when the Christian Democratic Party split in three in 1969. When Tomic was nominated to succeed Frei, most of the conservative members of the Christian Democratic Party voted for Alessandri, the right-wing candidate of the National Party. Tomic called for an extension of agrarian reform and for the nationalization of copper and large monopolistic sectors of the economy. In the 1970 election he won 28 percent of the vote to Allende's Popular Unity's 37 percent and Alessandri's National Party's 35 percent.

6. JAP stands for Juntas de Abastecimiento y Precios (Organizations of Provisions and Prices). These were neighborhood-based price control and distribution agencies that had been formed during Allende's Popular Unity government in order to combat the black market; they were used to ration and distribute scarce necessities.

7. Orlando Letelier, former Chilean ambassador to the United States and cabinet minister under Allende, was killed by a car bomb explosion in

Washington, D.C., on September 21, 1976. The bomb that killed him and his American coworker Ronni Moffitt had been planted by the American mercenary Michael Townley, acting on orders from the Secret Police in Chile. Spooner suggests the following motives for this crime: "Letelier, who had once worked for the Inter-American Development Bank, had been lobbying the multilateral lending agencies to suspend loans to Chile and had successfully campaigned in Holland for the cancellation of a $62.5 million mining investment in Chile. Worst of all, in view of the Chilean military, he had received a sympathetic hearing from influential members of the U.S. Senate, which passed a bill cutting off arms sales to Chile on June 16, 1976" (1994, 125).

8. MIR is Movimiento de Izquierda Revolucionario (Movement of the Revolutionary Left), an ultra-left party founded at the University of Concepción in 1965. MIR was not part of the Popular Unity coalition; it supported the Allende government only when doing so was absolutely crucial for political survival.

9. Manuel Contreras, a personal friend of Pinochet, was the director of the secret police network called DINA. The creation of DINA in 1974 marked a phase in the repression characterized by secrecy and disappearances. Contreras was also responsible for the death of Orlando Letelier in Washington.

Chapter 12. Elena Pinilla

1. Under joint Communist and Socialist leadership, an array of popular grassroots organizations such as Committees for the Homeless, Committees for Just Rents, and Committees for Neighborhood Health Care became the basis for the FLN, which was formed in the early 1950s.

2. When I was in Chile in 1993, several women explained to me that they were able to get divorced by finding loopholes in the marriage license and declaring the original document null and void.

3. La Jota refers to the Juventudes Comunistas de Chile (JCC), the Chilean Young Communists League.

4. Even at this writing, in 1997, Pinochet remains commander in chief. Although many of the reforms initiated by the second democratic government under President Eduardo Frei (1994-) have begun to show results, the families of the detained and disappeared have yet to learn the whereabouts of many loved ones. According to Thomas Writh, in the foreword to Sepúlveda 1996, "Despite the labor of the Chilean Commission on Truth and Reconciliation (Rettig Commission), which documented 957 individuals (the real number is undoubtedly much higher) who disappeared after detention during the dictatorship, not a single family has been successful in prosecuting the presumed perpetrators" (17).

5. The antiabortion law points to the deeply rooted patriarchal structure of policymaking in Chile, where laws are still made by a majority of men who are, for the most part, insensitive to issues related to women's health and particular needs. The Catholic Church is also influential in opposing legislation supporting the reproductive rights of women and the right to divorce.

Chapter 14. Rosa Alfaro

1. The FPMR, the guerrilla wing of the Chilean Communist Party, launched its first campaign for armed resistance against the dictatorship on December 14, 1983; it "took over a radio station in Santiago, and dedicated itself to the armed defense of the people. Within the next few months the Frente launched a series of attacks on electric power plants" (Schneider 1995, 173). Manuel Rodríguez was a leader of the Chilean Independence Movement. He was considered one of the most radical of the heroes of the Chilean Independence Republicans who fought against the Spaniards. He was assassinated. Albania was the name of a street in Santiago.

2. The regime sought to weaken the growing opposition of the youth active in the FPMR by killing off its most important leaders. Julio Guerra Olivares was only twenty-nine, was the father of a five-year-old daughter, when the military raided his apartment in Santiago and murdered him in cold blood—then claimed that they had killed him in self-defense, since he was supposedly harboring weapons there. The other eleven slaughtered throughout the night in Operation Albania ranged in age from twenty to thirty. A few were unemployed; two of the others were students; the oldest was a university economist; and the rest were in various trades such as engineering and construction. Three were women—two single, the married one pregnant—and seven of the eight men were, like Julio, the fathers of small children (a daughter was born to the youngest after his death).

3. Tucapel Jiménez was the president of Chile's public employees' union. He lost his job for supporting the "no" vote against Pinochet in 1980 and then became a taxi driver. After he publicly called for the creation of a national coalition to oppose the regime's economic policies in February of 1982, he was brutally murdered. As Spooner recounts, "On February 25, Jiménez's taxi was stopped by at least three men who pointed a gun at his head and commandeered his vehicle to a back road on the outskirts of Santiago. Jiménez, . . . who had opposed the Allende government and had publicly defended the new military regime before a United Nations labor conference, was shot five times in the back of the head" (1994, 174). The official investigation failed to identify the murderers. The regime spread the rumor that he had been killed in a domestic dispute involving another woman.

Chapter 16. Chiloé Sasso

1. Chiloé, Patricia Sasso's nickname, is an island in southern Chile.

2. It is important to note that although this informant defines herself as poor; according to Chilean standards she never lived in poverty. Her father was a miner and her mother a school teacher; therefore, her socioeconomic status was middle or lower-middle class. Someone living below the poverty line in Chile would definitely not have been able to take ballet lessons or study in the United States. But Chiloé Sasso attended a private school with children of the wealthiest class; constantly comparing their privileges and lifestyle with those of her own family, who managed only to make ends meet, contributed to her perception of herself as poor.

3. La Moneda is the Presidential Palace, located in the center of Santiago; it was bombed by the military during the 1973 coup.

4. ITT, International Telephone and Telegraph, was one of the U.S. companies that had been expropriated by the Allende government and was one of the powerful lobbies that supported the CIA planning of a military coup in Chile. In 1974, compensation agreements were reached with ITT, Anaconda, Kennecott, and others.

Conclusion: Self-Fashioning Through Narration

1. Smith 1988 offers a rigorous survey and critique of recent theories of subjectivity in the humanities and social sciences. He analyzes the notions of "the subject" presented through the political writings of Louis Althusser, the psychoanalytic writing of Jacques Lacan, and the philosophical work of Jacques Derrida. He draws attention to the specific ways in which feminist theories of subjectivity account for agency and political action and are linked to an emerging theory of social resistance.

2. See esp. Anzaldúa 1990 and Anzaldúa and Moraga, 1981. These anthologies offer both creative and theoretical writings that deal with the experiences of feminists of color living within the United States and document their struggles to combat racism, sexism, and class oppression as well as to negotiate their own multiple and sometimes conflicting alliances.

References

Ad Hoc Working Group of the United Nations. 1975. *Report of the Economic and Social Council* A-1028. New York.

Agosín, Margorie. *Scraps of Life: Chilean Arpilleras.* 1987. Trans. Cola Franzen. Toronto: Williams-Wallace.

———. 1993. "Women, Politics, and Society in Chile." Michigan State University Working Paper 235 (March).

Alegría, Claribel, and D.J. Flakoll. 1987. *They Won't Take Me Alive: Salvadoran Women in the Struggle for National Liberation.* Trans. Amanda Hopkinson. London: Women's Press.

Alexander, Robert. 1978. *The Tragedy of Chile.* Westport, Conn.: Greenwood Press.

Alvarado, Elvia. 1987. *Don't Be Afraid, Gringo: A Honduran Woman Speaks from the Heart.* Trans. and ed. Medea Benjamin. San Francisco: Institute for Food and Policy Development.

Angell, Alan. 1980. "Chile after Five Years of Military Rule." *Current History* 76 (Feb.): 58-61.

Anzaldúa, Gloria, ed. 1990. *Making Face, Making Soul/Haciendo Caras: Creative and Critical Perspectives by Feminists of Color.* San Francisco: Aunt Lute Books.

Anzaldúa, Gloria, and Cherríe Moraga, eds. 1981. *This Bridge Called My Back: Writings by Radical Women of Color.* New York: Kitchen Table.

Ayers, Brian. 1976. *The War That Never Was: An Insider's Account of CIA Covert Operation against Cuba.* New York: Bobbs-Merrill.

Barnet, Miguel. 1969. "La novela testimonio socio-literatura." *Unión* 4 (Oct.).

———. 1981. "The Documentary Novel." *Cuban Studies/Estudios Cubanos* 11 (Jan.).

Barrios de Chungara, Domitila, with Moema Viezzer. 1978. *Let Me Speak! Testimony of Domitila, a Woman of the Bolivian Mines.* Trans. Victoria Ortiz. New York: Monthly Review Press.

Barry, Tom, Beth Wood, and Deb Preusch. 1984. *The Other Side of Paradise: Foreign Control in the Caribbean.* New York: Grove Press.

Behar, Ruth. 1993. *Translated Woman: Crossing the Border with Esperanza's Story.* Boston: Beacon Press.

————, ed. 1995. *Bridges to Cuba/Puentes a Cuba*. Ann Arbor: Univ. of Michigan Press.

Berger Gluck, Sherna. 1991. "Advocacy Oral History: Palestinian Women in Resistance." In *Women's Words: The Feminist Practice of Oral History*, ed. Sherna Berger Gluck and Daphne Patai. New York: Routledge.

Berger Gluck, Sherna, and Daphne Patai, eds. 1991. *Women's Words: The Feminist Practice of Oral History*. New York: Routledge.

Beverley, John. 1993. *Against Literature*. Minneapolis: Univ. of Minnesota Press.

Beverley, John, and Marc Zimmerman, eds. 1990. *Literature and Politics in the Central American Revolutions*. Austin: Univ. of Texas Press.

Blanco, Hugo. 1973. *The Coup in Chile: Firsthand Report and Assessment*. New York: Pathfinder Press.

Blum, William. 1986. *The CIA: A Forgotten History*. London: Zed Press.

Boorstein, Edward. 1977. *Allende's Chile: An Inside View*. New York: International.

Bose, Christine E., and Edna Acosta-Belén, eds. 1995. *Women in the Latin American Development Process*. Philadelphia: Temple Univ. Press.

Bunster, Ximena. 1986. "Surviving beyond Fear: Women and Torture in Latin America." In *Women and Change in Latin America*, ed. J. Nash and H. Safa. Boston: Bergin & Garvey.

Cañadell, Rosa. 1993. "Chilean Women's Organizations: Their Potential for Change. *Latin American Perspectives* 20 (Fall): 43-60.

Carranza, Julio, Luis Gutierrez Urdaneta, and Pedro Gonzalez Monreal. 1995. *Cuba, La restructuración de la economía: Una propuesta para el debate*. Havana: Editorial de ciencias Sociales.

Castro, Fidel. 1981. Speech. *Granma Weekly Review*, April 21.

Castro Porta, Carmen. 1990. *La lección del maestro*. Havana: Editorial de Ciencias Sociales.

Chaney, Elsa. 1974. "The Mobilization of Women in Allende's Chile." In *Women in Politics*, ed. Jane Jaquette. New York: Wiley.

————. 1979. *Supermadre: Women in Politics in Latin America*. Austin: Univ. of Texas Press.

Chuchryk, Patricia. 1989. "Feminist Anti-Authoritarian Politics: The Role of Women's Organizations in the Chilean Transition to Democracy." In *The Women's Movement in Latin America: Feminism and the Transition to Democracy*, ed. Jane S. Jaquette. Boston: Unwin Hyman.

Clifford, James. 1986. "Introduction: Partial Truths." In *Writing Culture: The Poetics and Politics of Ethnography*, ed. George E. Marcus and James Clifford. Berkeley: Univ. of California Press.

————. 1988. *The Predicament of Culture*. Cambridge: Harvard Univ. Press.

Covarrubias, Paz. 1978. "El movimiento feminista chileno." In *Mujer y Sociedad*. Santiago: UNICEF Centro Estudios de la Mujer.

Darling, Lynn. 1995. "Havana at Midnight." *Esquire* (May), 96-104.

David, Henry. 1936. *The History of the Haymarket Affair*. New York: Monthly Review Press.

Debray, Regis. 1971. *The Chilean Revolution: Conversations with Allende*. New York: Random House.

Del Aguila, Juan M. 1994. *Cuba: Dilemmas of a Revolution*, 3d ed. Boulder, Colo.: Westview Press.

De Vylder, Stefan. 1974. *Allende's Chile: The Political Economy of the Rise and Fall of the Unidad Popular*. Cambridge: Cambridge Univ. Press.

Drake, Paul W., and Iván Jaksic, eds. 1991. *The Struggle for Democracy in Chile, 1982-1990*. Lincoln: Univ. of Nebraska Press.

Espín Guillois, Vilma. 1975. *Memories, 2nd Congress: FMC*. Havana: Orbe.

———. 1976. "Women in Revolutionary Cuba." In *Women in Latin American History: Their Lives and Views*, ed. June E. Hahner. Berkeley: Univ. of California Press.

———. 1990a. *La mujer en Cuba*. Havana: Editorial Política.

———. 1990b. *La mujer en Cuba: Familia y sociedad—Discursos, entrevistas, documentos*. Havana: Imprenta Central de las FAR.

———. 1991. "Interview with Vilma Espín by *Claudia*." In *Cuban Women Confront the Future: Vilma Espín*. Ed. Deborah Shnookal. Victoria, Australia: Ocean Press.

Feijóo, María del Carmen. 1978. "Las luchas feministas." *Todo es Historia* 128 (Jan.): 6-23.

Fisher, Jo. 1993. *Out of the Shadows: Women, Resistance, and Politics in South America*. London: Latin American Bureau.

Foner, Philip. 1970. *Autobiographies of the Haymarket Martyrs*. New York: Monthly Review Press.

———. 1973. *A History of Cuba and Its Relations with the United States*. New York: Monthly Review Press.

Foucault, Michel. 1980. *Power/Knowledge: Selected Interviews and Other Writings*. New York: Pantheon.

Franco, Jean. 1992. "Going Public: Reinhabiting the Private." In *On Edge: The Crisis of Contemporary Latin American Culture*, ed. George Yúdice, Jean Franco, and Juan Flores. Minneapolis: Univ. of Minnesota Press.

Franklin, Jane. 1997. *Cuba and the United States: A Chronological History*. New York: Ocean Press.

Fusco, Coco. 1995. "El Diario de Miranda/Miranda's Diary." In *Bridges to Cuba/Puentes a Cuba*, ed. Ruth Behar. Ann Arbor: Univ. of Michigan Press.

———. 1996. "Hustling for Dollars." *Ms.* 7 (Sept.): 62-70.

Garretón, Manuel Antonio. 1991. "The Political Opposition and the Party System." In *The Struggle for Democracy in Chile, 1982-1990*, ed. Paul Drake and Iván Jaksic. Lincoln: Univ. of Nebraska Press.

Geertz, Clifford. 1993. *The Interpretation of Cultures: Selected Essays*. New York: Basic Books.

Geiger, Susan N.G. 1986. "Women's Life Histories: Method and Content." *Signs: Journal of Women in Culture and Society* 11 (Winter): 334-51.

Gutiérrez, Gustavo. 1973. *A Theology of Liberation*. New York: Maryknoll Orbis Books.

Hahner, June, ed. 1976. *Women in Latin American History: Their Lives and Views*. Berkeley: Univ. of California Press.

Hall, Stuart. 1989. "Cultural Identity and Cinematic Representation." *Framework* 36: 68-81.

Harlow, Barbara. 1987. *Resistance Literature*. New York: Methuen.

Harris, Colette. 1995. "Socialist Societies and the Emancipation of Women." *Socialism and Democracy* 9: 91-113.

Hojman, David E. 1996. "Poverty and Inequality in Chile: Are Democratic Politics and Neoliberal Economics Good for You? *Journal of Interamerican Studies and World Affairs* 38 (Summer and Fall): 73-96.

Houser, Thomas. 1978. *The Execution of Charles Horman: An American Sacrifice*. New York: Harcourt Brace Jovanovich.

Huberman and Sweezy. 1969. *Socialism in Cuba*. New York: Monthly Review Press.

Jaquette, Jane. 1989. "Women and the New Democratic Politics." In *The Women's Movement in Latin America: Feminism and the Transition to Democracy*, ed. Jane S. Jaquette. Boston: Unwin Hyman.

Jara, Joan. 1984. *An Unfinished Song: The Life of Victor Jara*. New York: Ticknor & Fields.

Jara, René, and Hernán Vidal, eds. 1986. *Testimonio y literatura*. Minneapolis: Institute for the Study of Ideologies and Literature.

Kaminsky, Amy K. 1993. *Reading the Body Politic: Feminist Criticism and Latin American Women Writers*. Minneapolis: Univ. of Minnesota Press.

Keen, Benjamin, ed. 1991. *Latin American Civilization: History and Society, 1492 to the Present*. Boulder: Westview Press.

Kirkpatrick, Louis. 1968. *The Real CIA*. New York: Macmillan.

Kirkwood, Julieta. 1983. *La política de feminismo en Chile*. Documento de Trabajo 183. Santiago: FLASCO.

———. 1986. *Ser política en Chile: Las feministas y los partidos*. Santiago: FLASCO.

Klimpel, Felicitas. 1962. *La mujer chilena: El aporte femenino al progreso de Chile, 1910-1960*. Santiago: Andrés Bello.

Kozol, Jonathan. 1978. *Children of the Revolution*. New York: Delacorte Press.

Lage-Dávila, Carlos. 1995. "Speech Delivered at the Opening Ceremony of the 12th Havana International Fair, Oct. 30, 1994." *Cuba Update*, Feb.: 16-19.

Lancaster, Roger. 1988. *Thanks to God and the Revolution: Popular Religion and Class Consciousness in the New Nicaragua*. New York: Columbia Univ. Press.

———. 1992. *Life Is Hard: Machismo, Danger, and the Intimacy of Power in Nicaragua*. Berkeley: Univ. of California Press.

Larguía, Isabel, and John Dumoulin. 1985. "La mujer en el desarrollo: Estrategía y experiencias de la Revolución Cubana." *Casa de las Américas* 25 (March-April): 37-53.

Leiva, Alicia. 1987. "Las desigualdades en el trabajo de hombres y mujeres." *Coyuntura Económica* 14: 172-92.

Levinson, Sandra. 1995. "The CID-Gallup Poll." *Cuba Update*, Feb.: 7-9.

Lewis, Oscar, Ruth M. Lewis, and Susan M. Rigdon. 1977. *Four Men: Living the Revolution—An Oral History of Contemporary Cuba*. Urbana: Univ. of Illinois Press.

Little, Cynthia. 1978. "Education, Philanthropy, and Feminism: Components of Argentine Womanhood, 1860-1926." In *Latin American Women: Historical Perspectives*, ed. Asunsión Larvín. Westport, Conn.: Greenwood Press.

Loveman, Brian. 1979. *Chile: The Legacy of Hispanic Capitalism*. New York: Oxford Univ. Press.

———. 1988. "Military Dictatorship and Political Opposition in Chile, 1973-1986." In *Chile: Dictatorship and the Struggle for Democracy*, ed. Grínor Rojo and John J. Hassett. Gaithersburg, Md.: Ediciones Hispamérica.

MacEwan, Arthur. 1981. *Revolution and Economic Development in Cuba*. New York: St. Martin's Press.

Marín, Linda. 1991. "Speaking Out Together: Testimonials of Latin American Women." *Latin American Perspectives* 70 18 (Summer): 51-68.

Martí, José. 1975. *Inside the Monster: Writings on the United States and American Imperialism*. Ed. Philip Foner. New York: Monthly Review Press.

———. 1977. *Our America*. Ed. Philip Foner. New York: Monthly Review Press.

———. 1982. *On Art and Literature: Critical Writings by José Martí*. Ed. Philip Foner. New York: Monthly Review Press.

Masiello, Francine. 1990. "Women, State, and Family in Latin American Literature of the 1920s." In *Women, Culture, and Politics in Latin America*, Seminar on Feminism and Culture. Berkeley: Univ. of California Press.

Mates, Jessica. 1994. "For Cuba's Gays and Lesbians, Change Is in the Wind." *Gay Community News* 20 (June): 23-33.

Mattelart, Michele. 1977. *La cultura de la opresión femenina*. Mexico: Serie Era.

Menchú, Rigoberta. 1984. *I . . . Rigoberta Menchú: An Indian Woman in Guatemala*. Ed. Elizabeth Burgos-Debray, trans. Ann Wright. New York: Verso.

Miller, Francesca. 1990. "Latin American Feminism and the Transnational Arena." In *Women, Culture, and Politics in Latin America*, Seminar on Feminism and Culture. Berkeley: Univ. of California Press.

——, ed. 1991. *Latin American Women and the Search for Social Justice.* Hanover, N.H.: Univ. Press of New England.

Modlich, Reggie. 1993. "Cuba: Struggle for Development Is a Challenge for Women." *Women and Environments* 13 (Winter): 37-38.

Morales, Mario Roberto. 1994. *Señores bajo los árboles o brevísima relación de la destrucción de los indios.* Guatemala: Artemis-Edinter.

Murray, Nicola. 1979. "Socialism and Feminism: Women and the Cuban Revolution: Part Two." *Feminist Review*, no. 3: 99-108.

Mutchler, David E. 1971. *The Church as a Political Factor in Latin America: With Particular Reference to Colombia and Chile.* New York: Praeger.

Padula, Alfred, and Lois Smith. 1985. "Women in Socialist Cuba, 1959-84." In *Cuba: Twenty-Five Years of Revolution, 1959-1984*, ed. Sandor Halebsky and John M. Kirk. New York: Praeger.

Partnoy, Alicia. 1986. *The Little School: Tales of Disappearance and Survival in Argentina.* Trans. Alicia Partnoy with Lois Athey and Sandra Braunstein. San Francisco: Cleis Press.

Patai, Daphne. 1988. *Brazilian Women Speak: Contemporary Life Stories.* New Brunswick, N.J.: Rutgers Univ. Press.

Peretz, Don. 1986. *The Middle East Today.* 4th ed. New York: Praeger.

Personal Narratives Group, ed. 1989. *Interpreting Women's Lives: Feminist Theory and Personal Narratives.* Bloomington: Indiana Univ. Press.

Petras, James. 1973. "Chile after Allende: A Tale of Two Coups." *Monthly Review* 25 (Dec.).

Petras, James, and Morris Morley. 1974. *The United States and Chile: Imperialism and the Overthrow of the Allende Government.* New York: Monthly Review Press.

Politzer, Patricia. 1989. *Fear in Chile: Lives under Pinochet.* Trans. Diane Wachtell. New York: Pantheon.

Poniatowska, Elena. 1984. "Testimonios de una escritora: Elena Poniatowska en micrófono." In *La Sartén por el mango: Encuentro de escritoras latinoamericanas*, ed. Patricia Elena González and Eliana Ortega. Río Piedras, P.R.: Ediciones Huracán.

——. 1988. "And Here's to You, Jesusa." Trans. Gregory Kolovakos and Ronald Christ. In *Lives on the Line: The Testimony of Contemporary Latin American Authors*, ed. Doris Meyer. Berkeley: Univ. of California Press.

Pratt, Mary Louise. 1990. "Women, Literature, and National Brotherhood." In *Women, Culture, and Politics in Latin America*, Seminar on Feminism and Culture in Latin America. Berkeley: Univ. of California Press.

Rabinow, Paul, and Norma Haan, eds. 1983. *Social Science as Moral Inquiry.* New York: Columbia Univ. Press.

Randall, Margaret. 1981a. *Sandino's Daughters: Testimonies of Nicaraguan Women in Struggle.* Vancouver: New Star Books.

———. 1981b. *Women in Cuba: Twenty Years Later.* New York: Smyrna Press.

———. 1992. *Gathering Rage: The Failure of 20th Century Revolutions to Develop a Feminist Agenda.* New York: Monthly Review Press.

———. 1995. *Our Voices/Our Lives: Stories of Women from Central America and the Caribbean.* Monroe, Maine: Common Courage Press.

Reed, Gail. 1995. "Cuba's Economy 1995: Critique and a Crystal Ball." *Cuba Update*, Feb.: 10-13.

Rivero y Mendez, Isel. 1993. "Cuban Women: Back to the Future?" *Ms.* 3 (May): 15-17.

Rodríguez, Ana, and Glenn Garvin. 1995. *Diary of a Survivor: Nineteen Years in a Cuban Women's Prison.* New York: St. Martin's Press.

Rodríguez, Ileana. 1982. "Organizaciones populares y literatura testimonial: Los años en Nicaragua y El Salvador." In *Literatures in Transition: The Many Voices of the Caribbean Area*, ed. Rose Minc. Gaithersburg, Md.: Montclair State College/Hispamérica.

———. 1996. *Women, Guerillas, and Love: Understanding War in Central America.* Minneapolis: Univ. of Minnesota Press.

Rojas Sanford, Robinson. 1975. *The Murder of Allende and the End of the Chilean Way to Socialism.* New York: Harper & Row.

Salazar, Claudia. 1991. "A Third World Woman's Text: Between the Politics of Criticism and Cultural Politics." In *Women's Words: The Feminist Practice of Oral History*, ed. Sherna Berger Gluck and Daphne Patai. New York: Routledge. 93-106.

Salloum, Habeeb. 1996. "Cuba's Underground Economy on Guardalavaca Beach." *Contemporary Review* 269 (July): 1-5.

Schild, Verónica. 1994. "Recasting 'Popular' Movements: Gender and Political Learning in Neighborhood Organizations in Chile." *Latin American Perspectives* 21 (Spring): 59-80.

Schneider, Cathy Lisa. 1995. *Shantytown Protest in Pinochet's Chile.* Philadelphia: Temple Univ. Press.

Schultz, Donald E., ed. 1994. *Cuba and the Future.* Westport, Conn.: Greenwood Press.

Sepúlveda, Emma, ed. 1996. *We, Chile: Personal Testimonies of the Chilean Arpilleristas.* Trans. Briget Morgan. Falls Church, Va.: Azul.

Shnookal, Deborah, ed. 1991. *Cuban Women Confront the Future: Vilma Espín.* Victoria, Australia: Ocean Press.

Smith, Brian H. 1982. *The Church and Politics in Chile: Challenges to Modern Catholicism*. Princeton, N.J.: Princeton Univ. Press.

Smith, Lois M., and Alfred Padula. 1996. *Sex and Revolution: Women in Socialist Cuba*. New York: Oxford Univ. Press.

Smith, Paul. 1988. *Discerning the Subject*. Minneapolis: Univ. of Minnesota Press.

Sommer, Doris. 1991. "Rigoberta's Secrets." *Latin American Perspectives 70* 18 (Summer): 32-50.

Spooner, Mary Helen. 1994. *Soldiers in a Narrow Land: The Pinochet Regime in Chile*. Berkeley: Univ. of California Press.

Steenland, Kyle. 1977. *Agrarian Reform under Allende*. Albuquerque: Univ. of New Mexico Press.

Stone, Elizabeth. 1981. *Women and the Cuban Revolution: Speeches and Documents by Fidel Castro, Vilma Espín, and Others*. New York: Pathfinder.

Sweezy, Paul, and Harry Magdoff, eds. 1974. *Revolution and Counter-Revolution in Chile*. New York: Monthly Review Press.

Tarasov, Konstantin, and Vyacheslav Zubenko. 1984. *The CIA in Latin America*. Trans. Demitry Belayavsky. Moscow: Progress.

Valdés, Teresa. 1988. "Women under Chile's Military Dictatorship." In *Chile: Dictatorship and the Struggle for Democracy*, ed. Grínor Rojo and John J. Hassett. Gaithersburg, Md.: Ediciones Hispamérica.

Valenzuela, Arturo. 1978. *Chile: The Breakdown of Democratic Regimes*. Baltimore: Johns Hopkins Univ. Press.

Valenzuela, J. Samuel, and Arturo Valenzuela, eds. 1976. *Chile: Politics and Society*. New Brunswick, N.J.: Rutgers Univ. Press.

———. 1982. *Military Rule in Chile: Neo-Liberalism and Dictatorship*. Baltimore: Johns Hopkins Univ. Press.

———. 1986. *Military Rule in Chile: Dictatorship and Oppositions*. Baltimore: Johns Hopkins Univ. Press.

Valenzuela, María Elena. 1987. *La mujer en el Chile Militar*. Santiago: Ediciones Chile y América-CESOC.

———. 1991. "The Evolving Roles of Women under Military Rule," and "The Political Opposition and the Party System." In *The Struggle for Democracy in Chile, 1982-1990*, ed. Paul Drake and Iván Jaksic. Lincoln: Univ. of Nebraska Press.

Visweswaran, Kamela. 1994. *Fictions of Feminist Ethnography*. Minneapolis: Univ. of Minnesota Press.

Wald, Karen. 1989. "Cuban Women Face the Future." *Black Scholar* 20 (Winter): 14-16.

Watson, Lawrence C., and Maria Barbara Watson-Franke. 1985. *Interpreting Life Histories: An Anthropological Inquiry*. New Brunswick, N.J.: Rutgers Univ. Press.

Waylen, Georgina. 1992. "Rethinking Women's Political Participation and Protest: Chile 1970-1990." *Political Studies* 40 (June): 299-314.

WINN. 1994. Reports from Around the World: "Chile: The Struggle by Women to be Heard." *Women's International Network News* 20 (Spring): 74.

Yúdice, George. 1991. "Testimonio and Postmodernism." *Latin American Perspectives 70* 18 (Summer): 15-31.

Index